Catholicity and Pantheism.
ALL TRUTH OR NO TRUTH.

AN ESSAY,

BY

THE REV. J. DE CONCILIO,

OF THE PROPAGANDA COLLEGE,

PROFESSOR OF DOGMATIC AND MORAL THEOLOGY AND PASTOR OF ST. MICHAEL'S
CHURCH, JERSEY CITY.

NEW YORK:
D. & J. SADLIER & COMPANY,
31 BARCLAY STREET.
MONTREAL: CORNER NOTRE DAME AND ST. FRANCIS XAVIER STS.
1874.

Entered according to Act of Congress in the year 1873, by
D. & J. SADLIER & COMPANY,
In the Office of the Librarian of Congress at Washington,
D. C.

Printing Statement:

Due to the very old age and scarcity of this book, many of the pages may be hard to read due to the blurring of the original text, possible missing pages, missing text, dark backgrounds and other issues beyond our control.

Because this is such an important and rare work, we believe it is best to reproduce this book regardless of its original condition.

Thank you for your understanding.

TO HIS GRACE

JAMES ROOSEVELT BAYLEY,

Archbishop of Baltimore,

PRIMATE OF THE UNITED STATES OF AMERICA,

IN TOKEN OF

SWEET REMEMBRANCE OF HIS PATERNAL RULE.

AS A SLIGHT ACKNOWLEDGMENT OF

MANY PERSONAL ACTS OF KINDNESS,

THESE PAGES

ARE INSCRIBED BY

THE AUTHOR.

CONTENTS.

CHAPTER I.
PAGE.
Introduction, - - - - - - - 13

CHAPTER II.
Pantheism examined from the Ontological Point of View —the Infinite—Idea of the Infinite according to the Pantheist, - - - - - - - - 26

CHAPTER III.
The Problem of Multiplicity, - - - - - 53

CHAPTER IV.
The Blessed Trinity, or Multiplicity in the Infinite, - - 67

CHAPTER V.
Laws according to which the Mystery of the Trinity should be understood, - - - - - - 82

CHAPTER VI.
The Finite, - - - - - - - - 114

CHAPTER VII.
The Finite—Continued, - - - - - - 137

CHAPTER VIII.

Union between the Infinite and the Finite, or First Moment of God's External Action, - - - - - 164

CHAPTER IX.

Union between the Infinite and the Finite—Continued, - 195

CHAPTER X.

The Supernatural, or Sublimitive Moments of God's Action, - - - - - - - - - 230

CHAPTER XI.

Relations between the Sublimitive Moment and Substantial Creation, - - - - - - 269

CHAPTER XII.

The Cosmos in Time and Space, - - - - 302

CHAPTER XIII.

The Cosmos in Time and Space—Continued, - - 339

PREFACE.

THE present work consists of a series of articles, which we have at times published in the *Catholic World*, a magazine which since its first number has done so much honor to its editor and to the cause which it has undertaken to defend.

The aim which we have had in view, has been as much the refutation of Pantheism, as the satisfaction of a strong desire on our part of presenting the whole body of Catholic truths in all their universality, unity, grandeur, and beauty.

We are firmly convinced, with all the thinking minds of the century, that the form of controversy with the human mind, as exhibited in all the signs of the present time, must be thoroughly changed. Hitherto, we have endeavored to lead men's minds to Catholic truth by external evidence; we must now change our tactics and convince them by internal evidence.

When, at the dawn of Protestantism, the human mind rebelled against the authority of the Church, it did not and could not reject all other dogmatic truths, and the consequences resulting from them, by the action of which European society had been formed and which had been so deeply rooted in men's minds, as to become the very flesh and blood of Christendom. Men then unable to throw off the habit of thinking, which they had inherited from sixteen Christian centuries; a habit which had grown with their growth, and which everything around them, language, customs, laws, arts and sciences conspired to make deeper and deeper, were forced almost instinctively to admit most of revealed truth.

It was easy, then, for the controversialist to take a standing-point from the dogmatic truths fully admitted and agreed upon by his adversary, and to show how necessarily and logically they led to the admission of the authority of the Church. But the steady and swift work of three centuries of demolition, the action of that principle of disintegration proclaimed by Luther have not only eliminated from men's minds all dogmatic truth, but have given them a sceptical turn of mind, which will take nothing for granted, unless sifted to the very bottom, unless accompanied by internal evidence as far as the subject will admit.

In former times it was not difficult to convince a man who believed in the existence, and had a true idea, of God, who admitted the possibility of revelation, that of miracles and prophecies, how logically these things pointed out to the existence of an infallible authority, and led him necessarily to the Church. External evidence was, as it were, a home argument to him, because it chimed in and agreed with the bent of his mind. But now that he does not believe in, nor has a true idea of, God, who rejects scornfully all possibility of anything supernatural and superintelligible, it is impossible for us to follow the beaten track, but must find a new way of presenting the Catholic truths to him; that is to lay them out before him in all the internal evidence of which they are capable; internal evidence, which results not only from reasons, with which each particular truth may be supported, but that which emanates from the link by which all truths hang upon each other, from the bearing which they have on all the fundamental problems raised by the human mind; from the relations they possess with all the orders of human knowledge; in a word, do not present to man's mind all the truths of the Church only piecemeal, and, as it were, dissected (this has to be be done to obtain an accurate idea of them) but lay them out before him, as it were, in a beautiful panorama, one depending on the other, and all forming a most compact and harmonious whole; show him how the system fits his mind, and satisfies the best aspirations of his soul; inculcate upon him that the system alone is the type of all intelligibility, all life, all beauty, that it is the pattern and origin of all science, all action, all arts, and man's mind, which, after all, was made for truth, will naturally, and almost instinctively, embrace it. This is what we attempted to do in this work, of which only a portion of the first part appears now, under the title of *Catholicity and Pantheism*. We might have presented the whole body of Catholic truths, having no regard to errors, but we have preferred to compare them with error because the statement of error and its refutation, enables the reader the more easily to grasp the view of truth. Next, we have chosen Pantheism among all errors; because, first, it is the only error which is universal, and by its generality the natural-born enemy of Catholic truth, and consequently gives us the opportunity of raising and discussing all the fundamental problems of human knowledge. Second, Because Pantheism is the real practical error of the day, the last logical consequence of the principle of free examination. Let us understand it well: that which was foreseen by the Catholic geniuses, who first grappled with Protestantism, has come to pass. The principle of free examination carried to its furthest consequence, has resulted in making what was once Christendom disappear, and has created a new society, a new public opinion different from the heathen society of old only in the open effrontery of the assertion of its spirit.

The spirit of the old heathen society and of the new is the same—the *Deification of self and all its cravings*, with this difference: that men in the old heathen society were cumbered with a multitude of gross idols, in which they expressed and actualized, and as it were, incorporated the deification of self; but they would have blushed to admit that the external idol was a cloak for their interior egotism, and would never have acknowledged that in adoring Jupiter, Juno, Mars, or Venus, they were deifying and worshipping their own ambitious revenge, jealousy, or lust.

But such a disguise is unworthy of the present time. The men of this age openly and avowedly profess their deification, they profess in the light of the day in books, in speeches, in action, the divinity of their origin, the omnipotence of their power, the endless advance of their progress. It would be useless for us to bring forward proofs of this part. God is not forgotten to-day for a time, as in former Christian centuries, such as the middle ages, when they *sinned and feared God*. There is no God now to fear, or to offend, but man is the God, whom other ages have adored and everything the God of old, the universe must serve for the deification of man. Is there any supreme intelligence, publicly acknowledged by modern society, able to put any restraint on the intelligence of the individual or society? Is there any supreme and higher law publicly owned by modern society, fit to restrain the unbridled licence of the will of man, or of the all-powerful will of society? Is there any authority, publicly acknowledged, having a right to curb the all-powerful and grasping absolutism of the state? None of these things is acknowledged, but publicly and avowedly denied. Then the intelligence of man, his will, that of society, or of that state, are the only supreme absolute independent intelligence and will, the fountain of all laws, of all justice, of all right. Then the God of old, the supreme and absolute intelligence, giving laws to all finite intelligences was a mistake. Then the God of old, the supreme law, the absolute origin of all justice and right governing all finite will, was a blunder. It is the intelligence, the will of man, of society, of the state which are independent, self-existing, absolute, which are the only God; the God of old was a dream, a fancy of benighted ages, dispelled by the glare of the nineteenth century. What is this but Pantheism carried to its farthest consequences? Pantheism, then, is not an opinion of philosophers, it is not a system of books resting and gathering dust on the shelves of the scholar, it is a living, quickening, tremendous reality, a reality which is drying up and exhausting the very life of man, sapping the very foundation of society, demolishing the strongest and the most powerful state. We have no doubt that many seeing the title-page of our book will turn away as being something too abstract and too dry. It is so, but it undertakes to grapple with an error that is living and acting in our midst, and which, if not checked, will overthrow society and cast us into barbarism. And let none, especially Americans, think that they can grapple with it by other means, but that of dissecting philosophically its principles and opposing to it the only true principles which emanate from the Catholic Church alone. We have wondered of late at the Communist, and stood aghast at the so-called outrages which he committed. He has been schooled for the last century in believing that the God of old was a fable, and that man, society, the state, were God. He has been taught this in the most explicit terms, even as far as to be told that the God of old was the *Evil;* he has seen that doctrine carried out into practice in thousands and millions of facts by that society or state which ought to have protected him against it, and shall we complain because he has applied in his own favor the consequence of that doctrine and practices. I am as much God, says the Communist, to the rich, as you are, and I cannot see why I should not be as rich as you. I am as much God, says the Communist, to the state, and I cannot comprehend, why I should not have the same power and authority as you. This has happened abroad. Let us continue to educate the masses without religion or God; let us continue to give them erroneous, extravagant ideas of the rights of their intelligence, of their liberty, of what the power of man can achieve; let us give them a practical idea of Pantheism, as we are doing, without inculcating upon them the eternal and absolute rights of God; let us make them forget that they are creatures, and we shall soon have the same results which watered France with blood.

Our readers will see by these incontrovertible facts, the second reason why we have singled out Pantheism among all errors. Because it is the universal, the radical error pervading and permeating man, society, and the body politic. If man, society, or the state must be saved at all, it must be by returning to the fundamental truths of the Church. Pantheism or Catholicity, truth or no truth, life or death, for man and society.

Our work, naturally, will divide itself into several parts; as we shall compare Pantheism and Catholicity in all the principal orders of human knowledge. The portion of the first part which we publish now, is the principal one, as that which treats of the fundamental ontological questions. And should God grant us life and health, and should we receive encouragement from the public, we shall endeavor soon to complete this first part.

August 15th, FEAST OF THE ASSUMPTION OF THE B. V.

CATHOLICITY AND PANTHEISM.

CHAPTER I.

INTRODUCTION.

MAN is made for truth. The ray of intelligence beaming from his countenance and kindling his looks with life marks his superiority over all inferior creation, and loudly proclaims this fact. Intelligence must have an object; and what can this object be but truth? As a necessary consequence from this fact, it follows that error can be nothing else than fragments of truth; ill-assorted, improperly joined together. Error does not consist in what logicians call simple ideas, or self-evident propositions; but in complex ideas, the result of a long chain of syllogisms. Another consequence, closely allied to the first, is, that the greater the error, the more universal and more widely spread, the more particular truths it must contain. Or, if it does not contain a greater number of partial truths, it must either have the power of apparently satisfying a real and prevalent tendency of our mind, otherwise it would never exert dominion over the intelligence; or else it must possess the secret of awakening and alluring a true and imperative aspiration of our nature.

It is through these views that we have been enabled to explain to ourselves the prevalence of Pantheism. The simple utterance of the word Pantheism, the *Deity of everything*, would seem to carry its refutation with it, so plain and evident is its falsehood, so glaring its absurdity.

Pantheism, however, has been the universal error in time and space. In India, Persia, China, Greece, Rome, Pantheism flourished; now under a religious, and then under a philosophical form. After the Christian era it was the religion or system of those who did not understand the Christian dogmas as taught by the church; and the fathers of the first centuries, in battling against Gnosticism, Eclecticism, and Neoplatonism, were struggling with this old error of the world—Pantheism. Depressed for awhile by the efforts of the doctors of the church, it arose with fiercer energy under the forms of all those heresies which attacked the dogma of the Incarnation of the Word.

In the middle ages there were many philosophers who held Pantheism; and in modern times, since the dawn of the Reformation, it has become the prevalent, the absorbing error of the world. Always the same as to substance, it assumes every variety of form: now you see it in a logical dress, as in the doctrine of the German school; again it takes a psychological garb, as in that of the French school, with Cousin at its head; or it assumes a social and political form, as in the Pantheism of Fourier, Leroux, Saint Simon, and all the progressists of every color or shade; and finally, it puts on a ghostly shroud, as taught by the American spiritualists. Under whatever garb it may appear, it penetrates and fills all, and pretends to explain all. It penetrates philosophy, natural science, history, literature, the fine arts, the family, society and the body politic, and religion. It holds its sway over all, and exhibits itself as having the secret of good and evil. How is this to be explained? If the falsehood of Pantheism be so evident, whence is it that it is the universal error in time and space, and has made such ravages in man's intelligence? The greater its falsehood, the more inexplicable becomes its prevalence. Has the nature of man changed? Has his intelligence lost its object? It is true, man's intelligence is not perfect. Since the fall it is weakened and obscured, but doubtless it has not ceased and could not cease to be intelligence; truth has not ceased to be its natural essential object. How, then, are we to explain the prevalence of so mighty an error? By the fact that it is a system which by its generality seems to satisfy a supreme tendency of our mind, and to appease one of the most imperative cravings of our souls. Man's intelligence has a natural tendency to synthetize, that is, to bring everything into unity. This tendency arises both from the essential oneness of the mind and from the nature of its object. The object of the mind is being or reality in some form or other. That which does not exist cannot even be apprehended, and hence cannot be the object of the mind. To understand and to understand nothing is, at the same time, the affirmation and the negation of the understanding. Now, if the object of the intelligence, in order to be known and understood by the said faculty, must represent itself under the form of being or reality, it is under this respect necessarily one. Under whatever form it may exhibit itself, under whatever quality it may be concealed, it must always be reality or being, and, as such, one. But if being, reality, or unity, taken in the abstract, were the sole object of the intelligence, there would be an end to all its movement or life. All science would be at an end, because science is a process, a movement; and movement is not possible where an abstraction is the sole object of the mind. Being and unity, then, abstractedly considered, would be the eternal stupor of the mind.

This cannot be so, however. Intelligence is action, life, movement. Now, all this implies multiplicity; hence the object of the intelligence must also be multiple. But does not this second condition also destroy the former, which requires that the object of the intelligence should be one? Here reason finds a necessary, though, as we shall see, only an apparent contradiction, both in the logical as well as ontological order. In the logical order, because the intelligence seems to require unity and multiplicity as the conditions without which its action becomes impossible. In the ontological order, or the order of reality, because if the object is not at the same time one and multiple, how can those conditions of the mind be satisfied?

The intelligence, then, in order to live, must be able to travel from unity to multiplicity in an ascending or descending process, and to do so, not arbitrarily, but for reasons resting on reality.

In this lies the life of the intelligence; science is nothing but this synthetical and analytical movement. Let the mind stop at analysis or multiplicity, and you will give it an agglomeration of facts of which it can neither see the reason nor the link which connects them; and hence you place it in unnatural bonds, which, sooner or later, it will break—it matters not whether by a sophistical or a dialectic process. On the other hand, let it stop at unity, and you condemn it to stupor and death.

The foregoing ideas will explain the fact, how a particular error will either have a very short existence or fall into the universal error of Pantheism. For in this, so far as we can see, lies the reason of the universal dominion of Pantheism. Because it proposes to explain the whole question of human knowledge, it takes it up in all its universality, and the solution which it sets forth has all the appearance of satisfying the most imperative tendency of our mind. To be enabled to explain the numberless multiplicity of realities, no matter how, and, at the same time, to bring them into a compact and perfect whole, strikes to the quick the very essence of man's intelligence and allures it with its charms. If this be not the main reason of the prevalence of Pantheism, we acknowledge we do not understand how such a mighty error could ever take possession of man's mind; we are tempted to say that human understanding was made for falsehood, which is to deny the very notion of intelligence.

What Pantheism proposes to do for the mind, it also promises to do for the soul.

There is, in man's heart or soul, impressed in indelible characters, a tendency after the infinite, a craving almost infinite in its energy, such is the violence with which it impels the soul to seek and yearn after its object. To prove such a tendency were useless. That void, that feeling of satiety and sadness, which overwhelms the soul, even after the enjoyment of the most exquisite pleasure, either sensible or sentimental; the phenomenon of solitaries in all times and countries; the very fact of the existence of religion in all ages and among all peoples; the enthusiasm, the recklessness and barbarity which characterize the wars undertaken for religion's sake; the love of the marvelous and the mysterious exhibited by the multitude; that sense of terror and reverence, that feeling of our own nothingness, which steals into our souls in contemplating the wide ocean in a still or stormy night, or in contemplating a wilderness, a mountain, or a mighty chasm, all are evident proofs of that imperious, delicious, violent craving of our souls after the infinite. How otherwise explain all this? Why do we feel a void, a sadness, a kind of pain, after having enjoyed the most stirring delights? Because the infinite is the weight of the soul—the centre of gravity of the heart—because created pleasures, however delightful or exquisite, being finite, can never quiet that craving, can never fill up that chasm placed between us and God.

The pretended sages of mankind have never been able to exterminate religion, because they could never root out of the soul of man that tendency. I say pretended sages, because all true geniuses have, with very few exceptions, been religious; for in them that tendency is more keenly and more imperiously felt.

This is the second reason of the prevalence of Pantheism. To promise the actual and immediate possession of the infinite, nay, the transformation into the infinite, is to entice the very best of human aspirations, is to touch the deepest and most sensitive chord of the human heart.

Both these reasons we have drawn *a priori;* we might now prove, *a posteriori,* from history, how every particular error has either fallen into Pantheism or disappeared altogether. But, since this would carry us too far, we will exemplify it by one error—Protestantism.

The essence of Protestantism lies in emancipating human reason from dependence on the reason of God. It is true that at its dawn it was not proclaimed in this naked form, nor is it thus announced at the present time ; but its very essence lies in that. For, if human reason be made to judge objects which God's reason alone can comprehend, man is literally emancipated from the reason of God.

What does this supreme principle of Protestantism mean, that every individual must, by reading the Bible, find for himself what he has to believe?

Are the truths written in the Bible intelligible or superintelligible ; that is, endowed with evidence immediate or mediate, or are they mysteries?

If they be purely intelligible, endowed with

evidence mediate or immediate, there is no possible need of the Bible, for, in that case, reason could find them by itself. If they be mysteries, how can reason, unaided by any higher power, find them out? It will not do to say, They are written in the Bible, and reason has merely to apprehend them. Suppose a dispute should arise as to the right meaning of the Bible; who is to decide the dispute? Reason? Then reason must grasp and comprehend mysteries in order to decide the dispute. For none can be judge unless he is qualified thoroughly to understand the matter of the dispute. From this it is evident that to make reason judge of the faith is to make it judge of the mysteries of the infinite, and, therefore, is to emancipate the reason of man from subjection to the reason of God. Hence, Protestantism was rightly called a masked rationalism.

It soon threw off the mask. The human mind saw that it can never be emancipated from the reason of God unless it is supposed to be independent, and it could never be supposed independent unless it was supposed equal to the reason of the infinite.

The result of all this is necessarily Pantheism. And into Pantheism Protestants soon fell, especially the Germans, who never shrink from any consequence if logically deduced from their premises. Such was the latent reasoning of Fichte,

Schelling, Hegel, and others, in building up their form of Pantheism.

To understand is to master an object, to mould it so as to fit our intelligence. We can understand the infinite, we can master it. Therefore, we are at least equal to the infinite, " we are ourselves the infinite," we ourselves lay it down by a logical process. Hence the astounding proposal which Fichte made to his disciples, that the next day he would proceed to create God, was nothing else but the echo and logical consequence of the cry raised by the unfrocked monk of Wittenberg, proclaiming the independence of reason from the shackles of all authority.

On the other hand, the denial of human liberty and the absolute predestination of the Calvinists give the same result. If we are not free agents, if God can do what he lists with us, we are no longer agents in the strictest and truest sense of the word. Now, every substance is an act, a *monas*, a force; if, then, we are not agents, we are not substances, and hence we become qualities, phenomena of the infinite substance. All this as regards doctrine. But Protestantism ran into Pantheism by another road almost as soon as it arose, for the action of the feelings is swifter and more rapid than logic. Protestantism being rationalism in doctrine is necessarily naturalism with regard to the soul; and by presenting to the soul only nature, its authors left the craving after the supernatural and the infinite thirsty and bleeding. What was the consequence? Many Protestant sects fell into mysticism, which is but a sentimental Pantheism, a species of interior theurgy. History is too well known to render necessary any proof of these assertions. These are the consequences at which active minds must arrive when, in their researches, they do not meet with truth.

As to those minds which are not active, or not persevering in their inquiries, they fall into indifference, which is but a scepticism of the soul, as doubt is the scepticism of the mind.

Now, the question arises, What is the best method of refuting Pantheism? Many have been the refutations of Pantheism, but they are limited to pointing out the absurd consequences following from it, which consequences, summed up, amount to this: that Pantheism destroys and makes void the principle of contradiction in all the orders to which it may be applied; that is to say, it makes void that principle in the ontological order or order of realities, in the logical order, etc.

But, notwithstanding the truth and force of this refutation, we do not know that it has converted a single Pantheist. From the fact that Pantheism is more prevalent at the present time than ever it was, we should conclude that it has not. We say this with all the respect and deference due to those who have exerted their talents in the said arena. For we know that some of the noblest intellects have brought their energy to bear against this mighty error. But, if we are allowed to express our opinion, we say that all former refutations have been void of effect for lack of completeness, and in force of a determination on the part of their authors to limit themselves to the abstract order, without descending to particulars, and to the order of realities. The result was, that while Pantheism, without any dread of consequences, applied its principles to all orders of human knowledge, and to all particular questions arrayed under each order, and was, as it were, a living, quickening system—false, indeed, in the premises, but logical and satisfactory in the consequences resulting from those premises—the refutations of it, confined within the limits of logic, were a mere abstraction; true, indeed, and perfectly satisfactory to any one who could apply the refutations to all the orders of human knowledge, but wholly deficient for those who are not able to make the application. We think, therefore, that a refutation of Pantheism should be conducted on the following principles:

1st. To admit all the problems which Pantheism raises, in all the generality of their bearing.

2d. To examine whether the solution which Pantheistic principles afford not only solves the problem, but even maintains it.

3d. If it is found that the Pantheistic solution destroys the very problem it raises, to oppose to it the true solution.

These are the only true principles, as far as we can see, which will render a refutation of Pantheism efficient. For, in this case, you have, in the first place, a common ground to stand upon, that is, the admission of the same problems; in the second place, if you can prove that the Pantheistic solution of the problems destroys, instead of solving them, it will be readily granted by the Pantheist for the sake of the problems themselves. When you have done all this, you do not leave the mind in doubt and perplexity, but you present to it the true solution, and it will then be ready to embrace it.

A refutation conducted upon those principles we have attempted in the work we now publish.

We take Pantheism in all its universality and apparent grandeur; we accept all its problems; we examine them one by one, and we show that the Pantheistic solution, far from resolving the problems, destroys them; and we substitute the true solution. In a word, we compare Pantheism with Catholicity; that is, the universality of error with the universality of truth—the whole system of falsehood with the whole system of truth. We make them stand face to face, and we endeavor to exhibit them so plainly that the brightness and splendor of the one may thoroughly extinguish the phosphoric light of the other. We show the Pantheist that, if he ever wants a solution of *his* problems, he must accept Catholicity, or proclaim the death of his intelligence.

To do this it will be necessary for us to compare Pantheism and Catholicity in all orders; in the logical order, in the ontological order or the order of reality; and under this order we must compare them in the moral, social, political, and æsthetic orders. The truth of the one or the other will appear by the comparison.

It is true we undertake a great task; great especially as regards the positive part of the refutation. For it embraces the whole of theology; not only with relation to what is commonly regarded as its object, but in the sense of its being the supreme and general science, the queen of all sciences, the universal metaphysic in all possible orders. We own that we have felt the difficulty of such a task, and many times have we abandoned it as being far above our strength. But a lingering desire has made us return to the work. We have said to ourselves: Complete success and perfection are beyond our hope, but we can at least make the attempt; for, in matters of this kind, we think it well to reverse the wise maxim of the Lambeth prelates, and rather attempt too much than do too little.

As to the soundness and truth of our doctrine we never harbored a fear. We are a Catholic; and it is Catholic doctrine we explain in this book. The whole substance of it is held as revealed doctrine by the Catholic Church. It is true there are some opinions, which we have linked with the dogmas to give unity of science to the whole. But we have felt we had a right, as Catholic, to do so. We understand a Catholic's most essential privilege to consist in being beyond the pale of error. This *is* the only restraint which his reason receives. When the Church commands him to believe such and such a dogma, as revealed by God, she but shuts him out of error. So long, then, as he holds fast to these dogmas he enjoys the widest and the sublimest liberty—the liberty of the children of God, which lies in the impossibility of erring. Let the Catholic, therefore, keep his mind conformable to that of the Church, and then he may launch out in speculation full of daring and security.

We have tried to do so. But have we succeeded? We are not aware of having written anything contrary to any revealed truth. If it has escaped us without our knowledge, we unconditionally reject it, and submit the whole book to the holy Roman Pontiff in whom resides the fullness of the infallible authority founded by Christ on earth. In this spirit we cheerfully and manfully enter upon our task.

CHAPTER II.

PANTHEISM EXAMINED FROM THE ONTOLOGICAL POINT OF VIEW—THE INFINITE—IDEA OF THE INFINITE ACCORDING TO THE PANTHEIST.

THE infinite of the Pantheist is *something* stripped of subsistence, limits, determinations, definiteness, qualities, or quantity; it is devoid of all consciousness, intelligence, will, individuality; it is something hanging between reality and unreality, bordering on possibility and existence; it is not altogether actual or entirely possible, but that which is *in fieri*, or becoming; in a word, that which is both being and nothing. It is pure, unalloyed abstraction, without a mind which makes the abstraction.

We acknowledge that Pantheists do not all express themselves in the above manner with regard to the infinite; but, if we strip their systems of their various forms, all agree in presenting the same idea.

Whether, with the materialistic Pantheists of old, we call the infinite a common principle or seed of liquid nature, from which everything sprang up, and which is the substratum of everything; or whether we call it the *primitive number*, with the Pythagoreans; or we like to exhibit it as the first *unity* or *monas*, with Plotinus and the Neoplatonists; or we look upon it as the *infinite substance* of Spinoza; or finally, with the Germans, we prefer to call it the *ego* or the *absolute identity*, or the *ideal-being;* or the *impersonal reason*, with Cousin—all converge into this idea, that the infinite is something indeterminate, unconscious, impersonal; which, by an interior necessity, is impelled to unfold and develop itself, assuming all kinds of limitations and forms; and thus, from being undefined, indeterminate, abstract, it becomes real, defined, determinate, concrete; from being one, it becomes multiple. The genesis of creation in all its components, and the history of mankind, are the successive unfolding and realization of the infinite in a progressive scale. For, in its necessary development, it becomes matter, organism, sense; and in man it acquires intellect with the consciousness of itself. Here commence all the phases of the development of man recorded in history: phases of a progressive civilization, which are but necessary unfoldings and modifications of the infinite; and which will go on progressing perpetually, to what end, or for how long, Pantheists and progressionists are unable to determine.

By means of this theory of the infinite, they endeavor to réconcile reality with the ontological ideas of being, the infinite, substance, and the absolute. For they reason thus: The idea of being is essentially universal, and as such it must embrace all reality, and therefore it can be but one. The same must be said of the idea of the infinite. This comprehends everything, and therefore absorbs everything.

The reader can easily see, from what we have thus far said, that the first problem which Pantheism raises and which is to be solved, is the following: What is the nature of the infinite? We accept the problem, and shall discuss it by making the following inquiries.

1. Does the idea which Pantheism gives of the infinite really resolve the problem?

2. What is the true solution of the problem?

With regard to the first inquiry we answer that the idea of the infinite, as given by the Pantheists, when well examined, leads to one or two different conclusions:

1. Either it is the idea of finite being, and consequently requiring the existence of an infinite being as its origin.

2. Or, it is the idea of a mere abstraction, an absolute nonentity, and hence leading to absolute nihilism. In both cases Pantheism, instead of

resolving the problem, destroys it. We shall endeavor to prove both these propositions, assuming as granted that the principles of Pantheism are these two:

1. The infinite is that the essence of which lies in becoming.

2. It becomes multiplicity, that is matter, organism, animality, etc., by a necessary interior movement.

The pantheistic idea of the infinite leads either to the idea of God given by the Catholic Church, or to absolute nihilism. Proven by the first principle of the Pantheists.

Before entering upon the proof, we must lay down a few truths of ontology which are metaphysically certain.

First Principle. Being and actuality are one and the same thing.

The proof of this principle lies in the explanation of what actuality really means. Now, actuality is one of those ideas, called by logicians simple ideas, and which cannot be defined. We shall endeavor to explain it as follows.

Actuality is but a relation of our mind. When we think of a being, not as yet existing, but against the existence of which we see neither an interior nor an exterior reason, we call it possible being; and the perception of all this, in our mind, we call the perception of the *possibility* of a being.

But when we think of the being, not as possible, but as having, so to speak, travelled from possibility to real existence, we call that being *actual;* and the perception of the mind, the perception of the actuality of a being.

It is evident that actuality adds nothing to being, beyond a mere relation of our mind, which, comparing the being, as really existing, with its possibility, calls it *actual;* because it is existence in act, in contradistinction to possibility, which is power or potentiality.

Actuality, then, and being or reality are one and the same thing.

Second Principle. Actuality and duration are one and the same thing.

An act or being which does not last, not even one instant, is nothing; because our mind cannot conceive a being to exist, and have no duration whatever. Therefore an act or being necessarily implies duration, and they are therefore one and the same thing.

But it will be remarked: Are there no transitory acts? Do not all philosophers admit the existence of acts which are continually changing?

We answer, What is meant by a transitory act? Does it mean something which is continually changing, so much so that none of its elements has any duration whatever, not even for an instant; or does it mean that the parts or moments, if we may call them so, are in a state of continual transition? In both cases such acts do not and cannot exist.

Before demonstrating this, we observe that it was the ancient Italian school of Elea which, before every other school, raised the problem of transient acts, pointed out the great difficulty which existed in explaining their nature, and demonstrated the impossibility of their existence. To render the demonstration clear, we remark that a transient act may mean either one of two things: an act which is composed of different parts, each in continual transition; or an act which has a beginning, and after a certain duration, also an end. We admit the existence of such acts in the second sense and not in the first. For if an act continually changes, none of the states which it successively assumes have any duration whatever. Otherwise it would no longer be a transient act in the first sense. But that which has no duration at all cannot be considered to exist. Therefore an act really transient cannot exist. What, then, is a transient act? We have seen that it supposes something standing or lasting. But what lasts is immanent, that is, has duration. Therefore a transient act can only be the beginning or end of an immanent act, or, in other words, the beginning or end of duration. To illustrate this doctrine by an example: suppose I wish to draw a line on this paper. If all the points, of which the line is to be composed, were to disappear the very instant I am drawing them, it is evident I should never have a line. Likewise, if all the states, which a transient act assumes, are supposed to have no duration whatever, the act also can have no duration, and hence no existence. A transient act, then, is the beginning or end of an immanent act.

Having laid down the foregoing propositions, we come to the discussion of the pantheistic idea of the infinite.

What, according to Pantheism, is the idea of the infinite? Something the essence of which consists in becoming, in being made, *in fieri*. Now, we reason thus: a being the essence of which lies in becoming means either an act permanent and lasting, capable of changes, or it means something the essential elements of which are continually changing, and have, therefore, no duration whatever. If the last supposition be accepted as describing the pantheistic idea of the infinite, then the infinite is a sheer absurdity, an absolute nonentity. For, in this case, the infinite would be a transient act, in the sense that its essential elements are continually changing, and have no duration whatever. Now such acts are absolutely inconceivable. The mind may put forth its utmost efforts to form an idea of them, yet it will ever be utterly at a loss to conceive anything about them.

Pantheism, on this supposition, would start from absolute nihilism, to build up the existence of everything. On the other hand, if the second supposition be admitted, that the infinite is a permanent being, capable of changes and developments, then it is a transient act in the second sense, that is, the beginning or end of an immanent act; in which case we object to its being self-existing, and insist that it leads to the admission of the idea of the infinite as given by the Catholic Church. We demonstrate this from the ontological idea of immanent and transient acts.

If there be transient acts, there must also be immanent acts, because transient acts are the beginning or end of immanent acts. But no immanent act can be the cause of its end, because no act could be the cause of its cessation; nor can an immanent act be the cause of its own beginning, since in that case it would act before it existed.

It follows, then, that an immanent act cannot be the cause either of its beginning or of its end. But a transient act, that is, the beginning or end of an immanent act, must have a cause, by the principle of causality. If, then, the transient act is not caused by the immanent act, of which it is either the beginning or the end, it must be caused by another immanent act.

Now this immanent act, which causes the transient act, has either itself a beginning, in which case it would be preceded by a transient act, or it has no beginning at all, and consequently can have no end.

If it be caused by a transient act, we should be obliged to admit another immanent act; and, if we do not wish to admit an infinite series of causes, (which would by no means resolve the difficulty, but only increase it,) we must finally stop at an immanent act which has neither beginning nor end.

If it be not caused by a transient act, then we have already what we seek for; an act without beginning nor end.

But, the infinite of the Pantheists, if it be not a mere abstraction, an absolute nonentity, *is* a transient act.

Therefore, it leads to the admission of a purely immanent act. We present the same demonstration in another form, to make it more intelligible.

A transient act is the beginning or cessation of an immanent act.

Now, this beginning or cessation must have a cause, by the principle of causality. What can the cause be? It cannot be the same immanent act, of which the transient act is either the beginning or the end. Because, if the immanent act were the cause of its beginning, it would act before its existence; and if it were the cause of its end, its action would be simultaneous with its destruction or extinction, which is a contradiction in terms. On the other hand, it cannot be a transient act, because this *itself* must have a cause. Nor can it be another immanent act, which has a beginning or end; for in that case it would be a transient act. Therefore, it must be a purely immanent act, without beginning or end. In short, a self-existing transient act, such as the infinite of the Pantheists, is an absurdity, because this denotes an act which gives itself a beginning, or which gives itself an end. This beginning or end must be given it by another. Now, this second is either a purely immanent act, without beginning or end, or it has had a beginning, and may have an end. In the first supposition we have the Catholic idea of God. In the second we may multiply these causes *ad infinitum*, and thus increase *ad infinitum* the necessity of the existence of God to explain those existences.

We pass to the examination of the second leading principle of Pantheism, which is thus expressed. The infinite, by a necessary interior movement, becomes multiple.

How is this to be understood? If the infinite of the Pantheists, by a necessary interior movement, unfolds itself, and becomes multiple, it follows that it is the cause of transient acts. Our mind can attach no other signification to that principle, beyond that of an immanent act, producing transient acts. Now the question arises,

Is this ontologically possible? We insist that it is not, and lay down the following proposition: No being, which moves or unfolds itself, that is, which performs transient acts, can do so by its own unaided energy; but requires the aid of another being, different from itself.

An immanent act which produces a transient one does so either by an eternal act, also immanent, and in that case it cannot be the subject of the transient act produced; or it produces a transient act of which it is the subject—so much so that the transient act is its own act, as, for instance, the act by which a sensitive being feels a new sensation, or the act by which an intelligent being begets a thought, are transient acts, the one of the sensitive principle, the other of the rational being. These transient acts modify the subject which produces them, and effect a change in it.

Now, in the first case, if an immanent act which produces transient acts is eternal in duration, these cannot terminate in the subject, by the supposition. For, if the transient act were laid inside the permanent act, it would be its cessation, and in that case the act would no longer be eternal according to the supposition.

In the second place, if an immanent act becomes the subject of transient acts, or, in other words, modifies itself, a sufficient reason must be given, a cause of such modification, by the principle of causality. Why does it modify itself? What is the cause of such a change? The being or subject, or immanent act, does not contain the sufficient cause of the modification or change; because if it contained it, the act produced would be permanent, and not transient, that is, it would have always been in the immanent act. For it is a principle of ontology of immediate evidence that, given the *full* cause, the effect follows. Now the immanent act in question *was* before the transient act existed; therefore, the immanent act is not full and sufficient cause of the transient act which modifies it. If it is not the full and sufficient cause of its modification, it cannot modify itself without the aid of an exterior being. Now, this exterior being cannot be supposed to be of the same nature with the act in question, otherwise it would itself require aid. Therefore, it must be a being which does it by an eternal immanent act; and that Being is the *Infinite* of Catholic philosophy.

Applying this demonstration to the second principle of Pantheism, that the infinite, by a necessary interior movement, unfolds and develops itself, or modifies itself, it is evident that this second principle, like the first, is ontologically impossible; that the infinite must either be purely, simply, and eternally actual, or it cannot develop itself without the aid of another being of a different nature; consequently that the second Pantheistic principle is nothing else but the idea of finite being perfecting itself by the aid of the Infinite of Catholic philosophy.

In order that this conclusion may appear more evident, we subjoin another argument, more adapted to the comprehension of most readers.

According to the pantheistic hypothesis, the infinite, by a necessary interior action, is forced to expand, to develop itself. Now, we want to show that this it cannot do by its unaided energy. We prove it thus: This action of the infinite is a movement; we make use of the word movement in its widest signification, as meaning any action whatever. Now, this movement either existed always in the infinite or it had a beginning. In the system of the Pantheists it has a beginning because they hold that the infinite successively assumes different forms. There was then a time in which it did not move. Then the infinite had only the power, and not the act of moving; and when it *did* move, it passed from the power to the act.

It will not do for the Pantheist to endeavor to avoid this conclusion by saying that the movement of the infinite is eternal. Conceding that the movement is eternal, we ask, is the action only one, or is it multiple? In other words, is the full intensity of its energy concentrated in one movement, or is it divided? The Pantheist cannot, in force of his system, admit that the whole intensity of its energy is concentrated in a single movement; otherwise, the successive unfoldings were impossible; the unfolding would be instantaneous, and not successive.

The infinite, then, in its successive unfoldings, passes from the power to the act. Now, it is an ontological principle, as evident as any axiom of Euclid, that no being can pass from the power to the act, from quiet to movement, but by the aid of another being already in act. For power is, in relation to action, as rest is to movement. If the being is in rest, it cannot be in movement; if, on the contrary, it is in movement, it cannot be in rest. Likewise, if the being is supposed to act, it cannot, at the same time, be supposed to be in potentiality. A being in power and action, with regard to the same effects, is as much a contradiction as a being in rest and motion at the same time. To make this more intelligible, let us take an instance. Suppose the seed of a tree, say of a lemon: this seed is in potentiality to become a lemon. But it could never of itself become a lemon; because, if it could, it were already a lemon; it were a lemon, not in power only, but in act. To become a lemon it must be buried in the earth, it must go through the whole process of vegetation, and assimilate to itself whatever it needs from the earth and the air and the sun; and not until then can it be the fruit-tree we call lemon.

No being, then, can pass from the power to the

act, except by the aid of another being which is in act. Now, the infinite of the Pantheist is continually passing from the power to the act; from being indefinite and indeterminate, it becomes limited and determinate. Therefore it cannot do so but by the agency of another being, which is all action and no potentiality.

This being is God.

We have examined the first principles of Pantheism with regard to the infinite, and we have seen that a being the essence of which lies in being made, in becoming, either means something the essential elements of which are continually changing, so much so as to have no duration whatever, or it means a being which has a beginning and may have an end. In the first case, the infinite of the Pantheist would be a mere absurdity, a pure abstraction. In the second, it expresses nothing else but the idea of a finite being, and leads to the existence of a purely immanent being or act. Proceeding to discuss the second principle of Pantheism, that the infinite, by a necessary, interior movement, unfolds itself, we have demonstrated that this is impossible; that, granting the possibility of the infinite unfolding itself successively, this it could never do by its own unaided energy, but requires the help of another being. That, consequently, the second principle of the Pantheists leads also to the idea of God as proposed by the Catholic Church.

As a corollary following from the whole discussion, we draw the conclusion that the infinite is utterly inconceivable, unless it is supposed to be most perfect, most finished reality, if we may speak thus; that it is altogether absurd, unless it is supposed to be pure actuality, without the least mixture of potentiality; in a word, pure, simple action itself; in the language of the schoolmen, *actus purissimus*.

The discussion of the pantheistic idea of the infinite has led us to the main idea of the infinite as it is given by Catholic philosophy. We shall now proceed to fill up this idea and develop it to its utmost conclusions, so as to give an exact and full exposition of the doctrine of the infinite, as proposed by Catholic philosophy. The result of our discussion has been that the Infinite, or God, is action itself; or, in other words, pure actuality, an immanent act without beginning or end. Upon this we shall build the whole construction of the essential attributes and perfections of God, and admire how consistent, how logical, how sublime, is the Catholic idea of the Infinite.

I.

GOD IS NECESSARY BEING.

Necessary being is that the essence of which is one and the same thing with its existence; and, *vice versa*, the existence of which is one and the same thing with the essence, so much so that the idea of the one implies the idea of the other.

But God's essence is to be; for we have seen that he is actuality or reality itself. Therefore, God is necessary or self-existing being.

Hence the sublime definition he gave of himself to Moses: "*I am* WHO *am. He who is* sent me to you."

II.

GOD IS ETERNAL.

Eternity is duration without success or change; *duratio tota simul*, as the schoolmen would say. Hence it excludes the idea either of beginning or end. But duration and actuality are one and the same thing. Therefore actuality itself is duration itself; that is to say, duration without succession or change.

Now, God is actuality itself. Therefore he is eternal.

III.

GOD IS IMMUTABLE.

Immutability is life without succession or change; or, in other words, life without beginning or end, and without being subject to modifications. Now life is action. Action then, without succession or change, is immutability.

God is action itself. Therefore God is immutable.

IV.

GOD IS INFINITE.

Infinity is being itself with the exclusion of limits, that is, of not being; or, to express ourselves more intelligibly, it is being or perfection in its utmost and supremest actuality, excluding the possibility of any successive actualization, for the reason of its being already all possible actualization. Human language is so imperfect and so inadequate that, even in our efforts to avoid in the definition of the infinite all idea of succession or development, we are forced to make use of words which seem to suppose it. Those who are trained to think logically will grasp the idea without much effort; for the *being itself*, to the exclusion of not being or limitation, sufficiently and adequately define the infinite. Now, God, as action itself, is being itself.

Therefore, God is infinite.

V.

GOD IS IMMENSE.

Immensity is the presence of the whole being of God in his action.

This definition of immensity, being somewhat different in words from that commonly given by metaphysicians, requires explanation. Let the reader, then, pay particular attention to the following remarks.

Ubiquity implies residence of *being* in space, both spiritual and material. By spiritual space we mean the existence of different created spirits and nothing more.

By material space we mean the extension of matter.

That God can act on or reside in spiritual beings does not involve any difficulty.

But how can he reside in material space, space properly so called?

It is evident that a spiritual being cannot dwell in space by a contact of extension, since spiritual being is the very opposite of extension.

Therefore, a spiritual being can only dwell in space by acting on it.

The presence of the whole being of God in the action by which he creates, sustains, and acts in spiritual and material space, is ubiquity.

Immensity is the presence of the whole being of God in his action. The difference between the two lies in this; that ubiquity implies a relation to created objects, whereas immensity implies no such relation. We say, then, the presence of the *whole being* of God in his action, because God is pure actuality, action itself. If, therefore, in his action we did not suppose the presence of his whole being, we should establish a division in God; that is, we should suppose his being and his action to be distinct, which they are not, and this distinction would imply a development in

God, which is contrary to his being action or actuality itself.

It will easily be remarked that immensity is an attribute which flows immediately from the idea of God being actuality itself. We may therefore conclude that he is immense.

VI.
GOD IS ABSOLUTE SIMPLICITY.

Absolute simplicity, in its negative aspect, implies the absence of all possible composition or distinction in a being; the distinction, for instance, of essence and existence, of faculties and attributes.

Now, God is pure actuality, and this excludes all idea of such distinctions. Therefore, God is simplicity itself.

VII.
GOD IS ONE.

God is a necessary being, eternal, immutable, infinite, immense, all of which are sides of one idea—that of pure actuality.

Now, such a being can be but one, as is evident to every mind which understands the terms. God is therefore one.

Before we leave this part of the subject, let us compare both the pantheistic and the Catholic ideas of *God*, so that, when brought together face to face, they may appear in a better and more distinct light.

God, according to the Pantheists, is an eternal, self-existing *something*, devoid of all determination or limit, of all individuality, of all consciousness, of all personality, of all shape or form.

When well examined, the principle of the Pantheists presents no other idea to the mind than that of possibility, a kind of self-existent possibility, if we may bring together two terms which exclude each other.

Starting from this possibility, the Pantheists make it acquire determination, concreteness, consciousness, personality, by supposing an interior necessary force of development.

The Catholic idea of God is the very opposite of the pantheistic.

For, whereas they make God a possibility, something that is becoming, to be made; the Catholic Church exhibits him as reality, actuality, being itself. It is careful to eliminate from him the least idea of potentiality or possibility, of becoming something, or of being subject to development or perfection; because it insists that God is all reality, perfectly and absolutely actual. Any idea of further perfection is not only to be excluded from him, but cannot even be conceived; for the simple reason that he is all perfection, absolute, eternal perfection.

That this is the only reasonable idea of God is evident to every mind which is capable of understanding the terms. For happily it does not require a long and difficult demonstration to prove the falsehood and absurdity of the pantheistic, and the truth of the Catholic, idea of God. The understanding of the terms is quite sufficient.

Whoever says possibility, excludes, by the very force of the term, existence and reality. A self-existent possibility is a contradiction in terms; for possibility excludes existence, and self-existence implies it necessarily.

An eternal possibility is also a contradiction in terms; for eternity excludes all succession or mutation, and possibility implies it. An infinite possibility is yet more absurd; because infinite means absolute reality and actuality; possibility, on the contrary, implies only power of being.

But, on the contrary, how logical, how consistent, how grand, and how conformable to all ontological principles is the idea of God held by the Catholic Church! God is absolute, pure, unmixed actuality and reality. Therefore he is self-existing being itself; therefore he is eternal, because pure actuality is at the same time pure duration; therefore he is immutable, since pure actuality excludes all change and development; therefore he is infinite, because he is being itself, the essential being, *the* being; therefore he is simplicity itself, because a distinction would imply a composition, and all composition is rejected by actuality most pure, so to speak, unalloyed, unmixed.

The God of the Pantheist is a nullity, a negation; the God of the Catholic Church is really the Infinite. He is in himself whatever is real and actual in spirit, whatever is real and positive in matter, whatever is real and positive in the essence of all creatures. But he has all the reality of spirit without its limitation; all the reality of matter without its limitation; all the reality of all creatures without their limitation. All this reality in him is not such and such a reality; but he is all reality, pure, unmixed reality, without limit and without distinction.

What leads the Pantheists into the admission of their principle is a false, wrong idea of the infinite. They suppose, and suppose rightly, that the infinite must contain all reality; and seeing around them such a multitude of different beings or creatures, each one with its particular difference and individualization, they ask themselves the question, How can all these differences be concentrated in one being?—the infinite—and in endeavoring to resolve it they admit a first something undefined, indeterminate, which assumes gradually all these different forms.

What is this but a very material and vulgar idea of the infinite? That it was the idea of the first who began to philosophize is intelligible. But that modern philosophers should have no higher comprehension of the infinite, that they should not conceive how the infinite can be all reality, in its being without distinction, composition, change, or succession, is quite inconceivable; and is much less than we should expect from men boasting so loudly of their enlightenment.

Let them hear a Catholic philosopher of the middle ages upon the subject. After having demonstrated that whatever is real in the creature is to be found in God as the infinite and most perfect, he proposes the other question, How can all these perfections be found in God? and he answers, that they are necessarily to be found in God, but in a most simple manner, as one and single perfection. We subjoin his words:

"From what we have said, it evidently follows that the perfections of creatures are essentially unified in God. For we have shown that God is simple. Now, where there is simplicity there cannot be found diversity in the interior of the being. If, then, all the perfections of creatures are to be found in the infinite, it is impossible that they could be there with their differences. It follows, then, that they must be in him as ONE.

"This becomes evident, if we reflect upon what takes place in the faculties of comprehension. For a superior power grasps, by one and the same act of comprehension, all those things known, under different points of view, by inferior powers. In fact, the intelligence judges, by a unique and simple act, all the perceptions of sight, of hearing, and of the other senses. The same occurs in sciences: although inferior sciences are various in virtue of their different objects, there is, however, in them all a superior science which embraces all, and which is called transcendental philosophy. The same thing happens with relation to authority. For in the royal authority, which is one, are included all the other subordinate authorities, which are divided for the government of the kingdom. It is thus necessary that the perfections of inferior creatures, which are multiplied according to the difference of beings, be found together as one, in the principle of all things—God!"*

---

* St. Thomas's *Compendium Theologiæ*, cap. 22.

CHAPTER III.

THE PROBLEM OF MULTIPLICITY.

IN the development of the Catholic idea of God, which we have given in the previous chapter, we have met with no opposition from Pantheism.

Here, however, it raises the most difficult as well as the most sublime and profound question which can be proposed to human intelligence— the problem of multiplicity. We shall let a Pantheist propose it in his own words.

It will be remembered that the last of the attributes, which we vindicated as belonging to the infinite, was that of absolute unity. This attribute gives rise to the problem.

"What is unity," says Cousin, "taken by itself? A unity indivisible, a dead unity, a unity which, resting in the depths of its absolute existence, and never developing itself, is, for itself, as if it were not. In the same manner, what is variety without unity? A variety which, not being referable to a unity, can never form a totality, or any collection whatever, is a series of indefinite quantities, of each of which one cannot say that it is itself and not another, for this would suppose that it is one; that is, it would suppose the idea of unity; so that, without unity, variety also is as if it were not. Behold what variety or unity isolated would produce; the one is necessary to the other in order to exist with true existence; with that existence, which is neither multiple, various, mobile, or negative existence; nor that absolute, eternal, infinite existence, which is, as it were, the negation of existence. Every true existence, every reality, is in the union of these two elements; although, essentially, the one may be superior and anterior to the other. You cannot separate variety from unity, nor unity from variety; they necessarily coexist. But how do they coexist? Unity is anterior to multiplicity; how, then, has unity been able to admit multiplicity?"*

Again: " Reason, in whatever way it may occupy itself, can conceive nothing, except under the condition of two ideas, which preside over the exercise of its activity; the idea of the unit, and the idea of the multiple; of the finite and the infinite; of being and of appearing; of substance and of phenomenon; of absolute cause and of secondary causes; of the absolute and of the relative; of the necessary and of the contin-

---
* Cousin's *History of Modern Philosophy.*

gent; of immensity and of space; of eternity and of time.

"Analysis, in bringing together all these propositions, in bringing together, for example, all their first terms, identifies them; it equally identifies all the second terms, so that, of all these propositions compared and combined, it forms a single proposition, a single formula, which is the formula itself of thought, and which you can express, according to the case, by the unit and by the multiple, the absolute being and the relative being, unity and variety, etc. Finally, the two terms of this formula, so comprehensive, do not constitute a dualism in which the first term is on one side, the second on the other, without any other relation than that of being perceived at the same time by reason. The relation concerning them is quite otherwise essential, unity being eternity, etc.; the first term of the formula is cause also, and absolute cause; and, so far as absolute cause, it cannot avoid developing itself in the second term, multiplicity, the finite and the relative.

"The result of all this is, that the two terms, as well as the relation of generation which draws the second from the first, and which, without cessation, refers to it, are the three integral elements of reason. It is not in the power of reason, in its boldest abstractions, to separate any one of these three terms from the others. Try to take away unity, and variety alone is no longer susceptible of addition—it is even no longer comprehensible; or, try to take away variety, and you have an immovable unity—a unity which does not make itself manifest, and which, of itself, is not a thought; all thought expressing itself in a proposition, and a single term not sufficing for a proposition; in short, take away the relation which intimately connects variety and unity, and you destroy the necessary tie of the two terms of every proposition. We may then regard it as an incontestable point, that these three terms are distinct but inseparable, and that they constitute at the same time a triplicity and an indivisible unity." *

As the reader may have observed, Cousin raises the problem of multiplicity. He expresses it under a logical form, but the problem is a metaphysical one, and hence applicable to all orders, logical as well as ontological. It is raised by all Pantheists, whose words we abstain from quoting for brevity's sake; and, so far as the problem itself is concerned, it is a legitimate one; and every one, who has thought deeply on these matters, and is not satisfied with merely looking at the surface of things, must accept it.

Let us put it in its clearest light. The infinite, considered merely as unity, actuality, (all words which mean the same thing,) can be known nei-

---
* Lecture Fifth.

ther to itself nor to any other intelligence. It cannot be known to itself. For to know implies thought, and thought is absolutely impossible without a duality of knowing and of being known, of subject and of object. It implies an intelligence, an object, and a relation between the two. If, then, there is no multiplicity in the infinite, it cannot know itself. It is, for itself, as if it were not; for what is a being which cannot know itself?

Nor can it be known to any other intelligence; for mere existence, pure unity does not convey any idea necessary to satisfy the intelligence.

Moreover, the mere existence and unity of an object does not make it, on that account, intelligible. For an object to be intelligible, it is required that it should be able to act on the intelligence, such being the condition of intelligibility.*
Now, action implies already a multiplicity, a subject and the action. Therefore, if the infinite were mere pure unity, it could not be intelligible to any intelligence. But, in the supposition that there *is* a kind of multiplicity in the infinite, how would multiplicity be reconciled with unity? How would these two terms agree?

Multiplicity seems to be a necessary condition of the infinite, without which it would not be intelligible either to itself or to others. Absolute unity seems also to be a necessary attribute of

---

* See *Balmes' Fundamental Philosophy*, on Intelligibility.

the infinite, and yet these two necessary conditions seem to exclude each other. How, then, must we bring them together?

This is the problem to be solved; the grandest and most sublime problem of philosophy; which has occupied every school of philosophy since man began to turn his mind to philosophical researches.

The two great antagonists, Pantheism and Catholicity, give an answer to the problem, and it is the province of this chapter to discuss the two solutions, and see which of them can stand the test of logic, and really answer the problem instead of destroying it. We shall enter upon the discussion, after premising a few remarks necessary to the right understanding of the discussion.

The first remark which we shall make is to call the attention of the reader to the absolute necessity for the existence of the problem.

It is not Pantheism, nor Catholicity, which arbitrarily raises the problem; it exists in the very essence of being, in the very essence of intelligibility. Those philosophers who cannot see it may have taken a cursory glance over some pages of what purports to be philosophy, but they never understood a word of that which really deserves the name of that sublime science. We make this remark for two different reasons: First, in order to close the door to all the objections raised against the problem. For if it is demonstrated that a multiplicity is required in the infinite, then to raise objections against it only shows want of philosophic depth, but does not prove anything against the existence of the problem. We shall return to this subject. The second reason is a consequence of the first, to wit, that should we find that the answer to the problem is not as clear and evident as we might desire, we must not, on that account, reject the problem, but should be satisfied with the light that is afforded. This is but reasonable. Deny the problem we cannot. It follows, then, that we must be satisfied with an answer which, whilst it saves the problem, throws as much light on it as is possible, under the circumstances.

PANTHEISTIC SOLUTION OF THE PROBLEM OF MULTIPLICITY AND UNITY IN THE INFINITE.

Pantheism arrives at infinite unity by eliminating from it all possible determination, definition, reality, ideality, thought, will, consciousness; and rising from abstraction to abstraction, from elimination to elimination, from a more limited indefiniteness to a higher and broader and less restricted one, up to mere simple, unalloyed abstraction and unity.

All Pantheists follow the same process in order to arrive at unity. Cousin calls it dead, immovable, inconceivable; a thing existing as if it were not; the Being—Unreality of Hegel. But ascended to such a summit, all multiplicity eliminated, and pure unalloyed unity once found, how is multiplicity to be reconstructed? With the greatest ease in the world. Pantheists make this Being—nothing unfold and develop itself like a silkworm; alleging, as a reason for such development, an intrinsic necessity of nature, an imperative instinct which broods in its bosom.

Thus they reconstruct multiplicity by making the Infinite become finite, cosmos, matter, spirit, humanity, etc. Let us hear Cousin: "This is the fundamental vice of ancient and modern theories; they place unity on one side, and multiplicity on the other; the infinite and the finite in such an opposition that the passage from one to the other seems impossible."

And, after having remarked that this was the error of the school of Elea, he continues: "Immensity or unity of space, eternity or unity of time, unity of numbers, unity of perfection, the ideal of all beauty, the Infinite, the absolute substance, being itself, is a cause also, not a relative, contingent, finite cause, but an absolute cause. Now, being an absolute cause, it cannot avoid passing into action. If being, in itself alone, is given as absolute substance without causality, the world is impossible; but if being in itself is also a cause and an absolute cause, movement and the world naturally follow. The true absolute is not pure being in itself; it is power and cause taken absolutely, and, in *developing* itself, produces all that you see around you."

We quote Cousin in preference to others on account of his lucidity of style and expressions; but every one acquainted with the systems of the German Pantheists knows that their answer to the problem of multiplicity is substantially the same. We refer the reader, in confirmation of our assertion, to the excellent lectures on the systems of the German Pantheists, of Heinrich Moritz Chalybäus, professor at the University of Kiel.

Now, does the answer resolve the problem? Does it really conciliate unity with multiplicity in the Infinite? Does it really maintain intact the two terms of the problem? We think that it does not, and maintain that it destroys both terms of the problem.

The leading idea and principle of Pantheism is that unity is *becoming* multiplicity.

It is an existence in a continual *ex-sistere* in an emergence and manifestation.*

Now, who can fail to perceive that if unity is such, that is, unity when it is merely potential, when it has only the power of becoming, of passing into multiplicity, it is doubtless destroyed as soon as it passes from the power into the act; or, in other words, it is destroyed as unity when it becomes multiplicity? Strip this idea of a potential unity becoming actual multiplicity, strip

---
* Chalybäus' Lectures, etc.

it of all the logical phantasmagoria with which it has been adorned, especially by Pantheists of the German school, which phantasmagoria can only impose upon the simple, and you can see, as clearly as that two and two make four, that the whole thing amounts to nothing but to this: that unity vanishes as soon as it becomes multiplicity. It is with a special intention that we have made use of the simile of the silkworm. This poor creature too, like the unity of the Pantheists, has an instinct given it by God, of unfolding and developing itself, and the effect of its operation is the silk which serves to set off the beauty of man. But unfortunately, the process of development exhausts the little creature; for when it is completed, the poor creature dies, and its development is its death, and its production is its shroud; yet, it has this advantage over the unity of the Pantheists, that its remains continue to exist, whereas their unity evaporates completely in multiplicity. To speak more seriously, it is perfectly evident to every mind, that the answer of the Pantheists destroys the very problem it undertakes to solve. Unity is unity so long as it is a potency, a power of becoming; it vanishes as soon as it becomes multiplicity. Add to this, that their unity, to be infinite, must remain undefined, potential, and in the possibility of becoming; such being their idea of the Infinite For which reason they eliminate from it every limitation, all individuality, all thought, all consciousness. The natural consequence of this principle must be that it remains infinite so long as it is wrapped up in its vagueness and indefiniteness. Let it come forth from its indefiniteness, let it become definite, limited, concrete, and its infinity together with its unity is gone. It evaporates in the finite forms it assumes. On the other hand, let it remain absorbed in its indefiniteness, in its abstractiveness, and consequently, in its infinity, and multiplicity can no longer be conceived. It is absurd then to speak of multiplicity in the Infinite of the Pantheists, since it is clear that, when it assumes multiplicity, it can no longer be either infinite or one; and when it remains infinite it cannot be conceived as multiple. All this we have said, conceding the premises of Pantheism. But we have, in the first article, demonstrated the following principles: 1st. If the Pantheists take their unity in the sense of a pure abstraction, a transient act, the elements of which do not last one single instant, it is in that case an absolute nonentity, an utter unreality, and then it is useless to speak of multiplicity, since *ex nihilo nihil fit*.

2d. Or, they suppose their unity as something really existing, having the power of gradual development, and in that case we have demonstrated that such a being could not develop itself without the aid of a foreign being.

The premises of Pantheism then being false, the solution of the problem falls to the ground independently of its intrinsic value, if it have any, which we have shown it has not.

Pantheism cannot answer the problem of multiplicity. How can we then attain to its solution?

We answer: the Catholic Church resolves it, giving such an explanation of it as the finite and limited intellect of man may reasonably expect. For the Catholic Church does not pretend to give such a solution of the problem as to enable us thoroughly to understand it. She proceeds from two premises, to wit, that God is infinite, and that man, necessarily distinct from God, is finite, and therefore endowed only with finite intelligence. That these premises are true, appears evident from the demonstration we have already given, in which we have shown that the pantheistic idea of the infinite is the idea of finite being when it is not taken as meaning only an abstraction, a pure mathematical point. The ideas of the infinite and the finite exist, and therefore there must be also objects corresponding to these ideas. We shall return to this subject in a following chapter.

From these two ideas of the finite and the Infinite, it follows that man can never comprehend God; or, in other words, that the intelligence of man, with the relation to God as its object, must find mysteries or truths above and beyond its capacity. For, as it is absurd to shut up a body of large size in a body of much more limited size, supposing the present conditions of bodies not suspended, so it is absurd to suppose that the intellect of man, limited and finite, could grasp or take in God, who is infinite. We are aware of the opposition which is made by many to mysteries or super-intelligible truths; but we insist upon it, that all such opposition would vanish, if men would study philosophy more deeply and more assiduously. Why, a real philosopher, one who has sounded the depths of creation, and plunged into the profundity of the great ideas of being, of substance, of the absolute, of the infinite, the finite and the relative, into the ideas of eternity, of immensity, of immutability, of space and time, into the ideas of cause, of action, of movement; one who has entered into the labyrinth of his soul, and tried to catch the flying phenomena of its life, and to analyze all the fibres of its consciousness; such a one meets, at every step, with mysteries, and the more he digs into them, the profounder and the wider is the abyss lying at his feet. If we should meet with a man denying mysteries, and desirous to engage in a discussion, we would beg of him to go and first study the alphabet of philosophy.

The problem, then, proposing the reconciliation of unity with multiplicity in the Infinite, is held by the Catholic Church as a mystery, a truth which cannot be thoroughly understood by the human mind. But, notwithstanding all this, the solution which Catholic doctrine affords, though a mystery, is clear enough to be perceived, and distinct enough to make us see through the agreement of the two terms of the problem; so that, through the help of the Catholic Church, we shall have all the light thrown upon the problem in question which man may reasonably expect, seeing that the object of the problem is the Infinite, and the intellect apprehending it only limited and finite.

CHAPTER IV.

THE BLESSED TRINITY, OR MULTIPLICITY IN THE INFINITE.

GENERAL IDEA OF THE BLESSED TRINITY.

CATHOLIC doctrine admits that the most pure, simple, and undivided unity of the Godhead lies in its nature; but that this most simple nature is terminated by three real, distinct subsistences or persons, who form the only true and living Infinite. How this answer affords the solution of the problem will be seen in the course of this treatise, in which we shall endeavor to develop the idea of the Church in a scientific form. But, before we proceed to analyze it, we feel obliged to develop it in a cursory manner, in order to enable the reader to follow us in the analysis to which it will be subjected.

We say, then, that the essence of God, absolutely simple, is terminated by three real, distinct, opposite subsistences, which are a primary unbegotten activity, a begotten unintelligibility, an aspired goodness; all three in a state of personality. For this primary, unborn activity in the state of personality, in whom the whole Godhead resides, by understanding himself, begets a most faithful conception of himself, an intellectual utterance, a word or *logos*. Now, the nature or essence of intellectual conception or logos, consists in being the object conceived in the state of intelligibility. It follows, then, that the conception of the primary activity, in whom the fulness of the Godhead resides, is, in consequence, the Godhead itself in the state of intelligibility, whilst the conceiver is the Godhead itself, in the state of intelligent activity. Under this last *aspect*, to wit, of intelligent activity and of intelligibility, the conceiver and the conception are necessarily related to each other; a relation which arises from an opposition of origin, since the conceiver, as such, originating the conception, is necessarily opposed to it, and the conception, as such, by being conceived, is necessarily opposed to the conceiver. In this sense they are necessarily distinct from each other. It follows from this that each one has a concreteness of his own, a termination or a state, by whatever name it may be called; which concreteness is incommunicable to the other, and hence each one has the ownership of himself, and therefore is a person. For the first is the whole Godhead under the termination of unborn intellectual activity, which termination is strictly his own and incommunicable. The second is the fulness of the Godhead, under the termination of intelligibility or conception, which belongs to him alone, and is likewise incommunicable. But because in both resides the whole identical Godhead, though under a distinct, opposite, and relative termination, they are both one and the same God.

God conceiver and God conceived are, then, in nature and essence, one and the same; whilst as the conceiver and the conceived, they are two distinct persons; and in this sense, there is a necessary duality in the infinite. This duality is brought into harmony and unity by the production of a third termination, the Holy Ghost. The conceiver and the conceived necessarily love each other. This is the result of a metaphysical law of the act of intelligence, including subject and object; since to intelligence an object produces an inclination or attraction in the subject toward it. Now the two persons in the Godhead intelligence each other; therefore they love each other. It is, again, the nature of love that the object loved should abide in the subject loving, in a state of feeling or an actively attractive state, a state which human language cannot utter. The best expression we can find is, that the object should abide in the subject in the capacity of beatifying it. The Godhead, under the termination of conceiver, loves the Godhead under the termination of conceived; and, *vice versa*, the Godhead, under the termination of conceived, loves the Godhead under the termination of conceiver. The result of this operation is a third termination of the Godhead—the Godhead under the termination of love, goodness, or bliss, proceeding from the other two terminations, the conceiver and the conceived. This new termination being distinct from the two former, and opposed to them, inasmuch as it originates from them, is consequently its own, incommunicable to the others, and hence a person. But as it is the same identical Godhead, under the termination of love, the three are but one and the same God. Without these terminations of triplicity in the Infinite, God cannot exist or live. For what is a being without the knowledge of himself and without love? What is life but action? and action without a term originated is a contradiction in terms. The Godhead must, then, intelligence and love himself. The result of this are three terminations in the Godhead; a primary, unbegotten activity, a begotten intelligibility, an aspired goodness. That these three terminations do not break the unity of the Infinite will be manifest from the analysis to which we shall subject them.

We shall now proceed to vindicate the personality of the three terminations against a class of disguised Pantheists—disguised even to themselves—that is, the Unitarians.

Why should these three terminations in the Godhead be persons? Could not the Godhead understand and love itself without supposing three personalities?

We answer that without the admission of three persons in the Godhead, we should necessarily fall into the Pantheistic theory concerning God.

The Unitarians will concede to us that God must understand and love himself. Without this he were inconceivable. Now, we beg the Unitarians to tell us what this intelligence and love are? Are they only passing and transient acts or modifications, or are they faculties and attributes? What are they?

Besides essence and nature, which includes substance, our minds cannot conceive any other categories than the following:

1st. Attributes or perfections.

2d. Faculties.

3d. Acts of the faculties or modifications.

4th. Subsistence and personality.

Now, excluding subsistence and personality, the understanding and love of the Godhead must be either an attribute or faculty, or a transient act, or both of these together.

The Unitarians may demur at so many distinctions; but we would beg them to observe that when we see the most sacred dogmas, nay, the very pivot of knowledge, attacked by a flimsy and proud philosophy, we have a right to descend into the depths of science, and ask of the flimsy and boastful philosophy what it means when it attacks so sweepingly and so confidently. This remark has been forced from us by reading the following words of Channing: "We believe in the doctrine of God's unity, or that there is one God, one only. To this truth we give infinite importance, and we feel ourselves bound to take heed lest any man spoil us of it by vain (?) philosophy. This proposition, that there is one God, seems to us exceedingly plain. We understand by it that there is one being, one mind, one person, one intelligent agent, and one only, to whom underived and infinite perfections and dominion belong. We conceive that these words could have conveyed no other meaning to the simple and uncultivated people, who were set apart to be the depositories of this great truth, and who were utterly incapable of understanding those hair-breadth distinctions between being and person, which the sagacity of other ages has discovered."

We have read very few passages of other authors in which we find as much magisterial tone, sweeping assertion, profound ignorance of true philosophy, confusion worse confounded, as in these few lines of Channing.

Is it possible that Dr. Channing should call a hair-breadth distinction, that which lies between essence and nature, and personality? We suspect that the distinction between these terms being so nice, Dr. Channing never apprehended it; and without this elementary apprehension of the most fundamental notions of ontology, Dr. Channing should have kept his peace, and never have written a book touching mysteries, held and defended even unto death by thousands of the sublimest, the profoundest, and the most universal geniuses of Christianity; such men as S. Athanasius, S. Justin, S. Irenæus, S. Hilary, S. Augustine, S. Ambrose, S. Chrysostom, S. Jerome, S. Fulgentius, S. Thomas, Bossuet, Fénélon, Pascal, Leibnitz, etc. Before the testimony of such intellects, even the self-assurance of Dr. Channing should have hesitated. Dr. Channing, then, along with all those who hold his opinion, will be kind enough to tell us what they mean by God being one mind, one person, one intelligent agent. Are these things attributes, faculties, or acts? Let us define the terms, that the distinction which exists between them may be more manifest. An attribute or perfection is a partial conception of our minds, of a certain nature, and more particularly of the Infinite. The idea of the infinite implies all perfections. But as our limited minds cannot apprehend all that is contained in that idea at one intellectual glance, we are forced to apprehend it partially, and to divide it mentally, and to consider each side apart. The ideas or notions corresponding to all these apprehensions of the infinite, we call perfections or attributes. But let it be distinctly understood; ontologically, that is, in the order of reality, they do not exist out of, and are not distinct from, the essence of the Infinite. A faculty is the capacity of development in a being. An act is the transition from capacity into movement. Now, before we close with the Unitarians, we shall give the definition of individuality and personality as carefully and intelligibly as we can.

The last termination or complement of a being which makes it a unit, *in se*, separated or at least distinct from all other beings, which makes it *sui juris* and incommunicable to all others, constitutes what ontology calls individuality. To illustrate this definition, let us suppose our body in the two different states to which it is subject, when it is united to our soul, and when it is separated from it. It is evident that when my body is yet united to the soul, it is a corporal substance, but not an individuality, because it has none of those elements necessary to constitute individuality. It is not a unit *in se*, neither is it separated from any other being, because it is united to the soul, and hence it is communicable; and above all, it is not *sui juris*, since the soul possesses it as its most intimate and most subordinate organ and instrument. Let us take the other state of our body, when the soul has left it.

By this very fact, the body becomes an individuality, that is to say, a unit *in se*, distinct and separated from any other being, *sui juris*, and incommunicable. So true is this, that should that body in such a state, undergo any change, or do what we might improperly call an action, that change or action would be attributed to it, and to it alone.

For instance, suppose that body should fall and crush by its weight some living creature, we should say that body has killed that creature, because it *is* an individuality; whereas, suppose that same body, possessed of the soul, falling at night out bed, should kill by its weight that living creature, we could no longer say that body has killed, but we should say that man fell last night out of his bed, and killed, for instance, his child; because the union of the body with the soul as its most intimate organ, deprives it of its individuality, and consequently of solidarity.

Personality adds to individuality the element of intelligence, and consequently of self-consciousness.

A person, therefore, is a subtance, possessed of intelligence and self-consciousness, forming a unit *in se*, and hence being distinct from all others, having the ownership of himself, *sui juris*, and being the principle of imputability for all his actions.

If these notions, on which depend the whole field of ontology, which are the foundation of morality, of all social and political rights of man, on which the very bliss and ultimate perfection of man rest—if such notions are hair-breadth distinctions, we thank God that we are endowed with intelligence enough to apprehend them; else were a man to-morrow to force us into slavery, on the plea that we were only things, and not persons, we should be at a loss how to stop him, not being able, like Channing, to apprehend our own personsality, that supreme gift which makes us feel master and owner of ourselves and accountable for our actions.

Having premised these notions, we say the Unitarians, who grant that the Infinite is endowed with intelligence and will, must admit one of these three things: either the intelligence and will are perfections or attributes, or they are faculties, or they are persons. If they admit them to be perfections, they divide the Infinite; if they admit them to be faculties, they fall into Pantheism.

That is what we are going to prove in the following propositions.

First proposition: If intelligence and will were admitted to be mere perfections in God, the admission would imply a division in God and a breaking up of the Infinite.

Before we proceed to prove this proposition,

we premise that in the argument we take intelligence and will in action, and not in potentiality; in other words, we take them as acts, and not as faculties.

The reason is because, as we shall prove, there can be no faculties or potentiality in the Infinite. This premised, we lay down the undoubted ontological truth that between intelligence in act and the conception or interior *logos*, the result of intelligencing, there is and must be a real distinction. In other words, the intellect in act and the conception of the intellect necessarily imply a duality.

The reason of this is evident. First, because between the intellect in action and conception there is necessarily an opposition. The intellect in act, is such, inasmuch as it is not conception, and *vice versa*. Now, a real opposition implies, necessarily, a real distinction. Again, the conception or interior *logos* is to the intellect in action as the effect is to its cause, or, better, as the consequence is to its principle.

If, therefore, there were no real distinction between the intellect and the conception, there would be no real distinction between the effect and its cause, the principle and its consequence. Hence, thinking and thought are necessarily distinct. What is true of the act of thinking and of thought is true of the will and its *volition*, for the same reason. Hence it is evident that the intel lect in action, thought or the conception, the will in action and its volition, are necessarily distinct by their very ontological nature and relation. It follows, then, that if we admit them to be mere perfections of the Infinite, we would imply a real distinction in the essence of Infinite, in other words, a duality of essence; because a perfection in the Infinite is identical with essence, since we have said that perfections have no real existence *in re*, and are only partial conceptions of our minds, which cannot take in the Infinite at one intellectual glance.

Intelligence in action and conception, therefore, being considered as perfections, would be identical with the essence; and they requiring, in force of their metaphysical nature, a real distinction, the distinction would fall upon the essence of the Infinite. Any one versed in ontology will perceive this truth at a glance. Hence, Unitarians cannot say that the intelligence and the conception of the intelligence, the will and love in the Infinite, are mere perfections, without admitting a real distinction in the essence of the Infinite, and thus admitting a multiplicity of Infinites, which is absurd.

Second proposition: If Unitarians rank the intellect and thought, the will and its volition, of the infinite among faculties, they then fall into Pantheism.

Ontology, as we have said, defines a faculty to

be a force of development by union with its object.

Its notion implies three elements:
1. A force residing dormant in a being.
2. An object.
3. A union of force with the object, to render the development actual.

Applying this idea to the subject in question, every one can see at a glance that a faculty cannot be predicated of the Infinite without falling into Pantheism.

For it would be to admit in God a force of development, a capacity of unfolding, of actualizing himself.

Now, every faculty of development necessarily begins, from the minimum degree of actuality, to travel by progressive stages of unfolding to an indefinite maximum of progression. Hence, in the supposition, we should be forced to admit that God started from the minimum of life and action, and that he traveled through numberless stages of development, and will travel indefinitely through higher stages in the direction of a maximum of progress never to be attained. Now, this is almost verbatim the pantheistic theory of Hegel.

Every one who has read Hegel will have observed that his idea of the Infinite coincides perfectly with the above. For he starts from a minimum of reality, the *Being*, *Idea*, which, through a necessary interior movement, becomes matter, organism, animality, intelligence, etc.

It would not do for Unitarians to say that the argument does not apply to their system, since they admit a substance already existing and perfect as to being, only endowed with faculties. For, in the supposition, they would admit a finite, not an infinite being.

In a finite being we can conceive one already perfect in the order of existence, with faculties or force of accidental development. But we cannot say the same of the Infinite. The positive infinite, so to speak, is essentially actuality itself; hence, perfection itself, all terms which exclude and eliminate every possibility of development. If it be not that it must be the Infinite of Pantheism, a mere abstraction and unreality.

From what we have said, we conclude:

First, that the mystery of the Trinity is essentially necessary to the idea of God; that there can be no conception of Infinite actuality but through the supposition of three distinct terminations of the same essence.

Secondly, that Unitarians are absolutely powerless before Pantheism; nay, that their system is disguised Pantheism; and that by holding fast only to the unity of God, they sap the very foundation of the reality of the Infinite. The Infinite is essentially living. A living God is essentially conceiving himself by intellect. A subjective conception necessarily implies an objective conception. These two are absolutely and necessarily opposed to each other; and hence, really distinct. Again, a living God, who necessarily conceives himself, necessarily loves himself through his conception. Again, subjective love necessarily implies an objective love, and the two are essentially opposed, and hence distinct.

Thus we have three real distinct relations in the Infinite, a conceiver, a conception, and love.

On the one hand, these three relations cannot be either perfections or faculties; on the other, they cannot be denied of the Infinite without destroying the very idea of the Infinite. It follows, then, that they should be three terminations of the same essence.

The act of intelligence in God is so actual and perfect as to be in the very state of personality, intelligence itself. The product of this act is also so actual and perfect as to be conception itself, a personality distinct from the first. Love, the necessary production of both the intelligence and the conception, is also so actual and perfect, as to be love itself in a state of personality, three distinct subsistences of the same one infinite essence.

4*

CHAPTER V.

LAWS ACCORDING TO WHICH THE MYSTERY OF THE TRINITY SHOULD BE UNDERSTOOD.

We proceed, now, to lay down some general laws which govern, so to speak, the organism of the life of the infinite. The ignorance or the overlooking of these laws has ever caused those who plunged into the abyss of infinite life to search its genesis, to fall into one form or other of Pantheism, as will be seen in the course of this article.

The first and principal law may be enunciated as follows: *No other distinction can be predicated of the infinite, but that arising from the relative opposition of origin between the terms.**

We have already demonstrated that the life of the infinite is terminated by three distinct personalities, which establish a multiplicity in its

---

* Realis distinctio inter relationes divinas non est nisi ratione oppositionis relativæ. S. Th., S. T.; qu. 30, art. 2d.

bosom. A distinction, therefore, *must* be predicated of the infinite. But of what sort?

This distinction, in the first place, could not fall upon the essence without breaking its absolute simplicity. It must, consequently, be found among the terminations of the essence, or personalities. But, again, these three persons being possessed of the same identical essence, and thus participating in all its perfections, how can they be distinguished, one from the other? By a real opposition of origin. One person originates; the other is originated; as principle and term they are necessarily opposed to each other, and consequently distinct.

This law maintains both the unity and the multiplicity in the infinite. It maintains the unity; for the law does not require any real distinction between the persons and the essence, but only a distinction made by our reason to facilitate our apprehension; hence the three divine persons are truly and essentially the infinite. It maintains multiplicity, because the three divine persons are opposed on the ground of opposition of origin, and are consequently distinct. Here lies the whole difficulty, the reader will say; three things opposed one to another, and thus distinct from each other, how are they *one* in essence?

We might reply, in the first place, that the possibility of this is grounded on a psychological fact, which every one accustomed to reflection may easily ascertain. Take the operation of the human spirit. Man knows himself; in this fact the *me* enters twice; because the *me* is the subject which knows, and at the same time the object known. The *me* knowing is the being in the subjective form; the *me* known is the being in the objective form. Again, man loves himself through the idea of himself: the *me* here enters three times—the *me* under the subjective form of knowing and of loving; the *me* under the objective form of known; the *me* under the objective form of being loved. Nevertheless, all three are one and the same being; the *me* under the subjective form knows and loves the *me* under the objective form; a multiplicity and a unity which cannot be disputed; not only because of the testimony of consciousness, which avers to the fact, but because on this multiplicity and unity are founded two distinct sciences, psychology and ideology; psychology, which treats of the *me* as subject, of its nature and properties; ideology, which treats of the product of the *me*, or ideas.

This operation of man is an image of the genesis of God's life. The infinite knows and loves himself. Into this fact of his eternal life he enters three times; the infinite, so to speak, as subject knowing and loving himself; the infinite as object known; the infinite as object loved.

The infinite knowing himself is necessarily opposed to the infinite known, because it originates him by an intellectual operation; the infinite known is necessarily opposed to the infinite knowing, because originated by him. Again, the infinite loving himself and the infinite known (because the infinite cannot love himself except through the infinite known) are necessarily opposed to the infinite loved, because they originate him; the infinite loved is necessarily opposed to the infinite loving and known, because emanating from both. This relative opposition of origin causes a real distinction among the terms without breaking the unity of the essence.

But, the better to illustrate this law, and to show how well it maintains unity and multiplicity in the infinite, we shall here investigate the metaphysical law of the fact; that is, why and how things which are opposed to each other can harmonize and be brought into unity, in a third thing.

We have given an example of the fact in the operation of man; but let us give a few more instances to generalize it more and more. This fact is observed in both the ideological and ontological orders. First, as to the order of ideas. Two ideas, which in their own order are opposed to each other, harmonize and are brought together in a third idea. Take, for instance, the idea of substance and modification; substance conveys the idea of something subsisting by itself, that which requires no being to lean on in order to subsist. It means something standing permanent. The idea of modification is that of something which is not permanent in itself, but requires another being to lean on, to cling to, in order to subsist. The two ideas, as it appears, are directly opposed to each other, since their notions are contradictory; yet both ideas, contradictory one to the other in their own order, agree and are brought into companionship in the common idea of existence, one existing permanently, the other existing by leaning on another.

Moreover, take the transcendental idea of unity, truth, and goodness. Unity implies a negation of multiplicity, something undivided in itself and distinct from others. Truth implies a multiplicity, because it is essentially a relation of an object to an intelligence; *æquatio rei et intellectus*, as St. Thomas defines it. Goodness also implies a multiplicity, because it is essentially a relation of a being to a tendency or faculty.

These three ideas, contradictory or diverse, are brought into harmony in the common idea of being; for every metaphysician knows that unity, truth, goodness, are the transcendental qualities of being, and are identified with it.

The fact is therefore indisputable in the ideological order, that is, of ideas contradictory one to another or diverse, agreeing in a common idea. It is no less true in the order of reality, because ideology is founded on ontology. Take, for instance, a body; it has length, breadth, height, and depth. These qualities of bodies are contrary to each other in their own order, yet they harmonize in the body. Take the forces of attraction and repulsion; both are contradictory laws, yet both agree in the same body. Man harmonizes and brings together in himself the laws of movement, of vegetation, of animality and of intelligence, which are different and contradictory to each other. And in his spirit, as we have said before, he opposes himself as an object to himself, as subject without breaking the unity of the soul. Now wherein lies the reason of this fact? In the ideological order it lies in the universality of ideas; in the order of reality, in the intensity of being, or in the amount of perfection. A universal idea comprehends and harmonizes in itself inferior and more particular ideas, opposed to or different from each other; a more perfect being, or a greater reality harmonizes and brings together inferior qualities opposed to and diverse from each other, for the reason of its very intensity of perfection. A doctrine of St. Thomas beautifully illustrates this truth. He inquires into the distinction between intelligent and non-intelligent entities, and after having remarked that intelligent beings are distinguished from those not intelligent by this—that the second are only capable of containing their own forms or actuality, whereas the first, besides their own actuality, are capable of receiving the forms or actuality of other things, because in intelligent beings is found the ideal similitude of the object known, he alleges, as a reason for this distinction, contraction or limitation. "From this it appears," the concludes, "that the nature of unintelligen beings is more contracted and limited, while the nature of intelligent beings is endowed with the greater extension; hence the philosopher said that the soul is as it were every thing." *

This reason, however, which accounts for a more general idea or for a greater reality harmonizing in itself particular ideas or lesser realities opposed to each other in their own order, does not account for an opposition lying in the very bosom of a being. In other words, when the particular ideas and the lesser realities are taken as opposed to each other, they are considered distinct and apart from the general idea or greater reality. When they are harmonized in the general idea or greater reality, their limits and opposition are supposed to be eliminated; and this is the reason why the harmony becomes possible. But when the opposition is to be found in the same being, that is to say, when terms opposed to each other are not distinct from the general

---

* S. Th., S. T.; part. 1, qu. 14, art. 1.

idea or greater reality, but lie in its very bosom, then what is it that maintains both the opposition of the terms and the unity and simplicity of the being?

In this case, a relation of origin causes the opposition without breaking the unity of the being.

The same being supposed subsistent, being capable of intelligencing itself, can beget an ideal conception of itself; in other words, the same being can exist as object understood in itself, as subject understanding, as object loved in itself, and as subject loving. In this origination, the relation between the terms originated is true and real; because the being as subject, as such, is really opposed to itself as object, and truly relative to itself. The being could not be subject, without opposing itself as object to itself as subject. Yet this takes place without addition to or subtraction from the unity and the simplicity of the being; ontologically, the being is absolutely the same. What prevents us from perceiving this fully and clearly, is the action of the imagination and the essential condition of our intelligence, which cannot be exercised except by the help of a sensible phenomenon. Thus, when we strive to perceive a relation, it is pictured to our imagination as being something real, a kind of link or chain between the terms related. Now, when it is considered that this is only imaginary, and that ontologically a relation is nothing more than the attitude, to speak the language of schoolmen, of one object toward another it is evident that a being, capable of intelligence and of love, can oppose itself, as object, to itself as subject, without addition to or diminution from or breaking up of the simplicity of the being.

We conclude—particular ideas or lesser realities, opposed to each other, can be harmonized in general idea, or greater realities.

The metaphysical reason of this is, that opposition proceeds oftentimes from limitation, and that general idea or greater reality, by elimination of the limits, can harmonize things opposed in their own order. This reason is satisfactory when the particular ideas or lesser realities are considered distinct and apart from the general idea or greater reality; that is, they are opposed when distinct—the opposition vanishes when identified. But the reason is not satisfactory to explain how there may be terms distinct and opposed to each other in the same being, without breaking the unity of the being. The law of opposition of origin, and the relation resulting therefrom, fully explains and maintains both the multiplicity and the unity in the same being.

Applying these ideas to the infinite, it is evident that, the distinction of divine personalities taking place according to the law of opposition of origin, both the multiplicity of persons and the absolute simplicity of the divine essence are maintained. Because the distinction of the divine persons is caused by a relation of origin. Now, as we have seen, a relation of origin neither adds to nor subtracts from the essence; on the other hand, the relation between the terms is true and real. Consequently, the law of opposition of origin explains, as far as human intellect can fathom, how the distinction of the divine personalities can be maintained without at all detracting from the unity of the essence.

It will not do to say that theologians have imagined this law, to suit their systems. This law is given by the fact of human thought and by the ontological requirements of being. As we have already observed, being is essentially one, true, and good. Now these qualities at the same time are identified with being, because, when the mind tries to fathom them, it finds nothing added to being, and yet are they essentially a relation. Here we have identity and distinction, and nothing can explain it, as far as the mystery of being can be explained, except the law of opposition of origin. Our readers, from the above remarks, may see what becomes of that great objection, so often urged against the dogma of the trinity, and so many times disposed of by the doctors of the church, yet repeated again and again with the same assurance.

It is said, *quæ sunt idem uni tertio, sunt eadem inter se;* that is, things which are identical with a third thing are identical with each other. Now, the three divine persons, according to catholic doctrine, are identical with infinite essence; therefore they are identical with each other; that is, not distinct, and consequently cannot exist. Oftentimes, in thinking over this objection so triumphantly brought forward, we have thought of the well-known lines of Pope:

> "A little learning is a dangerous thing;
> Drink deep, or taste not the Pierian spring;
> Those shallow draughts intoxicate the brain,
> But drinking largely sobers us again."

For the principle, when examined carefully, does not apply to those cases in which a distinction is predicated of a being caused by a relation to itself.

For instance, upon that principle we might reason thus: things which are identical with a third thing are identical with each other. But height, length, breadth, and depth are one and the same thing with bodies; therefore, are identical among themselves; and all distinction between height and depth, length and breadth, is a pure figment; and architects, calculating the proportions of a building, would do well to remember the principle, for it would save them considerable time and trouble.

Again: unity, truth, and goodness are identical with reality. But those things which are identical with a third are identical with each other; therefore, unity, truth, goodness are identical among themselves, and it is the same thing to be one, true, and good, as to be. And all the different sciences formed on these relations of being are useless wastes of thought and meditation.

Moreover, the thinking and loving subject in man, the thought and the love, are identical with the soul; therefore, according to the said principle, there is no distinction between the thinking subject and the thought, and all ideology and grammar is nothing but useless pastime, and we could correctly say, the soul is a thinking subject—the soul is a thought.

The truth is, that the principle applies only to particular cases, and is by no means general; because, as we have demonstrated, being, in general, requires three distinct relations to be conceived, and which, remaining distinct among themselves, are yet identical with being.

The infinite being could neither be conceived, nor be actual, without three distinct relations, which must be identical with the essence, without ceasing to be distinct one from another. If its truth were general and it applied to all cases, it would abolish all distinction in the infinite being, and consequently, abolish its actuality and intelligibility, and leave it only as an abstraction —the Hegelian being—nothing.

Moreover, that the principle does not apply to the infinite is evident from the very enunciation and meaning of the principle. Things which are identical with a third are identical with each other. In the enunciation and in the meaning, the principle supposes a plurality, and, consequently, a distinction; for the gist of the principle is to compare a multiplicity to a unity. Now, who does not see that, if there were not a supreme identity and a supreme multiplicity beyond the sphere and subordination of this principle, the principle itself would be destroyed?

For if it be asked, what is the origin, the cause, and the supreme expression of plurality and distinction, which this principle supposes, we must rise to a supreme and typical distinction and identity, not subject to the principle; else we could never account for the existence of the principle.

The infinite is the supreme identity and the supreme multiplicity, the cause of all distinction and identity, and consequently, to it the principle cannot apply. We have followed the answer of Suarez to the above objection.

We conclude, therefore, that the first law governing the genesis of God's life is the law of opposition of origin, and that this law accounts both for the unity of essence and the trinity of persons in God.

We pass to the second law, which is as follows: *In the infinite, there must be a person who does not proceed from anything, and who is neither begotten nor made, but who subsists by himself.* The metaphysical reason of this law is, that there must be a first principle in everything, both in the ontological and in the ideological orders.

In the ontological order, because if every principle of reality, if every cause called for the existence of another to explain its existence, it is evident that there would be a process *ad infinitum* without explaining anything. For an infinite number of causes, each requiring another cause to explain their existence, would multiply, *ad infinitum*, the necessity of first cause, existing by itself and containing in itself the reason of its existence.

In the ideological order, because every science must have a principle which is not derived from any other, and which must be taken for granted, otherwise science would become impossible. Ask a proof and a demonstration for every principle, say of mathematics, and you will never be able to learn it.

Thus, in the genesis of infinite life, there must be a first person who subsists by himself, otherwise the life of the infinite becomes impossible.

But, besides this general reason which requires a first person underived from anything, there is a particular reason, more closely allied to the subject, which demonstrates it. Because, if there were not a first person in the infinite, not proceeding from any other thing, it would originate either from the essence or from another person. Now, it could not originate from the essence; because between the principle and its product there is a real opposition of origin; therefore, in the supposition, there would be a real opposition between the essence of the infinite and the first person. Now, the essence in question is infinite, and only the finite can be opposed to it. The first person, therefore, proceeding from the essence, would be finite and not infinite; that is, he would be a creature. Moreover, it would be impossible that the first person should proceed from the essence, because the essence without subsistence is an abstraction, and an abstraction could not originate a reality.

It could not proceed from another person, because, as we have remarked, this other person, unless subsisting of himself, would require another as his principle, and so on *ad infinitum*.

As a corollary of this law, it follows that whatever other persons may be supposed to exist in the infinite, they must originate from the first; because—no other distinction being possible in the infinite, but that arising from opposition of origin—it follows that, if there were other persons in the infinite, and if they did not originate from the first, they could not be opposed to it, and therefore they could not be distinguished from it; in other words, they could not exist.

A third law governs the life of the infinite; which, if possible, is yet more important than the former two. It is the law of immanence, which may be expressed in the following formula.

The action, by which the persons in the infinite are originated, terminates inside of the infinite, and is permanent, eternal, and complete.

Let it be observed that the action of an agent is always interior to it, because it is its own movement. But the product of the action is not always so; sometimes it is laid inside the agent; sometimes it terminates outside the agent. In the first case, the action is called immanent or interior; in the second, transient or exterior; not because the action is not always interior to the subject, but because the effect or term of the action is exterior or foreign to the subject. The first sense, then, in which the law of immanence is to be applied to the infinite is, that the terms of the action of the first person terminate inside the infinite; because, if they were to terminate outside of God, they would be something different from him, and consequently not divine persons, but finite beings.

But the law has a higher and more important bearing: it implies that the action by which the divine persons are originated is not transitory, successive, and incomplete, but permanent, eternal, and complete; because God is infinite actuality, or actuality itself.

Forget for one single moment to apply this law to the genesis of God's life, and you fall at once into Pantheism. For suppose the act, by which the divine persons are originated, to be transient, successive, temporary, incomplete, and it would follow at once that God is in continual development and explication. For He is either complete and perfect, or on the road to perfection. He is *in fieri*, or becoming.

And since, as we have often remarked, every development consists of different stages of explication, the last of which is always more perfect than those which precede it, it would follow that the genesis of God's life consists of a successive series of evolutions, the last of which is always more perfect than that which precedes it. Now, assuming the genesis of God's life at one determinate stage, and traveling backward to arrive at the first stage of explication from which He started, we should pass from a more perfect, defined, concrete stage of development, to one less perfect, less defined, less determinate, and thence to one still less so, until we should arrive at the most indeterminate, undefined, abstract stage of evolution; at the *least being*—the *being* not *being*, the first principle of Pantheism.

But, keeping in view the law of immanence, every one can see that God's action is supposed at once all perfect, complete, and adequate—in one word, eternal; and consequently every idea of development, progress, and succession is eliminated; and the consequence is, that the infinite is at once conceived as being infinite actuality; the first principle of Catholic theology—the precise contradictory of Pantheism.

Hence, according to this law, the first person is always originating, and his origination is always perfect; the others are always originated, and their existence is always perfect, adequate, and complete. We say *always* and *are originated*, not because the expressions convey the idea of eternal actuality and completeness, but because, our mind being measured by time, we can find no better words to exhibit the idea. Let this remark be made once for all.

A corollary of this law is, that whatever persons are originated in the infinite, being within the essence of God and terminating in Him, they are—*the infinite*, because nothing can be added to the infinite.

Fourth law: *In the infinite there are no more than two processions.*

By processions, we mean the origination of one person from another.

Now, that in God there are no more than two processions will appear evident, if we consider the proper operation of God. God is a spiritual nature; the proper operation of a spiritual nature is by intelligence and by will; therefore, the operation of God is by intelligence and by will, and consequently one origination is by the intelligence, the other by the will.

So far we have given those laws which govern, in general, the genesis of God's life. We must now proceed to those laws which govern the particular origination of each of the two divine persons.

Now, the law governing the origination of the second person is the law of intellectual generation. Generation implies the following elements: 1st, the production of a living being from a living principle; 2d, identity of nature between the two; 3d, this identity required by the very natural, essential, and direct tendency of the action by which the term is produced. It is according to these elements of generative law that the second person in the infinite is produced; and consequently he is really and truly the *Son* of God, as the producer is *Father*.

For the first person, whom we have said to be subsisting by himself, being intelligent activity, necessarily intelligences himself. He is the Godhead intelligencing himself.

Now, an object understood, inasmuch as it is understood, exists in the understanding in an intelligible state; for to understand means just to apprehend, to grasp intelligibly that which is understood.

The Godhead, therefore, is in himself as the Godhead understood in the Godhead understanding. Now, the object understood existing in the intelligence, is what is called mental word, intellectual conception, and by the Greeks, *logos*.

Hence in the Godhead exists the Godhead as mental word or logos. St. John, with a sublime expression, which electrified all the Platonic philosophers, began his Gospel thus: "In the beginning (the Father) was the Word."

This Word of the Godhead being conceived by an immanent act, an act which has neither beginning nor end, which is not power before it is act, is conceived therefore eternally, and consequently is coeternal with the conceiver. It is God or the infinite; because the first person, or intelligent activity, begets him by an operation which terminates inside himself, by the law of immanence; consequently the Word is identical with His essence, and is, therefore, the infinite.

Yet is he a distinct person from the first as Word.

For, although the intelligent activity and the Word are both God, yet are they distinct from each other by the law of opposition of origin, which implies that a term proceeding from a principle is necessarily opposed to it, and consequently distinct from it. Thus the intelligent activity, as principle, is necessarily opposed to the Word as term; and, *vice versa*, the Word as term is necessarily opposed to the intelligent activity as principle. In other words, the intelligent activity could not be what it is, unless it were the opposite of the Word, and this could not be the Word unless it were the very opposite of intelligent activity. Hence, to be intelligent, activity belongs so exclusively to the First, as to exclude any other from partaking in that distinctive constituent; and to be Word is claimed so exclusively by the Second, as to be attributed to no other. The result is a duality of terminations, possessed of the same infinite nature and its essential attributes, each having a constituent so exclusively its own as to be altogether incommunicable. Now, two terminations, possessed of the same infinite nature and its essential attributes, with a constituent so exclusively their own as to be attributed to no other, convey the idea of two persons. For what is a person? A spiritual being with a termination of his own, which makes him distinct from any other, gives him the ownership of himself, and renders him solidary of his action.

Now, the intelligent activity is a spiritual being, since he is the Godhead; is possessed of a constituent of his own, intelligent activity; has the ownership of himself; for, as intelligent activity, he is himself and no other, and cannot communicate himself; and is solidary of his notional action, that is, the action which constitutes him what he is: he is, therefore, a person.

Likewise the Word is a spiritual nature; for

he is the same Godhead as to substance; as a relation or Word, he is the owner of himself, incommunicable, and solidary of his notional action; hence, he is also a person.

In other words, the Godhead is an infinite spirit; all that constitutes him, both substance and terms of relation, is spirit. Consequently, each term of the divine relation, as such term, has an individuality of his own and, as infinite spirit, has knowledge and intelligence of himself; he beholds himself distinct from the other as term of relation, one with the other as substance. His distinction causes his relative individuality; consciousness and intelligence of his relative individuality make him a person.

Here an objection might be raised; to be a person implies, necessarily, to be intelligent, which is an essential attribute of spiritual being. Therefore the Word also must be intelligent, otherwise he would have neither knowledge nor consciousness of his individuality. But you have attributed intelligence to the first person as being his particular termination; therefore how can the Word be a person, if intelligence be the particular termination of the first? Either the Word is not intelligent, and then he cannot be a person, or intelligence is not the particular termination of the first, and in that case they cannot be persons, for they cannot be distinct.

The difficulty will vanish if it be observed that

we have not attributed intelligence to the first person as his particular termination, but intelligent *activity*.

A slight attention to the manner according to which the Word is produced in the infinite, will illustrate this distinction. The intelligence of the Godhead is infinite in its activity and actuality, as well as infinite in its term; which means that the Godhead understands itself infinitely, and an infinite term is the product of this intellection. Hence, once God has understood himself and conceived the expression of his intelligence, the activity is complete and fully terminated; consequently, the Word, the term of this intelligencing, has the Godhead with all its essential attributes communicated to him; except the activity of intelligencing, because the activity is complete in the production of the Word.

In other words, the act of the first person is eternal, complete, and perfect, by the laws of immanence. Its activity is fully and perfectly exercised in engendering the Word, hence it cannot be communicated. If it were communicated, it would argue imperfection and incompleteness in the act and in its term. In the act, for if any portion of activity remained to be communicated, the Godhead would not intelligence himself to the fullest extent of his infinity; in the term, because the Godhead not intelligencing himself to the full extent of his infinity, the intellectual utterance which would be produced would not fully and perfectly express the object.

Consequently both would be imperfect, incomplete, and potential. This happens in human conception. Our mind, being finite, that is, partial and imperfect, is forced to exert itself partially and conceive various mental words, which would not be the case if its activity were perfect and complete, as it is in the infinite.

This answers another objection which is brought forward by those who lose sight of the law of immanence in the divine operation. It is said, If the Word be intelligent, there is nothing to prevent his engendering another Word, and this second, a third, and so on *ad infinitum*.

The Word is intelligent, but not intelligent activity. When intelligence, so to speak, is communicated to him, it has been exercised in the engendering of himself; or better, the eternal immanent act of the intelligent activity communicating intelligence to the Word, is continually being exercised in the immanent engendering of the Word; therefore it cannot be communicated to him.* Hence that magnificent expression of the Scripture, "*Semel loquitur Deus.*" "*God speaks but once.*" But because the activity of engendering another Word is not communicated

---

* In Filio non habet *intellectus* illam veluti *virtutem* quia iam habuit actum sibi adequatum.—*Suarez*, De Trin., lib. i. cap. 7. v. 11.

to him, it does not follow that he is not endowed with the act of intelligencing the Father or himself; the Father as his principle, himself as the product of the Father. For it is one thing to be intelligent, another thing to be intelligent principle. To give some examples of this distinction. The architect of a building who has planned it, is the intelligent principle of the building; another, who understands the plan of the building, is the intelligent *beholder* of the building.

God is the intelligent cause of the world, man is the intelligent perceiver of the world.

There being, therefore, a distinction between intelligence as principle or cause, and intelligence as perception, one may easily conceive how the Word in the infinite may be possessed of intelligence, without being the principle of intelligence.

The Word, who is one Godhead with the first person, a distinct person himself, is also the substantial image of the first person. Because, in force of the act by which he is uttered, which is essentially assimilative, he is produced as the likeness of him whose expression and utterance he is; and as he is one as to substance with the conceiver, he is, consequently, his substantial image and likeness. We conclude, therefore, that the production of the second person in the infinite—resulting in a person, the substantial image of the conceiver, in force of the act of intelligencing by which he is produced, which is essentially assimilative—is governed by the law of generation ; and that, consequently, the first person in the infinite is *Father*, and the second, *Son*. " *Thou art my Son, to-day I have begotten thee.**"

The law by which the third person in the infinite is produced, is different from that which governs the production of the second.

The latter takes place according to the law of generation or assimilation; the former is subject to the law of aspiration, which must be understood as follows.

By his Word, the intelligent activity apprehends and conceives his infinite perfection and goodness. For the Word, as we have seen, is nothing but the infinite and most perfect expression or image of the intelligent activity, and as the intelligent activity is infinite perfection and excellence, so the Word is the utterance, the intellectual reproduction of that excellence and goodness. Hence the intelligent activity, by his Word, conceives and utters himself as infinite perception and excellence. But perfection or goodness *apprehended* is necessarily loved. For goodness, once apprehended, awakens the will, and necessarily inclines it toward itself; it necessarily attracts and affects it. The intelligent activity, therefore by apprehending himself through his Word as infinite perfection and goodness, necessarily loves himself.

---

* Ps. ii. 7.

Love implies the insidence or indwelling of the object loved in the subject loving. The intelligent activity, therefore, who necessarily loves himself through his Word, must be as object loved in himself as subject loving.

This love as object must be co-eternal with the infinite, because by the law of immanence which governs the genesis of infinite life, every origination in the infinite must be co-eternal with the infinite.

By the same law also, it must be identical and one with the infinite; because love, being originated by an immanent act, terminates inside of the infinite, and is, therefore, identical with the infinite. The love as object, therefore, is co-eternal and identical with the infinite; it *is* the infinite.

It is distinct from love as subject and from the Word, by the law of opposition of origin, which implies that a term which originates from a principle is necessarily opposed to it, and consequently distinct. Now, love, as object in the infinite, originates from the intelligent activity and from the Word. The intelligent activity, by apprehending himself, as infinite goodness and excellence, through his Word, loves himself. Hence, this love proceeds from both—the intelligent activity, who conceives his infinite goodness—the Word, who represents it, and makes it intelligible. This love-object is a third person. For, from what we have said, it appears that love-object is identical with the infinite, with the divine essence, and consequently partakes of all the infinite attributes of the essence; hence he is a spiritual and intelligent being; as distinct from both the intelligent activity and the Word, he is possessed of a termination exclusively his own, which makes him the owner of himself incommunicable and solidary of his notional action. Hence he is a person.

This third person, not being originated according to a likeness of nature, cannot, like the second person, be called son. He is the personal and subsisting love of the Father and of the Son; and as the object loved exists in the subject loving, as inclining, and in a certain manner as impelling, the subject toward it, as raising in the subject an attraction or aspiration toward it, hence the third person is called the living and subsisting Spirit of God.

The better to conceive this distinctive termination of the third term in the infinite, let us suppose an attraction between two persons. It is needless to remark that we use this term for want of a better and more spiritual one. Suppose, therefore, an attraction between two persons; do not make it an accident or modification, but substantial; carry it to its utmost perfection, actualize it *ad infinitum;* so that it may be able to return upon itself, to have consciousness of itself, to possess and own itself, and in this sense to feel itself distinct from and independent of all others—and you will have, as product, a subsisting or *personal* attraction, a third person.

Such is the idea we can form of the Holy Spirit. The Father beholds himself totally in the Son as an offspring of himself, and loves himself in his offspring, his perfect and substantial expression.

The Son beholds himself totally in the Father as his author, and loves the Father as his principle and origin. This common love, this mutual attraction, this aspiration of the Father toward the Son, and of the Son toward the Father, being infinite, is most actual, perfect, and complete —a living, subsisting attraction, with consciousness and the ownership of himself, as subsistence personifying their mutual love and binding both in one eternal tie of affection.

Hence, by this distinctive constituent of common love, the Spirit is the archetype of harmony and order; since in his personality he brings the opposition existing between the conceiver and the conceived into harmony and unity of love.

He is also the archetype of the *beautiful*, being the very beauty and loveliness of God.

Beauty, in its highest metaphysical expression, is variety reduced to unity, by order and proportion. Now, the Spirit harmonizes the reality and the intelligibility of God into a unity of love. Hence he is the beauty of the Father and the

Son—their personal and eternal loveliness; and as such, the archetype of the beautiful in all orders.

He is the very bliss of the infinite, because bliss is the perfect possession of infinite life. Now, it is in the production of the Spirit that the genesis of infinite life terminates and is complete. He is, then, the expression of the perfect possession and enjoyment of the infinite life—the living Blessedness of the infinite.

The last law which governs the mystery of God's life, and which is a consequence of all the laws we have explained, is the law of *insidence*.

This implies the indwelling of all the divine persons in each other. It is founded both on the community of essence and the very nature of personalities.

For the essence of the three divine persons, being one and most simple, it follows that they all meet in it, and consequently dwell in each other. On the other hand, what constitutes them persons is essentially a relation. Now, a relation necessarily asks for and includes the relative term. The intelligent activity is such, because in him dwells the Word, his infinite expression. The Word is such, because he is the expression of the intelligent activity, and dwells in him. The Spirit necessarily dwells in both, because he is the subsisting aspiration of the activity toward its conception, and of the conception toward its principle.

"Believe that the Father is in me, and I in the Father." (St. John.)

With these laws, we conclude the first part of the problem of multiplicity raised by Pantheism. It is true, as Pantheism affirms, that there must be a certain multiplicity in the unity of infinite essence. For, without a certain multiplicity, no being can exist or be intelligible. Pantheism, in giving such prominent importance to the problem, has rendered great service to philosophy and to religion, and has cut off, in the very bud, all those objections raised by the superficial reason of Arians or anti-trinitarians of old, or Unitarians of modern times. But, as we have seen, however able in raising the problem, Pantheism utterly fails in resolving it; and, in its effort to explain the problem, destroys both the terms to be reconciled. Catholicity, fully conscious of the immense value of the problem, unflinchingly asserts that it alone has the secret of its solution. Without at all assuming to explain away its super-intelligibility, it lays down such an answer as fully satisfies the mind which can appreciate the importance and the sublimity of the problem, and follow it into the depths of its explanation. The infinite, says Catholicity, is not infinite as an abstraction or potentiality, as germ as Pantheism affirms, which ceases to be infinite when it passes into multiplicity; the infinite is actually itself.

This actuality consists in a first personality unborn and unbegotten, with full consciousness of himself and his infinite perfection. This personality is active intelligence, and in intelligencing his infinite perfection, begets a conception, an intelligible expression of that perfection, a second person. The active intelligence loves his infinite personality conceived by him in his intelligence. This love is a third personality.

Three personalities or terminations of one infinite actuality: a multiplicity in unity; unity without being broken by multiplicity; multiplicity without being destroyed by unity.

Hence the infinite is not a dead, immovable, unintelligible unity, but a living, actual, intelligible unity; because it is unity of nature and a trinity of persons; because the unity falls in the essence, the multiplicity, in the terminations of the essence.

CHAPTER VI.

THE FINITE.

IN the pantheistic theory, the finite has no real existence of its own. It is a modification, a limit of the infinite. The sum of all the determinations which the primitive and germinal activity assumes, in the progress of its development, constitutes what is called cosmos. The interior and necessary movement of the infinite, which terminates in all these forms and determinations, is creation. The successive appearance of all these forms in this necessary development is the genesis of creation. The finite, therefore, in the pantheistic system, does not exist as something substantially distinct from the infinite, but is one form or other which it assumes in its spontaneous evolutions.

As the reader may observe, this theory rests entirely upon the leading principle of the system that the infinite is something undefined, impersonal, indeterminate, and becomes concrete and personal by a necessary, interior movement; a principle which, viewed in reference to the finite, gives rise to two others, first, that the finite is a modification of the infinite; second, that the finite is necessary to the infinite, as the term of its spontaneous development. Now, in the preceding articles, we have demonstrated, first, that the infinite is actuality itself; that is, absolute and complete perfection; second, that in order to be personal, he is not impelled to originate any modification or limit. Hence, two other principles concerning the finite, quite antagonistic to those of Pantheism. First, the finite cannot be a modification of the infinite, because perfection, absolutely complete, cannot admit of ulterior progress. Second, the finite is not necessary to the infinite, because the interior and necessary action of the infinite does not terminate outside of, but within himself, and gives rise to the mystery of the Trinity, explained and vindicated in the last two chapters. Consequently, his necessary interior action being exercised within himself, he is not forced to originate the finite to satisfy that spontaneous movement, as Cousin and other Pantheists contend. The finite, therefore, can neither be a modification nor a necessary development of the infinite. And this consequence sweeps away all systems of emanatism, of whatever form, that may be imagined. Whether we suppose the finite to be a growth or extension of the infinite, as the materialistic Pantheists of old seemed to imagine; or mere phenomenon of infinite substance, with Spinoza; or ideological exercise of the infinite, as modern Germans seem to think—according to the principle laid down, the finite is impossible in any emanatistic sense whatever. To any one who has followed us closely in the preceding chapters, it will appear evident that these few remarks absolutely dispose of the pantheistic theory concerning the finite, and close the negative part of our task respecting this question.

As to the positive part, to give a full explanation of the whole doctrine of Catholicity concerning the finite, we must discuss the following questions:

In what sense is creation to be understood?

Is creation of finite substances possible?

What is the end of the exterior action of God?

What is the whole plan of the exterior action of God?

Before we enter upon the discussion of the first question, we must lay down a few preliminary remarks necessary to the intelligence of all that shall follow.

God's action is identical with his essence, and this being absolutely simple and undivided, his action also is absolutely one and simple. But it is infinite also, like his essence, and in this respect it gives rise, not only to the eternal and immanent originations within himself, but also may cause a numberless variety of effects really existing, and distinct from him, as we shall demonstrate. Now, if we regard the action of God, in itself originating both *ad intra* and *ad extra*, that is, acting within and without himself, it cannot possibly admit of distinction. But our mind, being finite, and hence incapable of perceiving at once the infinite action of God, and of grasping at one glance that one simple action originating numberless effects, is forced to take partial views of it, and mentally to divide it, to facilitate the intelligence of its different effects. These partial views and distinctions of our mind, of the same identical action of God, producing the divine persons within himself, and causing different effects outside himself, we shall call *moments* of the action of God.

There are, therefore, two supreme moments of the action of God, the interior and the exterior. Whenever we shall speak of the action of God producing an effect distinct from and outside of him, we shall call it exterior action, to distinguish it from the interior, which originates the divine personalities. Moreover, we shall call exterior action of God, all the moments of it which produce different effects. We shall call creation that particular moment of his external action which, as we shall see, causes the existence of finite substances, together with their essential properties and attributes.

Now, as to the first question, in what sense can creation be understood; or, otherwise, what are the conditions according to which creation may be possible? On the following: First, the terms laid down by the action of God must be in nature distinct from him. Second, they must be produced by an act which does not cause any mutation in the agent. Third, therefore, they must be finite substances. For, suppose the absence of the first condition, creation would be an emanation of the divine essence; since, if the terms created were not different from the nature of God, they would be identical with it, and consequently creation would be an emanation or development of the substance of God. The absence of the second condition would not only render it an emanation of the substance of God—because, if creation implied a mutation in him, it would be his own modification—but it would render it altogether impossible, since no agent can modify itself but by the aid of another. If, therefore, creation cannot be either an emanation or a modification of God, it must be distinct from his substance. Now, something distinct from the substance of God, and really existing, and not a modification, cannot be anything but finite substance. Finite, because, the substance of God being infinite, nothing can be distinct from it but the finite;* substance, because something really existing, and which is not a modification, gives the idea of substance. Creation, therefore, cannot be understood in any other sense except as implying the causation of finite substances. But is creation of finite substances possible? In answer to this question, let it be remarked that the essence of a thing may have two distinct states: one, intelligible and objective; the other, subjective and in existence. In other words, all things have a mode of intelligible existence, distinct from the being by which they exist, in themselves; the one may be called objective and intelligible; the other, subjective. To give an instance, a building has two kinds of states: one, intelligible, in the mind of the architect; the other, subjective, when it exists in itself.

Now, the possibility of a thing to have a subjective existence in itself, depends upon the intelligible and objective state of the same thing. Because that only is possible which does not involve any contradiction. But that which does not involve any repugnance, is intelligible. Therefore the possibility of a thing implies its intelligibility, and its subjective existence depends upon its objective and intelligible state. This is so true, that the transcendental truth of beings, in their subjective state of existence, consists in their conformity with their intelligible and objective state. As the truth of a building consists in its conformity with the plan in the mind of the architect.

From these principles it follows that, in order to establish the possibility of the creation of finite substances, we must prove three different things: First, that they have an intelligible state; in other words, that their idea does not involve any repugnance. Second, that there exists a supreme act of intelligence, in which the intelligible state of all possible finite substances reside. Third, that there exists a supreme activity, which may cause finite substances to exist in a subjective state conformable to their objective and intelligible state.

When we have proven these three propositions, the possibility of creation will be put beyond all doubt.

Now, as to the first proposition, Pantheists have denied the possibility of finite substances. Admitting the general possibility of substance, they deny the intrinsic possibility of a finite one; and, as everything which is finite is necessarily *caused*, the whole question turns upon this — whether, in the idea of substance, there is any element which excludes causation and is repugnant to it. Every one acquainted with the history of philosophy knows that Spinoza coined a definition purposely to fit his system. He defined substance to be that which exists in itself, and cannot be conceived but by itself.* This definition is purposely insidious. That which exists in itself may have a twofold meaning; it may express a thing, the cause of whose existence lies in itself, a self-existing being; or it may imply a thing can exist without inhering in or leaning on any other. Again, that which cannot be conceived but by itself may be taken in a double sense—a thing which has no cause, and is self-existent, and consequently contains in itself the reason of its intelligibility; or it may signify a thing which may be conceived by itself, inasmuch as it does not lean upon any other to be able to exist. Spinoza, taking both terms of the definition in the first sense, had the way paved for Pantheism; for if substance be that which is intelligible by itself because self-existent, it is evident that there cannot be more than one substance, and the cosmos cannot be anything but phenomenon of this substance. Hence the question we have proposed: Is there, in the true idea of substance, any element which necessarily implies self-existence, and excludes causation? Catholic philosophy insists that there is none. For the idea of substance is made up of two elements: one positive, the other negative. The positive element is the permanence or consistence of an act or being—that is, the *existing* really. The second element is the exclusion or

---

* Eth. 1, Def. 1.

absence of all inherence in another being in order to exist.

Now, every one can easily perceive, that to exist really does not necessarily imply self-existence, or contradiction to the notion of having been caused by another. Because the notion of real existence or permanence of a being does not necessarily imply eternity of permanence, or, in other words, does not include infinity of being. If the permanence or real existence of a being included eternity of permanence, then it could not have a cause, and should necessarily be self-existent. But we can conceive a being really existing, which did not exist always, but had a beginning. The better to illustrate this conception, let it be remembered that duration or permanence is one and the same thing with being; and that, ontologically, being and duration differ in nothing. The permanence and duration of a being is, therefore, in proportion to the intensity of a being. If the being be infinite, the highest intensity of reality, the being is infinitely permanent; that is, eternal, without beginning, end, or succession. If the being be finite and created, the permanence or duration is finite also; that is, has beginning, and may, absolutely speaking, have an end. Everything, therefore, really existing without inhering in another, whether it be infinite or finite reality—that is, whether it have a cause or be self-existent—is a substance. If it be self-existent, it is infinite substance; if it be caused, it is finite substance.

This is so evident that none, slightly accustomed to reflect, can fail to perceive the difference between being self-existent and existing really. The two things can go separately without the one at all including the other. A thing may exist as really after being caused, as the substance which is self-existent and eternal, so far as existing really is concerned.

To show that the idea of substance, however, is such as we have been describing, it is sufficient to cast a glance at our own soul. It is evident from the testimony of consciousness, that there is a numberless variety of thoughts, volitions, sensations; all taking place in the *me*, all following and succeeding each other without interruption, like the waves of the ocean rolling one upon the other, and keeping the sea always in agitation. We are conscious to ourselves of this continual influx of thoughts, volitions and sensations; but, at the same time that we are conscious of this, we are conscious also of the identity and permanence of the *me* amid the fluctuations of those modifications. We are conscious that the *me*, which yesterday was affected with the passions of love and desire, is the same identical *me* which is to-day under the passion of hate. This permanence or reality of the *me*, amid the passing and transitory affections, gives the idea of substance or real existence; whilst the numberless variety of thoughts and feelings which affect it, and which come and go while the *me* remains, gives the idea of modification, or a thing which inheres in another in order to exist.

The above remarks must put the possibility of finite substance beyond doubt. But before we pass to the second question, we remark that any one sooner than a Pantheist could call in question the possibility of finite substance; because if, as we have demonstrated in the second chapter, the infinite of the Pantheists be not an absolute nonentity, a pure abstraction, it is nothing but the idea of finite being or substance. Hence, to prove the possibility of finite substance to the Pantheist, we might make use of the argument *ad hominem*. That which is intelligible is possible, by the principle of contradiction. But the idea of finite substance is intelligible to the Pantheists, being the foundation of their system; therefore, finite substances are possible.

Second question : Is there a supreme act of intelligence, in which reside all possible finite substances in their objective and intelligible state ?

The demonstration of the second proposition follows from that of the first.

For the idea of finite substance does not involve any repugnance, by the principle of contradiction. Therefore it is necessarily possible, as we have demonstrated. But that which is necessarily possible, is necessarily intelligible; because everything that is possible may be conceived. Therefore the idea of finite substance is necessarily intelligible, and may be conceived by an intelligence able to grasp the whole series of possible finite substances. But God is infinite intelligence, and as such is capable of apprehending all possible finite substances. Therefore in God's intelligence resides the whole series of possible finite substances, in their intelligible and objective state.

To render this argument more convincing, let us look into the ontological foundation of the possibility of finite substances. Finite substances are nothing but finite beings; consequently they are not possible, except inasmuch as they agree with the essence of God, which is the infinite, *the being*, and as such is the type of all things which come under the denomination and category of being. God, therefore, who fully comprehends his essence, comprehends at the same time, whatever may agree with it; or, in other words, comprehends all possible imitations, so to speak, of his essence; and consequently, all the possible imitations of his essence residing in his intelligence, there dwells at the same time the intelligible and objective state of all possible finite substances. St. Thomas proves the same truth with a somewhat similar argument. "Whoever," he says, "comprehends a certain universal nature, comprehends, at the same time, the manner according to which it may be imitated. But God, comprehending himself, comprehends the universal nature of being; consequently he comprehends also the manner according to which it may be imitated." Now, the possibility of finite substance is a similitude of the universal being. Hence, in God's intelligence resides the whole series of possible finite substances.

Third proposition: There exists a supreme activity which may cause finite substances to exist in a subjective state. For St. Thomas argues that the more perfect is a principle of action, the more its action can extend to a greater number and more distant things. As for instance, if a fire be weak, it can heat only things which are near it; if strong, it can reach distant things. Now, a pure act, which is in God, is more perfect than an act mixed of potentiality, as it is in us. If therefore by the act which is in us we cannot only produce immanent acts, as for instance, to think and to will, but also exterior acts by which we effect something; with much greater reason can God, by the fact of his being actuality itself, not only exercise intelligence and will, but also produce effects outside himself and thus be the cause of being.* The great philosopher Gerdii, appropriating this

---

* C. G. lib. ii. ch. 6.

reason of St. Thomas, develops it thus: " In ourselves, and in particular beings, we find a certain activity; therefore activity is a reality which belongs to the *being* or the *infinite*. The effect of activity when the agent applies it to the patient, consists in causing a mutation of state. The intensity of acts, depending on intelligence, has a force to introduce a mutation of state in the corporal movements. This may be seen in the real though hidden connection of which we are conscious to ourselves, between the intensity of our desires and the effect of the movements which are excited in the body; and better still, in certain phenomena which sometimes occur, though rarely when the imagination, apprehending something vividly and forcibly, produces a mutation of state in the body which corresponds somewhat with the apprehension of the imagination.* Now this change in the body, corresponding to what takes place in the fancy, that is, in the objective and intelligible state, shows that there exists a certain, though hidden, force and energy by which, from what exists in an intelligible state, may be introduced a mutation in the corresponding state of subjective existence. Therefore the efficacy of the supreme intelligence, being the greatest and the highest, in

---

* An imminent danger of being burned to death, vividly apprehended, has sometimes entirely cured persons altogether paralyzed and unable to move.

force of the supreme intensity of being which resides in it, may not only effect a change conformable to a relative, intelligible state in things already existing, but also cause them to pass altogether from the intelligible state into the state of existence. And, assuredly, if the finite intensity of desire and of imagination may produce an effort of corporal movement, the supreme intensity of the Infinite Being may, certainly, produce a substantial, existing being; since the supreme intensity of the Being bears infinitely greater proportion to the existence of a thing, than the intensity of desire does in relation to a corporal movement. The term therefore, of the supreme activity, is to effect, outside of itself, the existence of things which had only an intelligible and objective being in itself."*

It is well to remark here, that the supreme activity is not by any means determined necessarily to create; for the activity may be determined to a necessary operation, in that case only when the agent is actually applied to the subject capable of receiving a change of state. But creation is not the result of the application of the supreme activity to a subject co-existing with itself; because nothing co-exists originally with the supreme activity. Therefore creation cannot be an action determined by any necessity, but must depend only upon the energy or will of the supreme in-

---

* Gerdil, *Del Senso Morale.*

telligence in which the highest activity dwells. Hence it follows, that creation, as to its term, is not necessary, either because there is any principle in God impelling him necessarily to create, as we have seen, or because there is any principle outside of God forcing him to create; because outside of the supreme activity nothing exists. What is necessary about the creation of finite substances, is their intelligible and objective state, or their intrinsic possibility. For everything which does not imply any repugnance by the principle of contradiction, is intrinsically possible and intelligible. That which is intrinsically possible is essentially, necessarily, and eternally so. Consequently, the objective state of finite substances is necessarily so.

Pantheists, confounding the objective and intelligible state of the cosmos with its state of subjective existence; in other words, identifying the ideal with the real, the ideological with the ontological, have been led to admit the necessity of creation. This is particularly remarked in the systems of Schelling and Hegel; the one admitting, as first principle, the absolute identy of all things; the other identifying the *idea* with *being*. Both confounded the object and intelligible state of the cosmos with its state of subjective existence; and once the two are identified, it follows that, as the one, which is the intelligible, is necessary, eternal, and absolute, the other, the subjective, becomes also necessary and eternal; and hence the necessity of creation. Catholicity, on the contrary, carefully distinguishing between the ideal and the real, the objective and the subjective, and admitting the necessity and eternity of the first, because everything intelligible necessarily and eternally resides in the supreme intelligence, denies the necessity of the second, because of that very intelligible state which it admits to be necessarily and eternally so.

For a finite substance is not, and cannot be conceived as possible or intelligible, except it is supposed to be contingent or indifferent in itself to be or not to be, not having in itself the reason of its existence. This is the only condition according to which finite substances can be possible. Were it otherwise, were a finite substance supposed to be necessary, it would be self-existent, and have in itself the reason of its existence; and in that case it would no longer be finite, but infinite. To suppose, therefore, a finite substance not contingent is to suppose it necessary, is to suppose a self-existing finite substance, or, in other words, an infinite finite substance, which is absurd, and, therefore, unintelligible and impossible.

The intelligibility, therefore, or objective state of finite substances, which is necessary, eternal, and absolute itself, requires the contingency of their existence in a subjective state; and, consequently, their contingency is necessary because their intelligibility is necessary; and their creation is free, because whatever is indifferent in itself to be or not to be, absolutely depends, as to its existence, upon the will of the supreme intelligence.

An objection is here raised by Pantheists impugning the possibility of the creative act. It is as follows: Given the full cause, the effect exists. Now, the creative act, the full cause of creation, is eternal; therefore, its effect must exist eternally. But, an eternal effect is a contradiction in terms; because it means a thing created and uncreated at the same time. Therefore, creation is impossible in the Catholic sense, and can be nothing more than the eternal development and unfolding of the divine substance. Given the cause, the effect exists. Such an effect, and in such a manner as the cause is naturally calculated to produce, it is granted; such an effect and in such a manner as the cause naturally is not intended to produce, it is denied. Now, what is the cause of creation but the will of God? And how does the will naturally act, except by a free determination, and in the manner according to which it determines itself? Consequently, creation being an effect of the will of God, it will follow just when and how the will of God has determined it shall. Hence the will of God being eternal, it does not follow that the effect should be eternal also. In other words, given the full cause, the effect exists when the cause is impelled to act by a necessary intrinsic movement. But when the cause is free, and perfectly master of its own action and energy, the cause given is not a sufficient element for the existence of the effect, but, two elements are required, the cause and its determination, and the free conditions which the cause has attached to its determination. Nor does this imply any change in the action of God when creation actually takes place. For that same act which determines itself from eternity to create, and to cause substances and time, the measure of their duration, continues immutable until the creation actually takes place; and the creation is not an effect of a new act, but of that same immutable and eternal determination of God.

We conclude, finite substances are intrinsically possible; they have an intelligible and objective state in the infinite intelligence of God. God's infinite activity may cause them to exist in a subjective state conformable to their intelligible mode of existence. Therefore, creation in the Catholic sense is possible.

Before we pass to the next question, we must draw some corollaries.

First. God can act outside himself, since he can create finite substances with all the properties and faculties which are necessary elements of their essence, and naturally and necessarily spring from it.

Second. The creative act imlpies two secondary movements; one, called preservation, and the other, concurrence. Hence, if God does create, he must necessarily preserve his effects, and concur in the development of their activity. Preservation implies the immanence of the creative act, or the continuation of the creative act of God, maintaining finite substances in their existence. The necessity of this movement is proved by the following reason:

Every finite being is, in force of its nature, indifferent to be or not to be; that is, every finite being contains no intrinsic reason necessarily requiring its existence. Hence, the reason of its existence lies in an exterior agent or cause. But the finite being once existing, does not change its nature, but intrinsically continues to be contingent, that is, indifferent to be or not to be. Therefore, the reason of the continuation of its existence cannot be found in its intrinsic nature, but in an exterior agent; that is, in the action of the Creator. So long, therefore, as the action of God continues to determine the intrinsic indifference of contingent being to be or not to be, so long does the finite exist. In the supposition of the act ceasing, the finite would simultaneously cease to be.

Nor does this argument impugn the *substance* of finite beings. For, as we have seen, substance is that which exists really, though the reason of its existence lie in the creative act; whereas, what we deny here in the argument is the continuation of existence by an intrinsic reason, which would change the essence of the finite, and, from contingent, render it necessary.

The second moment of the creative act is concurrence. Finite substance is a being in the way of development; a being capable of modification. Now, no being can modify itself, can produce a modification of which it is itself the subject, without the aid of another being who is pure actuality. Therefore, finite substances cannot modify themselves without the aid of God. The action of God aiding finite substances to develop themselves, is called concurrence. We have already proved, in the second article, the principle upon which this moment of the action of God is founded. We shall here add another argument. A finite substance is a being in the way of development; a being in potency of modification; and when the modification takes place, it passes from the power or potency to the act. Now, no being can pass from the power to the act except by the aid of being already in act. Consequently, finite substances cannot modify themselves except by the aid of being already in act. Nor can it be supposed that finite substances can be at the same time in potency and in act with regard to the same modification; for this would be a contradiction in terms. It follows, then, that having power of being modified, they cannot pass from the power to the movement without the help of another being already in act. This cannot be a being which may itself be in power and in act, for then it would itself require aid. It follows, therefore, that this being, aiding finite substances to modify themselves, must be one which is pure actuality, that is, God.

Third corollary: From all we have said follows, also, the possibility of God acting upon his creatures by a new moment of his action, and putting in them new forces higher than those forces which naturally spring from their essence, nor due to them either as natural properties, attributes or faculties. For, if God can act outside himself, and effect finite substances distinct from him; substances endowed with all the essential attributes and faculties springing from their nature; if he can continue to maintain them in existence, and aid them in their natural development, we see no contradiction in supposing that he may, if he choose, grant his creatures other forces superior altogether to their natural forces, and, consequently, not due to them as properties or attributes of their nature.

For the contradiction could not exist either on the part of God or on the part of the creature. Not in the former, because God's action being infinite, may give rise to an infinity of effects, one higher and more sublime, in the hierarchy of beings, than the other. Not in the latter, because the capacity of the creature is indefinite. It may receive an indefinite growth and development, and never reach a point beyond which it could not go. Therefore, the supposition we have made does not imply any repugnance either in God or in the finite, the two terms of the question. Now, that which involves no repugnance is possible. It is possible, therefore, that God may act upon his creatures by a moment of his action distinct from the creative moment, and put in them forces higher than their natural forces, and not due to them as any essential element or faculty.

CHAPTER VII.

THE FINITE—CONTINUED.

WE pass to the next question: What is the end of the exterior action of God? God is infinite intelligence. An agent who acts by understanding must always act for a reason, which is as the lever of the intelligence. This reason is called the end of the action. Therefore, the external act, being the act of an infinite intelligence, must have an end, an object, a reason. So far everything is evident; but a very difficult question here arises: What can the end of the exterior action be? In the first place, it cannot be an end necessarily to be attained; for the necessity of the end would imply also the necessity of the means, and the external act in that supposition would become necessary. But suppose the end was not necessary. God, in that case, would be free to accept it; and in that supposition he would either act without a reason, or have another reason or object for accepting an end not necessary to be attained; which second reason would, in its turn, be either necessary or not necessary. If the former, the same inconvenience would exist which we have pointed out before; if the latter, it would require a third reason to account for the second; and so on *ad infinitum*. The answer to this difficulty consists in the following doctrine. The reason by which an agent acts may be twofold: one, efficient or determining; the other, qualifying the action without determining it. Ontologically speaking, every intelligent agent must act for a reason, but not always be determined to act by the reason. This is eminently true when the agent or efficient cause is the first and universal agent. In this case there would be a contradiction, if the first and universal agent were to act by a reason determining him to the act. For then the predicate would destroy the subject; that is, if the first and universal agent were to act by a determining reason, he would no longer be first, but second agent; no longer universal, but particular. Because in that case the final cause would move him, and thus he would neither be the first nor the cause of everything. This theory resolves the question of the end of the external act. There exists neither an intrinsic reason on the part of the agent to determine him to act outside himself, nor an exterior reason on the part of the term to impel him to act, as we have already demonstrated. Consequently, there can be no determining reason for the external act, and the act must determine itself. The efficient or determining reason of the external act is the choice of the act which is absolute master of itself; it lies in its liberty: and here applies with strict truth that saying, "Stat pro ratione voluntas." And necessarily so, since the first agent either determines himself without any efficient reason, or he is determined by the reason; and in that case he is no longer first, but second. But then God acts outside himself without any reason? Without any efficient and determining reason, independent of his own act, it is granted; without a sufficient reason to make the act rational, it is denied. If there be a reason which qualifies the act, it is sufficient and rational. Now, for instance, to create finite substances is to create substantial good; hence the act of creating them must be good, and therefore rational. And since every finite being, or its perfection, is good, inasmuch as it resembles the infinite goodness and perfection of God, it follows that, as St. Thomas says, the goodness of God is the end of the external act. *Divina bonitas est finis omnium rerum.*

The determination of the end of the exterior act, which is the goodness of God, as we have explained it, gives rise to another question, which has occupied the highest intellects among philosophers and theologians, and of which we must speak, to pave our way to lay down the whole plan of the exterior action of God, as proclaimed by the Catholic Church.

Finite beings are capable of indefinite perfection. An assemblage of finite beings would form a cosmos, or universe; and as they are capable of indefinite perfections, we may suppose an indefinite number of these, one more perfect than the other, all arrayed in beautiful order in the intelligence of the Creator, in which the intelligibility of all possible things resides. The question arises here, suppose God has determined to act outside himself, which of the whole series of the ideal world residing in his intelligence shall he choose? Can he choose any of them? Is he bound to choose the best?

The reader will remark that this question is different from that of the end of creation. The one establishes that God cannot be forced by any reason to act outside himself, else he would not be the first and universal cause. The other question that is proposed now, supposes that God has determined freely and independently of any reason to act outside himself, and asks whether God can choose any of the possible ideal worlds residing in his intellect, or is he forced to choose the best in the series?

Some philosophers, among whom are Leibnitz and Malebranche, contend that God is absolutely free to create or not to create; but once he has determined to create, he is bound to choose the best possible cosmos in the series. We shall let them expound their system in their own words.

"God," says Leibnitz, "is the supreme reason of things, because those which are limited, like everything which comes under our vision and experience, are contingent and have nothing in them which may render their existence necessary; it being manifest that time, space, and matter, united and uniform in themselves, and indifferent to everything, may receive every other movement and figure and be in another order. We must, therefore, seek for a reason for the existence of the world, which is the whole assemblage of contingent beings, and seek it in that substance which carries within itself the reason of its own existence, and which is consequently necessary and eternal.

"It is necessary also that this cause should be intelligent, because the world which exists now, being contingent, and an infinity of other worlds being equally possible, and equally claiming existence, so to speak, it is necessary that the cause of this world should have looked into all such possible worlds to determine upon one. This look or relation of an existing substance to simple possibilities can only be the intelligence which possesses their ideas; and to determine upon one, can only be the act of a will which chooses.

The power of such substance renders its will efficacious. Power has relation to being; intelligence, to truth; the will, to good. This cause, moreover, must be infinite in every possible manner, and absolutely perfect in power, in wisdom, in goodness; because it reaches all possibility. And as all this goes together, we can only admit one such substance. Its intelligence is the source of metaphysical essences; its will, the origin of existences. Behold, in a few words, the proof of one God with all his perfections, and of the origin of things by him!

"Now, this supreme wisdom, allied to a goodness no less infinite, could not fail to choose the best. For as a lesser evil is a kind of good, so a lesser good is a kind of evil; and there would be something to correct in the action of God, if there were a means to do better. And as in mathematics when there is neither a maximum nor a minimum—in fact, no difference at all—all is done equally, or when this is impossible, nothing is done,* so we may say the same in respect to perfect wisdom, which is no less regulated than

---

* If it is required, for instance, to draw the shortest possible line from the centre to the circumference of a circle, you may draw a line to every point of the circumference, and there is no reason why a line should be drawn to any one point rather than to another.

Or, if an object at the centre is attracted equally to every point in the circumference, it cannot move in any direction, but remains at rest.

mathematics, that if there had not been a best one among all possible worlds God would not have created any. I call world the whole series and collection of all existing things, that none may say that several worlds might exist in different times and places. For in that case they would be counted together as one world, or, if you prefer, universe. And although one might fill all time and space, it would always be true that they could be filled in an infinity of manners, and that there is an infinity of worlds possible; among which it is necessary that God should have selected the best, because he does nothing without acting according to supreme reason."* Malebranche, in his ninth metaphysical conversation, after having laid down the principle that the end of creation is the glory of God, concludes that God must choose the best possible cosmos, because thereby he would gain greater glory than if he chose any of the series. "That which God wishes solely, directly, and absolutely in his designs, is to act in the most divine manner possible; it is to impress upon his conduct, as well as upon his work, the character of his attributes; it is to act exactly according to what, and to all he is. God has seen from all eternity all possible works, and all possible ways of producing them; and as he does not act but for his own glory and according to what he is, he has determined to will that

---

* Leibnitz. Theod. P. 1, par. 8.

work which could be effected and maintained by ways which must honor him more than any other work produced in a different manner."

The principles of this theory are two. One is to admit a necessity on the part of God to choose the best possible world in the series; the other is to suppose from reason that there is a best possible cosmos, as Leibnitz does; in other words, it is to limit the question only to the creative moment, and not to the whole external action of God. Now, we think that both propositions are false. As regards the first, why should God choose the best? For three reasons, according to the German philosopher. The first is as follows: A lesser good is a kind of evil, if it be opposed to a greater good. But, if God chose any world of the series in preference to the best, he would prefer a lesser good to a greater; hence, he would prefer a kind of evil to good, and the world chosen would be a kind of evil. The major of the syllogism might be granted, though not perfectly correct, if a lesser good were opposed to a greater which must necessarily be effected, but not otherwise. Suppose, among a number of actions, one more perfect than the other, of which I am not bound to perform any, I choose to perform any of the series, rejecting all others; how would the action which I choose to perform be a kind of evil? If I was bound to perform the best, and preferred one which is less so, in a certain sense we might grant that the one I select is a kind of evil. But, when I am not bound to perform any, the one I choose, though not the most perfect, cannot change its nature of good because I might, if I preferred, perform a more perfect one. The argument, therefore, of Leibnitz, supposes what is to be proved, that God *was* bound to effect the best possible cosmos; for only in that case it might be said that he preferred a certain kind of evil to good. His second reason is not more solid than the first: If God did not choose the best, we might find something to correct in his action, because there would be a means to do better. We might find something to correct in the action of God, if, in the world he chose in preference to the best, there was something wanting in the attributes and properties required by its nature. But, if the world that God chooses is endowed with all its essential attributes and proper elements, certainly there would be nothing at all to correct in it. When that great Italian artist drew a fly upon the picture of his master, so true to nature that the master on coming home went right up to the canvas to chase it away, if any one holding the opinion of Leibnitz had told him, "There is something to correct in your fly, because you could have painted a madonna or a saint," the painter would certainly have been astonished, and his answer would have been, "I might do a greater and better work; but you cannot discover any defect in my fly, because you cannot deny that, though a fly, it is a masterpiece of art." The same reason holds good with regard to the subject in question. God might certainly do better; but, if he prefers not to create the best possible cosmos, and selects any of the series, if the one selected is endowed with all the elements its nature requires, it is perfect in its own order; and no one could discover any flaw or defect in it, but every one would be obliged to call it a masterpiece. The last reason of Leibnitz has much less foundation, and savors very strongly of Pantheism: If there had not been a best possible world in the series of all the possible ones, God would not have created any. This means neither more nor less than that the world, or the aggregate of all contingent beings, unless it had a kind of absolute perfection, would be impossible. It is tantamount to denying the very possibility of creation. Because a best possible world cannot be had; for the nature of all contingent beings is like number, which progresses indefinitely, without ever reaching to a number beyond which you cannot go. Consequently, the nature of contingent things, though capable of indefinite progress, is altogether incapable, ontologically speaking, of absolute perfection; a perfection which would be required to effect a world truly the best. If, therefore, such ultimate perfection is required in order that God may create, it is evident that creation is impossible, and that optimism runs into Pantheism. The argument drawn from the sufficient reason also fails. If God were to choose a cosmos less perfect in preference to one more perfect, he would have no sufficient reason for the preference. This argument fails, first, because a cosmos, the very best and most perfect, cannot be had, as we have hinted just now. Therefore, there is no necessity for any sufficient reason for choice. Suppose a series of worlds, one more perfect than the other, arrayed in the mind of God according to numerical order. If God were to choose the tenth in the series, there would be no sufficient reason for his preferring it to the eleventh; and, if he were to select this last, there would be no sufficient reason for his preferring it to the twelfth, and so on indefinitely; and as we cannot reach to a cosmos which would be the last and the highest in perfection, so there never could be a sufficient reason for the preference of any. Consequently, there being no sufficient reason for preferring any cosmos of the series, God is free to choose any.

In the second place, even if there could be a best possible cosmos, the reason alleged by Leibnitz would not, on that account, oblige God to choose it. For a reason may be objectively or subjectively sufficient; that is, its sufficiency may emerge from the object to be created, or from the agent. Now, granting the principle of the German philosopher, God might have a subjective reason to make him act according to the requirements of wisdom, even in preferring any cosmos of the series and rejecting the best. This subjective reason might be to show and to put beyond any possibility of doubt his absolute freedom and independence in the creative act. No optimist can deny that this may have been a sufficient reason for the creative act. Consequently, even granting the possibility of a best possible world, God was not bound to create it.

The reason of Malebranche is not more conclusive than those we have just refuted. God must prefer the best possible cosmos, because this alone would manifest his glory in the best possible manner. The argument would be conclusive, if it were proven that God does wish to, or must manifest his glory in the best possible manner. But this the French philosopher does not and cannot prove. Because the best possible manner for God to manifest his infinite excellence is, to cause an infinite effect. Now, this is a contradiction in terms.

The second position of the optimists to which we object is, to assume the possibility of a best possible cosmos, as Leibnitz does, from *reason*. Now, we contend that reason alone, unaided by revelation, proves decidedly the contrary; it proves that, ontologically speaking, a best possible cosmos cannot exist, and that, if there be a way by which to raise the cosmos to a certain ultimate perfection, or perfection beyond which it could not be supposed to go, this is altogether outside and beyond the province of reason alone, and must be determined by revelation. We have already alluded to this in the examination of the third argument of Leibnitz. The best possible cosmos implies a certain ultimate and absolute perfection. Now, ontologically speaking, this is impossible in finite beings. For the question here is between two extremes, the finite and the infinite. Between the two lies the indefinite. The first extreme, or the finite, may be supposed to ascend the ladder of perfection, or quantity of being, indefinitely, without ever reaching the infinite; because its nature is essentially immutable, as every other essence. Hence, suppose it as great in perfection as you can, it will be always finite, and consequently you may always suppose a greater still. Hence, admitting a series of numberless worlds one ontologically more perfect than the other, and you can never arrive at one of which you may say this is the best, because you can always suppose a better still.

St. Thomas with his eagle glance saw, centuries before, the birth of optimism, and refuted it triumphantly, in the following argument, similar to that which we have just given. Asking the question, whether the divine intellect is limited to certain determinate effects, he denies it thus: "We have proved," he says, "the infinity of the divine essence. Now, however you may multiply the number of finite beings, they can never approximate the infinite, the latter surpassing any number of finite beings, even if it be supposed infinite. On the other hand, it is clear that, besides God, no being is infinite, because every being comes under some category of genus or species. Therefore, no matter of what quality the divine effects are supposed to be, or what quantity of perfections they may contain, it is in the nature of the divine essence infinitely to excel them, and hence the possibility of an indefinite number of them. Consequently, the divine intellect cannot be limited to this or that effect."

This argument might be abridged thus: The nature of the infinite and of the finite being immutable, the infinite must always surpass, infinitely, the finite. Hence there can be no definite term assigned to the perfection of the finite, and consequently there cannot be a cosmos ultimate and absolute in perfection. Our reason, therefore, does not support the optimists in supposing a most perfect cosmos; on the contrary, it shows that, as to essence and nature, there cannot be a cosmos the perfection of which can be supposed to be ultimate, and in a certain manner absolute; in other words, limiting the question to the creative moment which effects ontological perfection only, a best possible cosmos cannot be had. Moreover, if there be a way by which to raise the cosmos to a certain ultimate and absolute perfection, reason can tell us also that it must be altogether supernatural, and to it superintelligible. In other words, this way must be a moment or moments of the action of God, distinct from the creative moment, and causing effects above and beyond the nature and essential attributes of every possible cosmos, ontologically considered.

For if this way of raising the cosmos to an ultimate perfection were the same moment of the action of God which creates essences and proper attributes, it could not correspond to the effect desired—that of raising the cosmos to a certain absolute perfection. Because, when we speak of a creative moment effecting essences and attributes, we consider the cosmos ontologically; and ontologically the cosmos cannot have an absolute and ultimate perfection. The creative moment creates substances and essential attributes; hence if the moment of raising the cosmos to an ultimate perfection were identified with the creative moment, it would always effect substances and essential attributes—that is, a cosmos indefinitely progressive—and could not give us a cosmos absolute in perfection. Therefore the moment or moments of the action of

God raising the cosmos to a certain absolute perfection must be distinct from the creative moment, and must produce effects above and beyond every possible cosmos, ontologically considered.

Now, that which implies a moment of the action of God, distinct from the creative moment and causing effects above and beyond every possible cosmos, is called supernatural, because beyond and above nature or essence. Therefore, the way of raising the cosmos to a certain absolute perfection must be supernatural in its cause and in its effects.

If supernatural in its cause and in its effects, it is evident that this way is superintelligible to reason. Because reason, being an effect of the creative moment, cannot understand that which is above and beyond it in its cause and in its effects.

Hence, reason cannot determine whether there is such a way, or what this way is; and must necessarily leave these two questions to be determined by revelation.

Another problem, closely connected with the one which we have just discussed, presents itself here. It is as follows: In the supposition that God could find a way by which to raise the cosmos to a certain ultimate perfection, it is asked whether the divine goodness, which is the end of the exterior action of God, contains in itself a principle of fitness and agreeableness to incline it to effect this best possible cosmos. This question, as the reader is aware, is altogether different from optimism. This opinion contends that God *must* create the best possible cosmos. The question we propose now asks whether divine goodness, which is the end of the external action of God, may be inclined to effect it in force of reason of fitness and agreeableness between divine goodness and the best possible production of it, a reason of fitness which implies no manner of obligation or necessity whatever.

We answer it affirmatively; it having the support of all Catholic tradition, and the proof of it is to be found in the very force of the terms— God is infinite goodness; in acting outside himself, he effects finite goodness. Now, finite goodness and infinite goodness are agreeable to each other; therefore, if there be a way of raising finite goodness to a certain absolute goodness, it will be most agreeable to infinite goodness.*

Before we enter upon the explanation of the whole plan of the exterior works of God, it is necessary to notice another point altogether within the reach and province of reason; this is, to assign some general laws which must govern the exterior action of God.

Reason, as we have seen, cannot of itself tell whether there may be a way of exalting the cos-

---

* S. Th. S. T. p. 3. q. 1.

mos to a certain ultimate perfection, and thus rendering it the best possible cosmos; again, reason cannot tell whether God has or has not chosen to effect it. But, admitting the supposition that there is such a way, and that God has perferred it, reason can assign some laws, which it conceives must necessarily govern his exterior action, if he chooses to effect the best possible cosmos. Nor is this going beyond the sphere or province of reason, or infringing upon the rights of revelation. Because, although the premises are superintelligible, and to be declared by revelation, yet the premises once given, reason may lawfully and safely deduce some consequences, evidently flowing from those premises. In this case, the premises would be superintelligible; the consequences springing from them altogether intelligible.

Reason, therefore, affirms that if God chooses to make the best possible cosmos, the effectuation of such cosmos must be governed by the laws of *variety*, of *unity*, of *hierarchy*, of *continuity*, of *communion*, of *secondary agency*. The first imports that, if God intends to effect the best possible manifestations of himself, to which the best possible cosmos would correspond, he must effect a *variety* of moments, a *variety* of species, of individuals under each species, except when the nature and the object of the moment admits no variety or multiplicity. St. Thomas proves the necessity of such a law by the following argument: "Every agent," he says, "intends to stamp his own likeness on the effect he produces, as far as the nature of the effect will permit, and the more perfect the agent, the stronger is the likeness he impresses upon his effect."

God is a most perfect agent; it was fitting, therefore, that he should impress his own likeness on his exterior works as perfectly as their nature would allow. Now, a perfect likeness of God cannot be expressed by one moment or species of effects; because it is a principle of ontology that, when the effect is necessarily inferior in nature to the cause, as in the present case of the cosmos with regard to God, the perfections, which in the cause are united and, as it were, gathered together into one intense perfection, cannot be expressed in one effect, but ask for a variety and multiplicity of effects. The truth of this principle may be seen in the following example. What is the reason that we must frequently make use of a variety of words to express one idea? The reason lies in the objective and ontological difference of the nature of the two terms. The idea is simple, spiritual, intelligible; words are a material sound. The one in its nature is far superior to the other; the idea is possessed of more being, more perfection than words. Hence the one cannot be expressed and rendered by the other, except through a variety and multiplicity of terms. Consequently this example illustrates the principle that, when an effect is inferior in nature to its cause, whatever perfections are found in the cause, as united and simplified in one perfection, cannot be rendered or expressed except by a multiplicity and variety of effects. What we have said of language may be affirmed of every fine art, as painting, sculpture, music, etc. The type which creates them is always one and simple; it cannot be expressed except in a variety and multiplicity of forms.

The best manifestations, therefore, of God's transcendental excellence cannot be rendered and mirrored except through a variety of moments, of species, and of individuals.

The law of variety asks for the law of *hierarchy*. For variety cannot exist except by supposing a greater or less amount of perfection in the terms composing the series, one being varying from the other by possessing a greater amount of ontological perfections. Now, by admitting a greater or less amount of being, we admit a superiority on the part of that which is endowed with more ontological perfection, and an inferiority on the part of that which is endowed with less; and each being composing the cosmos, keeping its own place according to the general order, and in relation to other beings, it follows that this superiority on the part of one, and inferiority on the part of the other, founded on the intrinsic worth of their respective essences, establishes and explains the law of hierarchy.

The third law is that of unity, which implies that the variety of the different moments composing the cosmos must be brought together so as to form a perfect whole. For, first, if the variety of moments, of species and individuals, is requisite in order to express the intensity of the ontological perfection and excellence of the type of the universe, which is the infinite grandeur of God, unity also, is required, in order to express the simplicity and entirety of the type. In the second place, what would be the cosmos without unity but a numberless and confused assemblage of beings? Hence, whatever may be the variety of the moments and species of the cosmos, they must necessarily be brought together as parts and components of one harmonic whole. The nature of this unity will be gathered from the explanation of the other laws. And first, it begins to be sketched out by the law of continuity. This implies that there should be a certain proportion between each moment of the cosmos, between one species and another, and between the degrees and gradations within the species, all as far as the nature of the terms will permit. Hence, the law embraces two parts:

1st. The necessity of the greatest number of

moments and of species, as much as possible alike to each other, without ever being confounded.

2d. The greatest possible number of gradations within the same species, in proportion as individuals partake more or less fully of the species.

To give an instance: the first part of this law explains why substantial creation is composed of, 1st, atoms which do not give any signs of sensitive life; 2d, of brute animals; 3d, of intelligent animals; 4th, of pure spirits. The second part of this law explains why each of the four species just mentioned is developed in gradations almost infinite—minerals composed and recomposed in all possible ways, manifesting forms, properties, and acts altogether different, and some so constantly as to defy any change from the force of nature so far known to man; hence, in force of that immutable type, they are taken by naturalists as so many scientific species, and are the fity-nine or sixty elements which chemistry so far enumerates; animals also, extending so gradually that the ladder of fixed marks, taken by natural philosophers as so many species, begins where the signs of life are almost insensible and dubious, and ends with man; nor is there wanting, as far as it may be known, any of the intermediate steps.

The pure spirits, as we know from revelation, are divided into choirs and legions innumerable, whose successive gradations in quality and number, to us unknown but certain, are unfathomable; and it is most probable that the ladder of pure spirits is higher, beyond measure, than that which we observe in the sensible universe, and that one spirit is far more superior and distant from another spirit than one star from another.

The necessity of this law springs from that of unity. For, if the type of the cosmos be one, each moment and species representing, as it were, a side of that type, there must be as much affinity and proportion between each moment and each species as to pave the way for the law of unity to represent and mirror the entirety and oneness of the type. We say as much affinity as it is possible to produce, because between each moment and each species there is necessarily a chasm which no continuity or affinity can fill up. For instance, between pure animality and pure intelligence there is necessarily a chasm. Man, placed between the two, draws them together as much as possible; yet the necessary distance marking the two distinct natures cannot by any proportion be eliminated, else the natures would be confounded and destroyed.

But variety, brought together by the law of continuity, cannot sufficiently exhibit unity. Hence the necessity of a fourth law, that of *communion*.

This law implies, 1st, that the terms of the cosmos should be so united together as to act one upon the other, and serve each other for susteance and development; 2d, that, founded on the law of hierarchy, inferior beings should be so united to superior ones as to be, in a certain sense, transformed into them, the distinctive marks of their respective natures being kept inviolate.

This law, in both its aspects, we see actuated in the visible universe. Thus man has need of food, which is administered to him by brutes and the vegetable kingdom; he has need of air, to breathe; of light, to see; of his kind, to multiply and to form society. All other animals have need of beings different from themselves to maintain their own existence; and of their like, to multiply their species. The vegetable kingdom needs minerals, earth, water, and the different saps by which it lives. If vegetables did not expel oxygen and absorb carbonic acid, air would become unfit for the respiration of animals; and these sending back, by respiration, carbonic acid, supply that substance of which plants stand in need. Everything, moreover, in the world serves for the development and perfection of man, both as to his body and as to his intellectual, moral, and social life. Every inferior creature is transformed into man. The same animal and vegetable kingdom which, transformed into his blood, sustains his life, helps him for the development of his ideas and his will. The reason of this law, which may be called the law of life, is, that the unity of the cosmos should not be only apparent and fictitious, but real. Now, a real union is impossible if the terms united exercise no real action upon each other, and do not serve for the maintenance and development of each other.

Finally, the law of communion calls for the law of secondary agency; that is, the effects resulting from the moments of the exterior action of God should be real agents. For no real union and communion could exist among the terms of the external action unless they really acted one upon another; any other union or communion being simply fictitious and imaginary. Hence Malebranche, in his system of occasional causes, where he deprives finite beings of real agency, has not only undermined the liberty of man, but destroyed the real communion among creatures, and marred the beauty and harmony of the cosmos. To represent the cosmos as a numberless series of beings united together by no other tie than juxtaposition, and by no means really acting upon each other, is to break its connection, its its real and living unity; is to do away with the whole beauty and harmony of that hymn and canticle which God has composed to his own honor and glory.

We come now to the last question: What is the whole plan of the exterior action of God?

We have seen that if there be a way by which to effect a cosmos endowed with a certain absolute perfection, that it would be most agreeable to infinite goodness, the end of the exterior action of God. We have seen, moreover, that whether there be such a way, and what this way is, must be determined by revelation. The Catholic Church, therefore, the living embodiment of revelation, must answer these two problems.

It answers both affirmatively. The most perfect cosmos is possible. God has effected it, because most agreeable to his infinite goodness.

What is this cosmos? We shall give it in the following synoptic table.

God's exterior action divided into:

The hypostatic moment;

The beatific, or palingenesiacal moment;

The sublimative moment;

The creative moment.

The terms corresponding to each moment of the action of God are:

The Theanthropos, or Jesus Christ, God and man, centre of the whole plan;

Beatific cosmos;

Sublimative cosmos;

Substantial cosmos.

Individual terms of each cosmos:

1. Beatified angels and men;
2. Regenerated men on the earth;
3. Angels, or pure spirits;

Men, or incarnate spirits;
Sensitive beings;
Organic beings;
Inorganic beings.

As each moment of the action of God, as the creative, implies two subordinate moments, preservation and concurrence, it follows that each moment of the action of God implies its immanence and concurrence, though in Theanthropos it takes place according to special laws. Hence,

Hypostatic immanence and concurrence;
Beatific immanence and concurrence;
Creative immanence and concurrence.

CHAPTER VIII.

UNION BETWEEN THE INFINITE AND THE FINITE, OR FIRST MOMENT OF GOD'S EXTERNAL ACTION.

THE result of our preceding chapter was a supreme duality—the infinite and the finite. The one absolutely distinct in nature from the other. The first self-existing, necessary, eternal, immutable, infinitely perfect, and absolutely complete and blessed in his interior life; the other, created, contingent, mutable, imperfect, and on the way to development. How can this duality, so marked and so distinct, the terms of which are so infinitely apart, be harmonized and brought together into unity.

Such is the fifth problem which Pantheism raises, and which it undertakes to solve.

Let us investigate more deeply the nature of the problem.

We do not now inquire whether there be any

kind of union between the infinite and the finite, because they are already united by means of the creative act.

The infinite creates the finite, sustains and directs it, three moments which constitute the finite and cause it to act. This is the first and fundamental union between the infinite and the finite. After what union, then, do we seek when the problem is raised, Is there a union between the infinite and the finite already perfect as to being, or, in other words, between the infinite and the finite already united by the creative act?

We inquire after a union which may mark and express the highest possible elevation of perfection which the cosmos, or the assemblage of all finite beings, may attain; and as the finite, as we shall see, cannot acquire its highest possible perfection except by a union with infinite perfection, it follows that the problem inquires after the highest possible union between the infinite and the finite.

We shall, according to our wont, give the Pantheistic solution of the problem, and then subjoin the answer of Catholicity. The Pantheistic solution is as follows: The infinite is the highest possible indetermination and indefiniteness in the way to development. It becomes definite, and concrete in the finite, and this by a gradual process.

First, it assumes the lowest possible form of

existence in the mineral kingdom. Then it begins to show life in the vegetable kingdom. It acquires sensation and perception in the animal, and shoots up into intelligence and consciousness in humanity. Yet is this intelligence and consciousness essentially progressive, and begins from the minimum degree to rise to the highest. This principle explains all the stages of more or less civilization of which history makes mention. At first the infinite acquires those faculties in humanity which border on and are more akin to the senses, such as the imagination and the fancy; hence the primitive state of nations is marked with very imperfect development of the reasoning faculties, and with a superabundance of imagination; consequently, this primitive state abounds in national bards, who discharge all those offices which, in nations more civilized, are fulfilled by others, such as historians, orators, etc. It is also the age of myths, when people with young and robust fancy are apt to give flesh and blood and personality to any striking legend in vogue, until the legend, so dressed up and personified, is misunderstood for a historical fact and real person. Then, in proportion as the development advances, the infinite acquires a better explication of the reasoning faculties, and hence the ages of philosophy. Of course the development is gradual and slow, and is perfected by time and continued development, until the infinite arrives not only to the fullest explication of the reasoning faculties, but also to the full conciousness of its infinity, and of its eternal duration.

The infinite, arrived at the fullest explication of its intelligence, and to the full consciousness of its infinity, is humanity, or the cosmos arrived to the highest possible perfection. This humanity, dressed up by the imagination of the people, with the individuality and personal traits, is the Christ, or the myth which Christians adore.

"The subject of the attributes," says Strauss, "which the church predicates of Christ, is not an individual, but a certain idea, though real, and not void of reality, like the Kantian ideas. The properties and perfections attributed to Christ by the church, if considered as united in one individual, the God-man, contradict each other, but may be reconciled in the idea of the *species*. Humanity is the collection of two natures, or God made man; that is, *the infinite spirit transformed into a finite nature who is conscious of his eternal duration*. This humanity is begotten from a visible mother and an invisible father, that is, spirit and nature. It is that which performs miracles, enjoys impeccability, dies, and rises again, and goes up to heaven. Man, believing in this Christ, and especially in his death and resurrection, may acquire justification before God."[*]

---

[*] Strauss, *La Vie de Jesus*, Par Littré, Paris.

According to Pantheism, then, the infinite, acquiring the full consciousness of his infinite perfections in humanity, is the highest possible perfection of the cosmos, and the union therefore, between the two is the union of *identity*.

We are dispensed from attempting any refutation of this theory, seeing that it rests on premises which we have already demonstrated to be false and absurd. We only beg the reader to observe how utterly futile and useless is this theory for the solution of the problem which has called it forth. The problem is, how to raise the cosmos to the highest possible perfection, or, in other words, how to establish the highest possible union of the finite and the infinite, from which the highest possible perfection of the finite may result.

Pantheism answers by proclaiming the absolute identity of the infinite and the finite, by marking the highest possible perfection on the cosmos, when the infinite in its finite form of development acquires a consciousness of its infinity. Now, it is evident in this answer that one term of the problem is swept away, that no real cosmos exists, that it is but a phenomenon of the infinite, and that, consequently, in the Pantheistic solution the problem of the highest possible union of the infinite and the finite cannot exist, because the second term of the union does not really exist.

In the preceding article we raised the question, Is there a means by which to raise the cosmos to the highest possible perfection, a perfection almost absolute and beyond which we cannot go? And we answer that the problem cannot be solved by human reason, being altogether superintelligible, and that the solution of it must be left to the Catholic Church the repository of divine revelation.

Now, the church answers the problem by laying down the first moment of the external action of God, the hypostatic moment. By it the human nature, and through it the cosmos, is elevated to the highest possible perfection—a perfection beyond which we could not go; and thus the problem is resolved, and the aspiration of the finite to the highest possible union with the infinite is satisfied. That the reader may fully understand the doctrine of Catholicity in answer to the problem, we shall beg leave to recall a few principles which will pave the way to the very heart of the answer.

1st. Every work of God, before it exists in itself, has an objective existence in God's word.

We remarked, in the sixth chapter, that every contingent being must have a two-fold state of existence, one objective, the other subjective. The objective is the ideal and intelligible state of every being residing eternally in the mind of God. Now, all God's ideality or intelligibility is centred in the Word, whose constituent is to be the very ideality or intelligibility of God. Consequently, the cosmos, before it exists itself, has an objective and intelligible state of existence in the Word. In other terms, the Word is the subsisting and eternal intelligible expression of everything that God is, and every thing that resides within God. He is, therefore, essentially the expression of all divine ideas. Now, all the works of God are a divine idea. Therefore, the Word by his personal constituent is the representation, the type of the general system of God's external works.

2d. All the works of God, inasmuch as they reside in the Word in a typical state, are infinite.

For whatever is within God is identified with his essence, which is absolute simplicity. Therefore, the cosmos, in its typical state residing in the Word, resides in God, and is thus identified with the essence of God, and is consequently infinite. St. John, with the sublimest expression ever uttered by man, renders this idea when he says, "All that was made in him (the Word) was life,"[*] indicating that the Word, consisting of all the intelligibility of God and that which was made belonging to the ideality and intelligibility of God, was the very life of the Word, and consequently infinite.

---

[*] We read this passage as St. Cyril of Alexandria, St. Augustine, Beda, and others read it.

3d. The Word is not only the type but the efficient cause of the cosmos. The truth of this follows from the essential relation of the Word to the Father.

The Father, knowing himself, knows also whatever is possible. But whatever he knows he utters and expresses by his Word. Therefore, the Father, through his only Word, utters himself and things outside himself. But his utterance of creatures is also the cause of their subjective existence, since God is pure and undivided act. Consequently, through his single Word he affirms himself and his exterior works and consequently the Word is also their efficient cause.

4th. The external action of God tends to express, exteriorly, the divine idea of the cosmos, as perfectly as it is uttered interiorly.

We have shown in the preceding chapter that, although it was not necessary that God should effect the best possible cosmos, for the reasons which we have therein given, yet it was most agreeable to the end of creation that God should effect the best possible cosmos. Now, the best possible cosmos is evidently that which draws as near as possible to its intelligible and typical state. Consequently, the external action of God has a tendency to express, exteriorly, the divine ideas as perfectly as he utters them interiorly. St. Thomas proves the same truth with a somewhat similar argument. Every agent, he says, intends to express his own similitude (the interior idea) on the effect he produces, and the more perfect is the agent, the better and stronger will be the similitude between him and his effect. Now, God is most perfect agent. It was, therefore, most agreeable to him to stamp his own similitude on his external works as perfectly as possible; that is, it was most agreeable to him to render his external works as like their typical state as possible.

5th. This supreme or best possible expression of the typical state of God's external works could not be substantial or ontological.

We have seen that the typical state of the cosmos, residing eternally in the word of God, is identified with him, and is therefore infinite. It follows, therefore, that if we suppose a supreme, substantial, and ontological expression of this typical state, we must suppose a supreme substantial and ontological expression of the infinite. Now, this is absurd; because a supreme and ontological expression of the infinite would be the very substance of God. On the other hand, the expression requiring necessarily to be created, would be essentially finite. Consequently, on the supposition, we should have a finite infinite substantial expression of God, which is a contradiction in terms.

6th. The supreme expression cannot be effected except by an incorporation of the infinite into the finite.

Having excluded the identity between the finite and infinite natures, an identity which would be a necessary consequence if the expression were substantial and ontological, if a supreme expression of the infinite is to be effected, if the cosmos, in its subjective state, is to be elevated and made as like as possible to its typical state, there are no other means of effecting this than by an incorporation of the infinite into the finite. For let it be remembered that the finite, in force of its nature, is indefinitely progressive. You can add perfection to perfection, but unless you transform it into the infinite, it will never change its nature, and will continue to be finite. Thus, the only possible way of elevating it to the highest possible perfection, is to raise it to a union with the infinite greater than which you cannot conceive.

7th. This union or incorporation must be effected by the Word.

Because, first, the Word is the natural organ between the Father and his exterior work, since, with the same utterance, the Father speaks himself and his external works. Secondly, this union is required in order that the external works may draw as near to their typical state as possible. Now, the Word is the living and personal typical state of the cosmos, the intelligible life of the external works; it is necessary, therefore, that *he* should enter into the finite, and bring into harmony the interior infinite type of the cosmos, with its finite external expression ; unite together the ideal intelligible state with the real subjective state of the cosmos.

From all we have said, it follows that all the external works reside in the Word; that inasmuch as they reside in the Word in their typical state, they are his very life, and consequently infinite; that the Word is not only the typical but efficient cause of the cosmos; that the external act tends to express exteriorly the typical state of the cosmos as perfectly as it is uttered interiorly; that this supreme expression could not be substantial and ontological; and that, consequently, the only means of effecting it was an incorporation of the infinite into the finite, to be executed by the Word as the natural organ between God and his external works.

Now, this is the answer which Catholicity affords to the problem, What is the union by which the finite attains its highest possible perfection?

It answers in the sublime expressions of the Eagle among the Evangelists, and which resume, in a few words, all we have hitherto said.

"In the beginning (the Father) was the Word.

"And the Word was with God.

"And the Word was God. The same was in the beginning with God. All things were made *by him*, and without him was made nothing.

" That which was made in him was *life*.

" And the Word was made *flesh*, and dwelt among us."*

The Word of God, the subsisting ideality of the Father, the living type of his external works, united himself to human nature, the micro-cosmos, or abridgment of the cosmos, in such a close and intimate union as to be himself the subsistence of human nature, and thus exalted the cosmos to its highest possible perfection. This union of the Word with human nature is called hypostatic or personal union.

We must now study its nature and properties, draw the consequences which flow from it, and point out how well it answers all the requisites and conditions of the problem.

And in the first place, we remark that the subsistence of finite beings is also contingent and variable. We have before given an idea of subsistence and personality; but we beg leave to recall a few ideas about these most important notions of ideology, that the reader may better perceive in what the nature of the hypostatic union really consists. We shall explain the following notions: possibility, actuality, nature, substance, subsistence, and personality.

Possibility is the non-repugnance of a being. It is intrinsic or exterior. When the essential elements which constitute the idea of a being do

---
*St. John i.

not clash together or contradict each other, the being is intrinsically possible. When, besides the intrinsic possibility, there exists a principle which may give the being actual existence, the possibility is external.

The intrinsic possibility of a being in the mind of the cause or principle of this being is called intelligible actuality. Actuality or existence, properly speaking—that is, subjective actuality—is the existence of the being outside of the intelligent cause which perceives it; or, in other words, the external expression of the intelligible actuality.

Nature is the radical, interior principle of action in every existing being.

Substance is the existing of the being in itself, or the permanence and duration of a being in itself. Now, a being which is a substance may be united with another substance, and the union may be so close that one of them may become the natural, inseparable, intrinsic organ of the other. In this case the being which is thus united with the other and has become the organ of the other, although not ceasing to be a substance, possesses no subsistence of its own. What, then, is the subsistence of a being? It is not merely the existing in itself; it is the exclusive possession of the existing in itself and whatever flows from this exclusive possession. A being is possessed of existence in itself and of its operations, when the union of which we have spoken does not exist. But whenever such union exists, though the being continues to be substance or to exist in itself, it has yet no exclusive possession of itself.

Hence, subsistence is defined the last complement of a substance which makes it an independent whole, separate or distinct from all others; makes it own and possess itself, and renders it responsible for its operations. Personality adds to this the element of intelligence; so that a person is that supreme and intelligent principle in a being which knows itself to be a whole, independent of all others; which enjoys the possession of itself, and is responsible for its actions. Consequently, every substance which is complete—that is, detached from and independent of all other substances in such a manner as to constitute a whole by itself, and alone to bear the attribution of its properties, modifications, and functions—is a subsistence.

The subsistence or personality of a contingent being is also contingent, and may be separable from it so as to give rise to a two-fold supposition, either that the contingent being never had a subsistence of its own, or, if it had, it may be deprived of it, and its own subsistence may be substituted by another.

In the first place, we remark, in vindication of this statement, that it is possible that any substance could really exist without a subsistence. Because, as we have said, subsistence is the last complement of substance, and consequently without it the substance could not be actual, but would be a mere abstraction. That for which we contend in the proposition just laid down is, that it is not necessary that a substance should have a subsistence of its own, but that it may subsist of the subsistence of another.

For it is evident that every being comprised within the sphere of the contingent and the finite may cease to be a whole by itself, and may contract with a nature foreign to itself a union so intimate and so strong as to depend on this foreign nature in all its functions and its states, and no longer to bear the attribution and solidarity of its actions and modifications. If, for instance, a hand detached from the whole body were to trace characters, this action would be attributed to it exclusively; it would be a subsistence, a whole by itself, and we should say, *That hand writes*. But if it should become a part of, and we should consider it as dependent on, a human nature and will, it would then lose the solidary attribution of the function of which it is the organ; and then we could no longer say, *That hand writes;* but, *That man writes*.

A contingent substance may be deprived of the possession of its subsistence by a union with a substance even inferior in nature to itself. Because its superiority over this nature would not prevent its being dependent on it in its functions and in its states, as is the case with the human soul, which presides over the body, which produces in it continual changes, and which, in spite of the excellence which distinguishes it from the mass of matter which it animates, yet depends on the body in its most intimate situations, and finds itself bowed down by the continual evil which it suffers thereby.

Hence is it that in man the possession of subsistence belongs neither to the soul nor to the body, and there is no other subsistence in him but the sum of the two natures of which he is composed, but the whole of the two extremes united together, and which is at the same time spirit and body, incorruptible and corruptible, the intelligent and the brute.

Hence, neither the soul nor the body are denominated separately by their respective functions; but it is the whole man who receives the attribution and the different appellations of the actions and states of either nature, and we say, man thinks, man walks, man wills, man grows. Consequently that axiom, *Actiones et denominationes sunt suppositorum*, Actions are to be attributed to the subsistence. We remark, in the second place, that in the infinite alone the subsistence and personality is necessary, and consequently can never be separated from him or be dependent on any other. Because in this order personality affects a nature essentially complete, total, and of its own intrinsic nature absolutely independent in its action and in its eternal and immutable state, of all external substance.

It follows, therefore, that if a divine personality enters into a finite nature, it must necessarily preserve its own subsistence, since it is evident that, if a divine person is united to a created nature in a manner so close and intimate as to form one single individuality, the created nature, in force of the principles above stated, would have no individuality of its own, and the divine personality would, in such case, necessarily be the supreme and independent principle constituting the new individual, the infinite term and completion of the two natures. Now, such is the hypostatic union. The infinite person of the Word united to himself human nature in a manner so close and intimate as to form one single individuality, Christ Jesus, the Theanthropos; so that the human nature of Christ had no subsistence of its own, but subsisted of the personality of the Word. Hence, in Christ the Word of God was the only supreme and independent principle, who knew himself to be a whole apart, composed of the human and divine natures, who bore alone the attribution and solidarity of the actions springing from either nature, and who was, consequently, the only person in Christ.

But to make the nature of the hypostatic union more intelligible to the reader, we shall dwell upon it a little longer.

We may reduce all the unions between the infinite and the finite to three. The first is the action of God creating finite substances, maintaining them in existence and directing all their movements, permitting, however, their defects and shortcomings.

This is the first and fundamental union between the infinite and the finite. It begins the moment the finite is created, and continues in existence by preservation and concurrence. All this in the natural order. In the supernatural order there is also a first and fundamental union, as we shall see, by which the action of God effects, as it were, a new and superior term, preserves and directs it in its development. Thus, the first union between the finite and the infinite is the action of God effecting a finite term, maintaining it in existence, and directing it in its development, both in the substantial and the sublimative moments. However, this union not only leaves whole and entire the individuality and subsistence of the two terms united, but is not even so close and intimate as to prevent the finite term of the union from occasionally failing in its action, and of falling short of the aim to which it naturally tends. Hence a second and more excellent species of union. By it the infinite is so closely united with the finite as not only to preserve it, and to direct it in all its actions, but also to prevent it from falling into defects and errors.

This second kind of union, though, as it is evident, far exceeding the former in intimacy and perfection, since it implies an extraordinary employment of activity on the part of the infinite, and a special elevation of the finite, is yet not so close as to deprive the finite term of its own subsistence and individuality.* We may, therefore, conceive a third kind of union, whereby an infinite personality may be united to a finite nature so closely and so intimately as not only to move and direct it in all its actions, as not only to prevent it from falling into failings and imperfections, but as to make it the *intrinsic instrument*, the *intimate organ* of his own infinite action in such a manner as to form of the finite nature and of the infinite personality a new and single individuality.

This supposition is eminently possible. For, on the one hand, the infinite personality being possessed of infinite energy, and, on the other, the finite nature being endowed with an indefinite capacity of sublimation, nothing can detain the first from communicating itself to the second with such energy, power, and intensity of com-

---

* This species of union is what, in theological language, would be called confirmation in grace, and took place in the Blessed Virgin and in some saints.

munication as to render it its own most intimate and dependent organ of action. In fact, let the communication of an infinite person to a finite nature be carried to its highest possible degree of union short of absorbing and destroying the real existence of the finite, its substantiality, so to speak; let this finite nature be, accordingly, raised to the highest possible intimacy with the infinite person; let the latter take such intense possession of the former as to make it its own intrinsic organ, the immediate and sole instrument of his own infinite operation, and what will the result be? Why, that the finite nature will no longer possess itself, no longer form a whole by itself separated from and independent of any other; no longer bear the attribution of the actions springing from its nature; in short, it will no longer be a subsistence and an individuality by itself, but will form one single individuality with the divine person, or rather the infinite person will be the only single subsistence of the two natures united, the infinite and the finite. The finite nature in this supposition would stand, with regard to the infinite person, in the same relation in which our body stands with regard to our soul. For the union of body and soul, which constitutes the individual called man, takes place according to this kind of union. The soul is united to the body in a manner so close and so intimate as to render the body its own most intrinsic, dependent instrument, the organ of its operations in such a manner that, in force of this operation, the body does not possess itself, does not form a whole apart, nor is it accountable for the actions which immediately flow from its nature. In other words, it has no subsistence of its own, but subsists of the subsistence of the soul. The result of this union is possessed of one subsistence and forms one person.

The Incarnation of the Word is like to this union, hence called hypostatic or personal union. The second person of the Trinity united himself to the entire human nature, constituted of body and soul, in a manner so close and intimate as to be *himself* the subsistence of the human nature; the latter never enjoying a subsistence of its own, because, contemporaneously to the very first instant of its existence, it became the internal, the immediate, and the most intimate organ of the Word of God, and subsisted of the subsistence of the Word, so that it never bore the attribution and solidarity of those actions which have an immediate origin in human nature, but the attribution and solidarity, and, consequently, the moral worth, of those actions, belonged to the personality of the Word, according to the axiom that *Actiones sunt suppositorum.*

Hence the union between the Word of God and his human nature was not a moral union, which always implies the distinct individuality and personality of the two terms united, as Nestorius thought, and many would-be Christians of the present day seem to hold.

Nestorius was ready to grant that the union between the Word and human nature was as high and intimate as possible, so far as moral union can permit; but never would he concede that it was any higher than simple moral union, which kept whole and entire the two individualities united. Consequently, he admitted two persons and two individualities in Christ—the *Word* of God and the man called Christ. From which theory it follows that our Lord was a mere man —a saint, if you will, the highest of all saints, yet simply a man.

Catholic doctrine, on the contrary, teaching that the union of the Word and the human nature was personal, inasmuch as the divine person of the Word was the subsistence in which his human nature subsisted, teaches consequently, at the same time, that in Christ there is one person, one individuality—the divine personality of the Word; that therefore Christ, the new individual, is God, being the second divine person, in which both his divine and human nature subsist. Nor was the human nature of this new individual so absorbed by the divine personality as to cease to be a substance, as Eutyches affirmed, who upheld, it would seem, a fusion and a mixture of the two natures altogether inconceivable and absurd.

From all we have said we may form quite an accurate idea of what the hypostatic union really means. It is the union, or the meeting, so to speak, of the human and divine natures in one single point of contact, the infinite personality of the Word of God; the human nature having no personality of its own, but subsisting of the identical personality of the Word.

The new individual possessed of the divine and human nature in the unity of the single personality of the Word is Jesus Christ.

To complete now the idea of the hypostatic union, we shall point out some consequences which evidently flow from that union:

1. We should consider that nature being transmitted through generation, and Christ being possessed of two natures, the human and the divine, it is necessary to admit in him a twofold generation: one eternal, according to which he received the divine nature from the Father; the second temporal, by which he received his human nature from the Virgin Mother.

2. As nature is the radical principle and source of operation in every being, it follows that, as Christ is possessed of two natures, we must predicate of him a double operation—one human, the other divine.

3. In force of the same principle, we must predicate of him whatever necessarily belongs to the two distinct natures. Hence, as intelli-

gence and will, together with their respective perfections, belong both to the human and to the divine nature, it is clear that we must attribute to Christ, first, a divine intelligence and a divine will with their perfections, such as infinite wisdom and knowledge, infinite holiness, goodness, justice, etc.; second, a human intelligence and a human will, together with the perfections of these faculties, as knowledge, wisdom, etc.

4. As actions, though immediately proceeding from nature, are to be attributed to the subsistence and personality, because nature could not act without being possessed of subsistence, and as the subsistence or personality of both natures of Christ is one—the personality of the Word of God; and as this personality is infinite, it follows that the actions of Christ, whether immediately springing from his human nature, or proceeding from his divine nature, have all an infinite worth and excellence, on the ground of the infinite worth of the person to whom they must be attributed. This principle, so evident, and grounded on the axiom of ideology to which we have alluded—*Actiones sunt suppositorum*—has been denied by some, especially Unitarians. But happily the most abstract principles of ideology have such a bearing upon human dignity that it is easy to refute such would-be philosophers on the strong ground of the dignity of the human species. Let us give an instance. How are the

actions immediately proceeding from the corporal nature of man, such, for instance, as those of locomotion, distinguished from the actions of locomotion in the brutes? And why is it that the actions of locomotion of the first may attain the highest and most heroic moral worth, while the same actions in the brute may never have a moral dignity? Ontologically they are the same. An animal may move its foot; I may do the same; both movements may save the life of a man. In me, the stirring of my foot may have the dignity of a moral and heroic action. In the brute, it can never have it. What causes the difference? The difference lies in the fact that I am a person, the brute is not. I, being a person, the supreme, first, and independent principle of action of both my natures, corporal and spiritual, it follows that all actions radically flowing from either of my natures are to be attributed to me as person, as the supreme and independent principle of them; and as I, as a person, am capable of moral dignity, all the actions, whether proceeding from my corporal or my spiritual nature, become capable of moral worth and dignity.

In Christ, the personality or the supreme and independent principle of action of both his natures, human and divine, being one, it is evident that whether his actions radically proceed from his human nature, or spring from his divine nature, they must all be attributed to his one and single person ; and as the person is infinite, the worth and dignity of all his actions is simply infinite. As in man the personality of both corporal and spiritual natures being capable of morality, the action springing from either nature may have a moral dignity and worth. We shall conclude this article by answering a few objections raised by Unitarians against the hypostatic union. We shall take them *verbatim* from Dr. Channing's lecture on *Unitarian Christianity:*

"According to this doctrine (the doctrine of those who hold the hypostatic union), Jesus Christ, instead of being one mind, one conscious intelligent principle, whom we can understand, consists of two souls, two minds : the one divine, the other human ; the one weak, the other almighty ; the one ignorant, the other omniscient. Now, we maintain that this is to make Christ two beings. To denominate him one person, one being, and yet to suppose him made up of two minds infinitely different from each other, is to abuse and confound language, and to throw darkness over all our conceptions of intelligent natures. According to the common doctrine, each of those two minds in Christ has its own consciousness, its own will, its own perceptions. They have, in fact, no common properties. The divine mind feels none of the wants and sorrows of the human, and the human is infinitely removed from the perfections and happiness of the divine. Can you conceive of two beings in the universe more distinct? We have always thought that one person was constituted and distinguished by one consciousness. The doctrine that one and the same person should have two consciousnesses, two wills, two souls infinitely different from each other, is we think an enormous tax on human credulity."*

---

* *Unitarian Christianity, p.* 196.

We are not, of course, aware from what source or teachers Dr. Channing learned the doctrine of the hypostatic union. Of one thing we are fully assured, that the Catholic Church never taught, first, that in Christ there are two souls. He is endowed with a human soul belonging to the human nature of which he is possessed. The infinite and divine nature of the Word, of which Christ is also possessed, has never, in theological language, been called a soul, nor can we denominate it by that name except in loose and metaphorical language, unworthy of a philosopher and theologian who is stating points of doctrine.

Again, the Catholic Church never taught that the human soul of Christ was ignorant. This may have been the opinion of those from whom Dr. Channing may have drawn the theory of the hypostatic union; but in stating a doctrine in which all Christendom concurs, Protestant as well as Catholic, we should have thought it more honest if Dr. Channing, not satisfied with his own teachers, would have taken the pains to ascertain what two hundred and fifty millions of Christians hold about it.

The first real objection of Dr. Channing is as follows:

"We maintain that this (to attribute to Christ two natures in one person) is to make Christ two beings."

The same looseness and want of accuracy of philosophical language. What does Dr. Channing mean by *being?* If by being is meant nature, of course we do all attribute to Christ two natures, the human and the divine.

If by being is meant person, we deny flatly that to attribute to Christ two natures is to make him two persons.

Let the reverend doctor prove the intrinsic impossibility of two distinct natures being united in one single subsistence and person, and then we shall grant him that Christ, being possessed of two natures, is two persons also. But such impossibility can never be demonstrated; for the fact of the union between soul and body in man, in the unity of one single personality, is a contradiction to all such pretended impossibility. We have, moreover, shown in the course of this chapter the intrinsic possibility of such supposition.

Dr. Channing continues.

"To denominate him one person, one being, and yet to suppose him made up of two minds infinitely different from each other, is to abuse and confound language, and to throw darkness over all our conceptions of intelligent natures."

If our reverend opponent chooses to look with contempt and slight on all distinct and accurate notions of ideology, which he calls, in another place, vain philosophy; if he prefers to form crude and undigested ideas; if he will not sound to the very depth the nature, the faculties of intelligent beings, their acts, the genesis of their acts, their distinctions from other faculties and their acts; but loves rather to argue from ideas common to men who have never thought and thought deeply on these subjects, and distinguished them carefully, and classified them, is it any fault of ours if, when we propound the true philosophical doctrines about these subjects, Dr. Channing's ideas should become confused, and that darkness should spread over that which was never clear?

"According to the common doctrine, each of these two minds in Christ has its own consciousness, its own will, its own perceptions. They have, in fact, no common properties. Can you conceive of two beings in the universe more distinct."

If by being the doctor meant natures, we cannot conceive any thing in the universe more distinct, for which reason Catholicity teaches that there are two *distinct* natures in Christ.

If by being the doctor means that those two natures must make two persons, we cannot grant the assertion, and ask again for proofs.

"We have always thought that one person was constituted and distinguished by one consciousness."

This is the only show of reason we can find in the whole passage we have been refuting; and we have no hesitation in affirming that, if our opponent thought that one person is constituted by one consciousness, in the sense that when an intelligent nature is endowed with consciousness it must necessarily possess a personality of its own, so that consciousness and personality may be said to be identical, as the doctor supposes, he was wrong in thinking so, and should study more deeply into the distinctive essence of consciousness and personality. We may make the following suppositions, according to true ideology:

1st. An intelligent nature, having consciousness of itself, may have a personality of its own, as is the common case in human nature.

2d. An intelligent nature, having the consciousness of itself, may be deprived of its own personality and subsist of the personality of another, simply because consciousness and personality are two distinct things, and may either go together or be separated, without one being affected by the other.

Personality is the last complement of an intelligent nature, by which it forms a whole apart from all others, possessing itself, and being solidary of its actions.

Consciousness, or the *me*, is nothing more than the notion of an intelligent activity which perceives the identity of itself, thinking and reasoning with the act which perceives such identity. It rises in man in that first moment on which he becomes aware that the act which perceives the reasoning activity is not something different from itself, but something identical with the reasoning activity. In that first instant in which he perceives himself, man may pronounce, I.

He that says I, in uttering that monosyllable

testifies of being conscious that there is an activity, that this activity is the same which reflects, speaks, and announces itself, perceiving this activity.

Now, it is evident that the two notions of personality and consciousness are absolutely distinct, and as such they may be separated; and that the one can exist without the other in the sense already explained. Consequently, supposing an individual composed of two natures, one divine, the other human, both brought together in the unity of one divine person, it follows that the divine nature has consciousness of itself; in other words, is conscious that there is an infinite activity which perceives itself, and is conscious of the identity between the activity and the perception of that activity. It follows, in the second place, that the human mind of the human nature has also a consciousness of itself; that is, that in itself there is a finite activity, and that activity perceives itself, and is concious of the identity between the activity and the act of perception.

The divine nature in this one divine person would be conscious of being that supreme and independent principle of action of the natures; whereas the human nature would not be conscious of being such a supreme and independent principle of action, but dependent and subject.

CHAPTER IX.

UNION BETWEEN THE INFINITE AND THE FINITE —CONTINUED.

IN the preceding chapter we unfolded the nature of the hypostatic moment, the solution which the Catholic Church gives to the problem of the highest sublimation of the cosmos. In the present we shall point out the consequences which flow from that moment, in order to put in bolder relief the nature of the exaltation which has thereby accrued to the cosmos.

For the sake of perspicuity, we shall bring those consequences under the following heads:

1. Consequences of the hypostatic moment, viewed in reference to the external action, as the effective typical and final cause of the cosmos.

2. Consequences of the hypostatic moment, considered respectively to the nature, properties, and action of the cosmos, as abridged in the human nature of the Theanthropos.*

---
* From two Greek words, theos, God, and anthropos, man.

3. Those which relates to the other moments and persons of the cosmos.

4. Those which affect the Theanthropos himself, in relation to the other moments and persons of the cosmos.

With respect to the consequences of the first class, it is evident that the efficient typical and final cause of the external works is absolutely and simply infinite. No real distinction can be made between God's essence and his action, between his interior and exterior action. Any distinction between these things would imply potentiality and imperfection, and would throw us back into Pantheism.

God's essence, therefore, his interior and external action, are, ontologically speaking, one and the same. Now, God is absolutely infinite; the effective typical and final cause of the cosmos is thereby absolutely infinite. In other words, the cause which calls the cosmos to being is endowed with infinite energy; the cause which serves as its exemplar and pattern, and which the cosmos must delineate and express, is the infinite perfections of God; the cause which inclines God to effect it is the infinite and transcendental excellence of his being, as capable of being communicated. Now, a cause infinite in every respect would naturally claim a term corresponding to the intensity of the action. It is upon this principle that Pantheism has been framed. An infinite cause claims a term also infinite. Now, an effect infinite in its nature is a contradiction in terms; therefore the work is and can be nothing more but a phenomenon of the infinite.

If Pantheists had paid attention to the Catholic theory, that the action of God, because infinite, is distinct in two moments, the one immanent and interior, the other transient and exterior; that the same action in the first moment is absolute and necessary, and gives rise to the eternal originations which constitute infinite life; that the same action in the second moment is absolutely free, and consequently master of the intensity of its energy, free to apply as much of that energy as it chooses; they would have seen that the above principle applies to the first but not to the second moment, and that therefore their theory rests on a false assumption.

However, though Pantheism rests on a false assumption, it cannot be denied that there is a certain fitness between an infinite cause and an effect, as much as possible corresponding to the infinite energy of the cause; and that consequently the external action of God, because infinite, is for that very reason inclined to effect the best possible cosmos, a cosmos almost infinite in its perfection; an infinite energy has a tendency to effect an infinite term; an infinite typical perfection, to realize an infinite expression; an infinite yearning of communication, to impart itself in a manner the most exhaustive possible.

This fitness of proportion between cause and effect is so evident as to baffle all doubt; yet the necessary distinction implied by the very nature of cause and effect, a distinction of infinite superiority on the part of the one and infinite dependence and inferiority on the part of the other, in the present case is that which gives rise to the problem which may be formulated as follows: given the infinite superiority of the cause of the cosmos, and admitting the essential inferiority of the effect, how to exalt the effect to a perfection almost absolute, and draw it as near the perfection of the cause as possible, without destroying the absolute and necessary finiteness of the effect.

The hypostatic moment is the sublime and transcendental answer which God has given to the problem. For in that mystery the cosmos, as abridged and recapitulated in human nature, without ceasing to be what it is, without losing its essence and nature, is exalted to the highest possible perfection, by a union of subsistence with the Infinite himself. Nay, the infinite subsistence and personality of the Word is the subsistence and personality of the human nature assumed; so that the human nature, though real and finite, is at the same time the nature of the person of the Word, and consequently partaking of all the dignity, perfection, and excellence of the Word. In other terms, the cosmos, as abridged in the human nature of Christ, is *deified*, not indeed by a change in its ontological being, but by the highest, strictest, and closest communication and union with the Godhead. For, next to the identity of nature, we can conceive of no closer union or communication than that which exists between two distinct natures completed and actualized by the same identical subsistence.

Now, this identity of subsistence communicates to the inferior nature all the worth and dignity of the superior; and consequently the human nature of Christ, and hence the cosmos which it abridges, are, as it were, deified in such a manner as to exchange the denomination of attributes, and we can call man God, and God man.*

Thus the tendency of the infinite cause of the external works is fully satisfied. The infinite energy of the efficient cause has for its term an object perfectly corresponding to the intensity of its energy; since it terminates in an object absolutely infinite—the *Word* completing the two natures, the divine and the human; an individual who is very God as well as very man.

---

* We could not say the human nature is divine, nor could we say the human nature is God, or *vice versa ;* but we can only predicate the concrete terms of the concrete. The metaphysical reason is, that the foundation of this interchange of names and properties of both natures lies in their being both concrete in the subsistence of the Word. If we consider them abstractly, they are separate, and consequently cannot interchange attributes.

The typical cause is even better satisfied, so to speak. It tends to express itself exteriorly, as perfectly as it exists interiorly. By the hypostatic moment, the same identical type of the cosmos, its intelligible and objective life enters to form part of the cosmos, the interior *logos* or *schema* is wedded to its exterior expression in the bond of one subsistence, and is at the same time type and expression, objective and subjective life. Unlike other artists, who must necessarily regret the impossibility of their impressing on the external work, be it marble or canvas, the interior conceptions of the mind, as fully and as perfectly as they conceive them interiorly, the divine artist of the cosmos found a means whereby to unite, to bring together type and expression, the intelligible and the subjective, the original and the copy, in one identical person; so that in the person of the Theanthropos, as you admire the art so exquisitely divine in the copy, you are dazzled by the effulgence of the type which dwells and shines forth in it; as you wonder at the exactness of the created expression, you can see the original conception also, blended together in one common subsistence.

The end also of the external work is fully attained. For in the hypostatic moment the infinite and transcendental excellence of God is communicated in a manner beyond which you could not go; God in this moment yielding himself so far as to make his own subsistence common to human nature, and thus making it share in his infinite dignity, attributes, and the very name of God.

We shall allude to one consequence only of the second class; those having reference to the sublimation of the cosmos; and that is the life of the cosmos.

Life is action and movement. Those beings which act not, exist but do not live. If, therefore, the action of the cosmos has been elevated to the highest possible perfection by the hypostatic moment, it follows that its life also has been exalted.

Now, though action originates in the nature, which is the first principle of action in a being, yet its ontological worth and dignity it receives from the subsistence or person, because the nature would be an abstraction, a possibility, without the subsistence.

In the case, therefore, of an individual in whom the nature is inferior, and the subsistence, which actualizes and completes the nature, is superior, in the scale of being, the actions primarily originating from nature as their first root have all the ontological worth of the subsistence, and not of the nature.

Consequently, all the human actions of Christ, primarily originating in his human nature, partake of the ontological dignity and value of his person, and not of his human nature; just because his human nature is completed by and subsists in the personality of the Word.

Now, this personality is infinite; infinite, therefore, is the ontological worth of the human actions of Christ.

And if we consider, as we have already remarked, that human nature is a recapitulation of all the elements of the cosmos, since it shares the spirit, intelligence, and will with the angelic nature, sensible apprehension with animal nature, life with the vegetable nature, and locomotion with inorganic nature, it follows that all the actions of the cosmos are recapitulated in human nature, and that consequently they are exalted to an infinite worth and dignity in the human nature of Christ, which is completed by his infinite personality.

The consequences of the third class will better explain and develop this exaltation of the life of the cosmos. The object of the external action consists in manifesting the infinite excellence and perfections of God. This creation does in two different ways: 1st, ontologically, the very nature of the cosmos being an expression, a likeness of the infinite. This function is discharged indistinctly both by intelligent and unintelligent beings.

2d. But this function, by which unintelligent creatures unconsciously manifest in their nature and properties the excellence of God, in intelligent creatures is necessarily a moral act, and gives rise to the virtue of religion; because intelligent creatures cannot possibly fail to perceive the relation which binds them to their creator, and to feel the duty of acknowledging it.

Hence, religion is an absolute duty for intelligent beings; so necessary and absolute that the opposite assertion would be a contradiction in terms.

To say a creature, is to affirm a being created by God with the express purpose of manifesting his perfections; to say intelligent, is to affirm a creature able to perceive this relation, and able to fulfil the purpose which it perceives was intended by the creator. To absolve, therefore, intelligent creatures from the duty of religion, is to affirm and deny in the same breath that they *are* intelligent creatures.

Hence, they must necessarily perceive and will the relation in which they stand to their creator, and consequently be religious by force of their very nature and existence.

The whole cosmos must pay to God, its creator, the homage of religion; unintelligent creatures by unconsciously portraying his perfections; intelligent creatures, by acknowledging the same with their intelligence and will.

Now, this first function of the cosmos, this primary act of its life, is elevated to the highest possible perfection through the hypostatic moment. For through this moment the external religion of the cosmos is elevated to the dignity and grandeur of the internal religion.

Philosophers and theologians do not treat of the existence of the eternal and objective religion, as often as they do of that religion which expresses the relations between the creator and his creatures, and might be styled external and temporal religion. But every thing temporal is the counterpart of something eternal; every subjective existence has an intelligible objective existence in eternity, a type without which its subjective existence were inconceivable.

Religion, then, must have its type in God: in his infinite essence must be found those eternal laws which render temporal religion possible.

What is there in the essence of the infinite which constitutes religion, and establishes its laws?

The eternal religion is the life of God, its laws the laws of the genesis of his life.

God is a living, personal being. He is unborn, unbegotten, intelligent activity; first termination of the Godhead. By one eternal, immanent glance of his intelligence he searches, so to speak, and scrutinizes the innermost depths of his essence, and thus comprehends himself, that is, conceives and utters himself interiorly.

This infinite, most perfect utterance and intelligible expression of himself is a second termination of the Godhead; the Word, who portrays and manifests the Godhead intelligibly; as the first person is the actuation of the Godhead under the termination of intelligent, primary, independent activity and principle.

This duality of terminations is brought into harmony by a third person, the result of the action of both. For between the intelligent principle, uttering himself intelligibly, and the utterance, the term of that intellectual conception, there passes necessarily an infinite attraction, a blissful sympathy, an unutterable complacency.

The Father beholds as in a bright, clear stream of infinite light the unspeakable beauty and loveliness of his infinite perfections, and utters them to himself, and delights in that utterance. The Son beholds himself as the most perfect, the consubstantial representation of the sublime excellence of the Father, and takes complacency in him as the principle of his personality.

This common complacency, sympathy, attraction, love, bliss, is the third termination of the Godhead, the Holy Spirit, the breath of the love of both, the personal subsisting attraction of the Father and of the Son, the person who closes the cycle of God's infinite life.

This is the eternal, immanent, objective religion. For what is religion in its highest metaphysical acceptation? It is the intelligible and loving acknowledgment of the infinite nature and attributes of God. Now, the Word is the infinite, substantial, and intelligible acknowledgment of the Father; the Holy Ghost is the infinite, substantial, loving acknowledgment of both. Therefore, the eternal mystery of the life of the infinite, the Trinity, is also the eternal objective religion by which God acknowledges, appreciates and honors himself.

It might be objected to the soundness of this doctrine, that one of the relations, which is the principal and fundamental in religion, the relation of dependence, is wanting in the life of the infinite, and that consequently that life cannot be taken as the eternal type of religion.

In the metaphysical idea of religion, dependence is necessary as the fundamental relation upon which all others rest. Because religion is essentially an acknowledgment of one person from another. Therefore, the person who acknowledges himself as indebted to another for something must, by that very fact, be dependent upon him. The intelligible acknowledgment means that one intelligent being perceives with his mind that he stands indebted to another for something, and consequently depends upon him for that thing. The practical or loving acknowledgment conveys the idea that the person who has perceived his standing indebted to another for something, acts in such a manner as to express by his action his sense of the dependence. Religion is therefore an intelligible and practical dependence of one person upon another.

But this relation of dependence does not necessarily imply the idea of inferiority in the hierachy of being upon the part of the person who is dependent, and a like superiority on the part of the person who is acknowledged. A dependence of origin or procession, without including any inferiority on the part of him who is dependent, is fully and absolutely sufficient in the metaphysical idea of transcendental religion.

The reason of this lies in the very nature of transcendental religion or acknowledgment. By this we seek the highest possible, the most perfect idea of acknowledgment, which necessarily implies an equality between the person who acknowledges and the person who is acknowledged. Otherwise, without the equality the acknowledgment would fall short of the perfection of the object acknowledged. Now, an inferiority of nature and attributes in the person who acknowledges would destroy the equality and imply an inferiority of acknowledgment, and consequently would not represent the idea of the highest, most perfect acknowledgment and religion.

The Son, therefore, depending upon the Father as to his origin, though absolutely equal to him in nature and attributes, and being the intelligible, infinite expression of the perfections of the Father, is by force of his very personality, the subsisting, living, speaking acknowledgment of the Father.

The Holy Ghost, depending upon the Father and the Son as to origin, though perfectly equal to them as to nature, and being the loving expression of the infinite goodness of both, is, by force of his very personality, the living, practical recognition of the Father and of the Son.

The eternal life of God, therefore, is the eternal typical religion. It is the only true religion in the transcendental meaning of the term. Because the more perfect is the recognition, the more adequate it is to the object, and the more it approaches to metaphysical truth, which lies in the equation of the type with its expression. It is the only religion worthy of God. For religion, as we have said, is the intelligible and practical recognition of God. Now, every one can see that such recognition, to be worthy of God, must be absolutely perfect. The intelligible recognition must imply such an idea of God as to be absolute utterance of his nature and perfections; the loving recognition must love God in the most perfect and absolute sense of the word. Now, God being infinite, an infinite, intelligible recognition, an infinite, practical, loving acknowledgment only can be worthy of him. He alone can know and love himself as he deserves. To draw then, nearer to our subject, we inquire, Is temporal religion worthy of God? And we observe, before answering the question, that by temporal religion we do not mean that recognition of God which results from the ontological essence of all the beings of the cosmos, but that voluntary and reflex acknowledgment which created spirits, whether men or angels, are bound to pay to their maker. We ask, therefore, is the acknowledgment which created spirits pay to God worthy of him, worthy of his infinite and transcendental nature and perfections? Evidently not. Because the intelligence of the cherubim, however high and lofty, and soaring as far above the intelligence of inferior created spirits as the eagle's flight over all the feathered tribes; the love of the seraphim, however intense, however deep, however tender, however ardent, are merely and simply finite. On the other hand, what is the intelligence and love of men compared with those of the heavenly spirits, who are so near the supreme intelligence and love, when compared to us, and yet so far from it, when compared with God?

The religion, therefore, of all created spirits is not proportionate to its object; it falls infinitely short of the merits of God. Hence the cosmos, of which created spirits form the best part, with the exclusion of the Incarnate Word, cannot properly discharge the first and paramount duty of the creature, the homage of acknowledgment and adoration to its creator.

But let the Word, the eternal mediator between God and the cosmos, let the intelligible and objective life, the type of the cosmos, enter into it, and the worth of the nature and the acts of the cosmos shall be exalted, elevated, changed, transformed; and it can then pay to God a tribute of recognition fully, perfectly, and absolutely worthy of him.

For the Theanthropos—the God-Man, who is possessed of infinite intelligence, and can comprehend God as far as God is intelligible, who is possessed of infinite will, and can love God as far as God is amiable, can recognize him, acknowledge him, theoretically and practically as perfectly as he deserves, with absolute equation. And the human nature of the Theanthropos, though in itself finite in its essence and in its acts, can likewise render to God a homage fully and perfectly worthy of him. First, because the acts of the Word of God, honoring the infinite majesty theoretically and practically in an infinite manner, are acts also belonging to human nature, are its own acts, so to speak; because they are acts of its own personality, and human nature can say to God, I honor thee with the acts of my own person, and they are infinite. Secondly, because even the acts springing immediately from human nature, and consequently in themselves finite, in force of the union of these same acts with the divine personality in whom they subsist; and human nature can say to God, I honor you with my own acts of worship and acknowledgment. In both cases, therefore, whether we look at the acts of the Theanthropos springing from his divine nature, or at those proceeding from his human nature, they are of infinite value, by force of the unity of his divine person; and consequently the Theanthropos can recognize God in an infinite manner, a manner absolutely worthy of God. This is what makes the Mass the supreme act of worship in the Catholic Church. But of this hereafter.

The cosmos, then, recapitulated in the human nature of Christ, is enabled to worship God as he deserves; the temporal religion of the cosmos is wedded to the eternal; and the Godhead is worshipped in his cosmos with the same perfect homage of recognition as he receives from eternity in the bosom of his interior life. The Word, as infinite recognition of the Father, is the eternal mediator of religion between the Father and the Holy Ghost. The Word incarnate is the mediator of religion between God and his cosmos.

All angels and men, and to a certain degree all creatures, all persons, all individualities, from the highest pinnacle of creation down to the farthest extremities thereof, united in a particular manner, which shall be hereafter explained, with the

Theanthropos, and partakers of his mind, of his will, of his affections, of his heart, of his life, can raise to God a canticle of acknowledgment fully worthy of him, perfectly equal to that which rose up silently in the bosom of the infinite, when, in the day of his eternity, he uttered his infinite word, and breathed his spirit and recognized himself very God.

Who will not admit a dogma which elevates the cosmos to such a height of dignity? And what can Pantheism offer in its stead? It can destroy both temporal and eternal religion, by identifying both terms, the cosmos and the infinite, and thus rendering a true acknowledgment of God impossible. But it can never impart that true exaltation, that high dignity to the cosmos, which the Catholic doctrine of the hypostatic moment affords. God acknowledges himself infinitely from all eternity, by uttering a perfect intellectual expression of himself, and by both aspiring a loving recognition of themselves. We creatures are enabled to acknowledge him as he acknowledges himself; the only recognition worthy of him. The Word, by becoming incarnate, enters into the choir of creation, and takes its leadership; brings into it the harmonies of the bosom of God, and on a sudden the music and the songs of the cosmos rise up to the height of its leader, and mingle with the harmonies of eternal life.

Before we pass to other consequences of the incarnation, we shall point out a corollary, among all others, which follows from the doctrine above stated, and which, though of the highest importance, is lost sight of both by apologists and rationalists.

This corollary is, that the Christian religion, as Christ founded it, is a *cosmological law*, and can no more be lost sight of by the philosopher than by a Christian himself.

For according to the actual plan of the cosmos, the plan which God selected, God was not satisfied with that finite, imperfect, natural acknowledgment which created spirits might render to him. But, as he was pleased not to leave the cosmos in its natural conditions, but raised it to the highest possible dignity by a union with the divine personality of the Word, so he was not satisfied that the acknowledgment which is due to him as the creator should be that natural, imperfect, finite acknowledgment which created spirits could, with their natural force, render to him, but willed that their acknowledgment should, by a union with the Theanthropos, be exalted to the dignity of the infinite acknowledgment which he renders to himself from all eternity.

This is a law of the actual cosmos which God selected, and it is as much a law, an integral part of its constituents, as any natural law which we may discover. God selected such a cosmos that we might pay to him a recognition true and worthy of him.

Now, Christianity, as Christ founded it, is the religion of all created persons in time and space, who, united to the Theanthropos by a particular mode of union, worship God with and through the Theanthropos; that is, worship God as he deserves. Consequently Christianity is a law of the cosmos, an integral constituent of that cosmos which God selected, and hence true, elevating, and imperative.

True, because it is a religion the acts of which are fully adequate to the object, since in it God is worshipped as perfectly as he deserves.

True, because, religion implying a knowledge of God, in Christianity knowledge is imparted to the minds of its followers fully adequate to the object known, in its origin, in its mode of communication, and its end. In its origin, being derived from the Theanthropos; in its mode, being imparted by a peculiar operation of the Theanthropos; and in its end, as tending to gradual development, until it has reached the fulness of knowledge, which may be imparted to a pure creature in palingenesia, the final regeneration of spirits in eternity.

True, because, religion implying operation and action, action is imparted in the same manner as knowledge.

Elevating, because it is evident that that aim

of Christianity is to raise human persons from their natural state, from their natural operation, to a superior state and operation through the Theanthropos.

Imperative, because, God having made Christianity a law of the cosmos, which he selected, it is not free to a moral agent to accept or reject it, but all must accept it as a law of the cosmos which no one may contravene.

Hence rationalists, and infidels, and indifferentists, in rejecting Christianity or in being indifferent to it, reject a law of the cosmos, a law which is as essential to the entirety of the cosmos, which God chose, as the law of gravitation or locomotion; and in reasoning upon the cosmos, after rejecting Christianity, rationalists and indifferentists should say, "I do not reason on the actual cosmos that God has selected; I reason on a cosmos of my own creation; I limit it, I contract it, I debase it, as it pleases my fancy; and yet, after that, I insist on retaining the name of philosopher."

We pass to the other consequence. The tendency of the exterior act is to form the cosmos, and especially created intelligences, into a universal society. We could prove this by the consideration of the efficient, typical, and final cause of the external act; but prefer to show it only from the typical cause, or objective life of creation.

The objective life of the cosmos is the life of

the infinite intelligibly expressed in the Word. Now, God's life is essentially one, absolute, most perfect, universal society. One is the nature of the infinite terminated and concreted by three distinct subsistences—the Beginning, the Word, the Spirit. One and identical is their intelligence and will; because intelligence and will, being an attribute of nature, as the three divine personalities partake of the same nature, they are at the same time endowed with the same identical intelligence and will.

One and identical is likewise their life and bliss; because the life and bliss of the infinite consists in knowing and loving himself, in which operation the three divine personalities share, in force of the identical absolute intelligence and will with which they are equally endowed. They are finally one by their common and reciprocal indwelling in each other; because the beginning is Father, inasmuch as his eternal Son dwells in his bosom. The Son is such, inasmuch as he is related to the Father, and dwells in him. The Spirit is such, inasmuch as he is related to both, and dwells in both.

The Trinity, therefore, is the type of one universal perfect society, because the three divine persons are associated by the unity and identity of nature, of attributes, of life, of happiness, and by a common indwelling in each other.

Now, the Trinity, as intelligibly mirrored in

the Word, is the objective life of the cosmos, or its typical cause. On the other hand, we have shown that the plan which God has chosen in his works *ad extra* is that which draws the subjective cosmos as near in perfection to its intelligible and objective life as possible.

The cosmos, therefore, in force of its typical cause, is called to represent the one most perfect universal society of the three divine persons as perfectly as possible.

This were impossible except by the admission of the existence of the Theanthropos into creation. For, once admitting the existence of the Theanthropos, we see that the eternal society of the three divine persons, as mirrored intelligibly in the Word, the very typical cause of the cosmos, has come in contact with the cosmos itself, by the closest, most intimate society—the same identical subsistence: the eternal and interior society is externated, and the cosmos and the infinite society of God form one single society in the identity of the person of the Word. Man and God are one single society in Christ. Unite now all created spirits and persons to this externation of the typical cause, by a principle of which we shall speak in the next chapter; unite their nature to his nature, their intelligence to his intelligence, their will to his will, their life to his life, their bliss to his bliss; and we shall have one universal society, partaking of the nature, the intelligence, the will, the life, the bliss, of the Theanthropos; and thus not only united with each other, and meeting each other in one common medium and centre, but also presenting a divine society whose bond of union is the intelligence, will, life, bliss of the Theanthropos communicated to them all; and through him and by him ushered into the eternal society of the Trinity.

This is the idea expressed in the sublime prayer of our Lord, when he said, Father, keep them in thy name whom thou hast given me, that they may be one as WE also are. And not for them only do I pray, but for them also who through their word shall believe in me; that they all may be one, as thou, Father, in me, and I in thee; that they also may be one in us, I in them, and thou in me, that they may be made perfect in one: that the love wherewith thou hast loved me may be in them, and I in them.*

This consequence of the hypostatic moment affords the cosmological reason of the truth, the divinity, the imperative necessity of the Catholic church.

For the Catholic Church is nothing else but the society of all the persons of the cosmos elevated in Christ and through Christ to the eternal typical society of the Trinity, by a community of supernatural intelligence, will, life, bliss, imparted to them by the Theanthropos, to whom

---

* St. John, ch. xvii., *passim*.

they are united, travelling centuries and generations to add new members to this universal society of all ages, until the number of members being complete, it shall cease its temporal action, and rest in eternity. This is the only true view of the Catholic Church. Men imagine it to be an afterthought, a thing begun nineteen centuries ago. The Catholic Church is a cosmological law; and hence *necessary, universal, imperative*. God in acting outside himself might have chosen to effect only substantial creation; but having once determined to effect the hypostatic moment, to cause the Theanthropos to form the exalting principle, the centre, the mediator of the cosmos, he could not but carry out to their fullest expression those relations which result from that moment. Now, the Catholic Church is the necessary consequence of the hypostatic moment. The Word, the type of the universe, is united to its expression in the unity of his divine personality, and is thus placed at the very centre of the universe, as that in which all things are consolidated. It follows, therefore, that all created persons must hover around about their centre, must be put in communication with him, united to him as their centre and mediator by a communion of intelligence, of will, of life, of bliss, and thus be associated with each other, and united with the eternal archetypical society—the Trinity.

This gives as a result a society of all created

persons united by the bond of the same theanthropic intelligence, will, life, and bliss.

Now, such is the Catholic Church. Therefore it is a cosmological law in the present plan of the exterior action of God; and as a cosmological law is *universal*, extending to all times and places, *divine* in its origin and action, and *imperative*, so the Catholic Church is essentially *universal* in time and space; *divine* in its origin and action; *imperative*, enforcing its acceptance and adhesion on every intellect which can contemplate the plan of the exterior works of God.

Hence Protestantism is not only a theological error, but a philosophical blunder.

God effects the hypostatic moment, and makes the Theanthropos the centre of the cosmos, and of the best part of the cosmos—men. He could not be their centre unless they were united to him by intelligence, will, and life. And they could not be united to him unless they were united to each other by a common theanthropic intelligence, will, and life, etc.* And the question being of incarnate spirits, this union of intelligence, will, and life could not be possible, except it were visible and external.

Hence, it is a necessary consequence of the hypostatic moment that men should be united in one universal, visible, and external society. Pro-

---

* The idea comprehends other conditions which it is not necessary to unfold now.

testantism, admitting the hypostatic moment, denies the consequence which so evidently flows from it, and denies by its fundamental principle a society of intelligence, and of will, and of life, and also the visibility, the externation of such society, and takes refuge in an individual union between himself and Christ, and says, by the same principle, "I have a right to form an intelligence of my own, in no way connected with the intelligence of other created persons. I have a right to follow laws which I shall individually find out and proclaim. I have a right to have a life exclusively my own, and no interchange shall pass between me and others."

Hence the absolute falsehood of Protestantism, which ignores the existence and qualities of this supreme cosmological law.

The cosmological law is *one*. Protestantism is *multiform*. The cosmological law is *universal*. Protestantism is *individual*. The cosmological law is *communicative* and *expansive*. Protestantism is *egotistical*

What is more remakable still is the astounding pretension of Protestantism to having enlightened and elevated mankind. Enlightened mankind by ignoring the plan of the universe in its beauty, in its harmony, in its whole! Elevated mankind by proclaiming individualism and egotism in the face of the one great life-giving law of a common universal society!

We would beg our Protestant readers to ask themselves the following questions:

Is it true that God made Christ, the Word incarnate, the centre of the cosmos, and hence the centre of all created persons?

Is it true that, in consequence of this, created persons should be united to him by partaking of his intelligence, will, and life?

Is it true that, in force of this union, all created persons become united to each other in force of the principle that two things united to a third are united to each other?

Is it true that God has effected all this in order to elevate human society to the society of his eternal life?

Is it not true that the Catholic Church is nothing but that?

Then the Catholic Church is *cosmological law, one, divine, universal, imperative.*

We pass to the fourth class of consequences, those which regard the Theanthropos in relation to all the moments and persons of the cosmos.

1. The Theanthropos was intended by God before and above all other works.

Every one is aware that an intellectual agent, in effecting his works, follows a different order from that which he pursues in planning them; in other words, the order of execution which an intellectual agent follows is in the inverse ratio of the order which he follows in idealizing them. In an architect's mind the end and use of a building is first in order, and he idealizes and shapes his building according to the object intended. In the execution of the work the order is inverted, the building is effected first, the object and use are attained afterward.

The order followed in idealizing a work is called by schoolmen the order of *intention;* that which is pursued in executing the work, the order of *execution.* When we say, therefore, that the hypostatic moment and the Theanthropos are the first of God's external works, we mean, of course, in the order of intention; we mean that they were intended by God first and before every other work when he resolved to act outside himself;[*] so that the incarnation was determined upon, not only independently of the sin of man, but would have taken place even if man had never fallen.[†]

The metaphysical reason of this consequence is found in the relation which means bear to the end. It is absolutely necessary that an intellectual agent should intend primarily and chiefly that object which is best calculated to attain the end he has in view in his action; which best ful-

---

[*] "Dico Deum primaria intentione, qua voluit se creaturis communicare, voluisse mysterium Incarnationis et Christum Dominum ut esset caput et finis divinorum operum sub ipso Deo." (Suarez, *De Incarnatione*, Disp. v. sect. ii.)

[†] Suarez, Ibidem.

fils his intention and is the most appropriate and nearest mean.

Now, the hypostatic moment, and consequently Christ, attains better than any other moment or individual the object of the external action of God, as we have shown. Therefore Christ was intended by God first and above every other work.

This consequence is poetically described by the inspired author of the Proverbs, in those beautiful lines so well known:

"The Lord possessed me from the beginning of his ways, before he made anything from the beginning.

"I was set up from all eternity, and of old before the earth was made.

"The depths were not as yet, and I was already conceived; neither had the foundations of water as yet sprung out.

"The mountains with their huge bulk had not as yet been established; before the hills I was brought forth.

"He had not made the earth, nor the rivers, nor the poles of the world.

"When he prepared the heavens, I was present; when with a certain law and compass he inclosed the depths," etc.*

2. Consequence. The Theanthropos is the secondary end of God's external works.

For, in a series of means necessary to the end, that which is first and chief is also end in respect to the other means. Christ, therefore, being the first and chief means to attain the end of the external act, is also end in reference to the other moments, and consequently the secondary end of

---
* Prov. ch. viii.

the cosmos. "All things," said St. Paul to the Corinthians, "are yours; and you are Christ's, and Christ is God's.

3. Christ is the secondary type of the cosmos. Ontologically speaking, the end determines and shapes the nature and perfections of the means, and bears to the means the relation of type and exemplar. Now, Christ is the secondary end of the cosmos; he is, therefore, the secondary model and type of the exterior works; in other words, he is the best and supremest expression of God's infinite excellence, the archetype of the cosmos; therefore he is also the secondary type of the cosmos.

4. Christ is the universal mediator between God and his works.

As in the bosom of God the Word is the medium in the genesis of his eternal life, the link which connects the Father and the Spirit; so, outside of God, the incarnate Word is the mediator, the medium universal and absolute, between God and his works, the link connecting the infinite and the finite.

For, in the first place, the very nature of the hypostatic moment makes him such. He is the *Word*, that is, the very Godhead, with his infinite nature and perfections, under the termination of intelligibility.

He is man, comprehending in his human nature all the various elements of substantial creation.

Both the Godhead and the human nature subsist of that one termination of intelligibility. It is evident, therefore, that the incarnate Word is essentially, by the very nature of the hypostatic union, the medium between the infinite and the finite.

Moreover, every intellectual agent is linked to his work by the type of it existing in the intelligence, without which knowledge the agent could never communicate with his work. The divine Artist of the cosmos, therefore, is in communication with it by the eternal cosmic type residing in his essence—the Word. Now, Christ is the Word incarnate, and, as such, is the type of the cosmos hypostatically united to its expression, the intelligible and objective life personally linked to the subjective. He is, therefore, the medium between the objective and subjective cosmos, and consequently between the cosmos and God.

Hence Christ is essentially the mediator of creation, both in the natural and supernatural moment; inasmuch as by him and through him all things were made in both orders.

He is essentially the mediator of the continuation of existence in both orders; since the same action, by which all things were made, through him continues to hold them in existence.

He is essentially the mediator of the action of creatures in both orders; since the same action by which all things are made to exist, and to continue in existence through him, incites them to action and aids them to develop their faculties. He is essentially the mediator of perfection and beatitude; because the same action, which incites and aids all existences, both in the natural and supernatural order, to develop their faculties, must also perfect them, and bring them to their final completion. And in the very act of beatitude, when the dawn of the vision of God shall flash before the mind of created spirits, the Theanthropos shall be the mediator between them and the superabundant and dazzling effulgence of the infinite, by aiding and invigorating their intellect with the light of glory.

"In him (Christ) were all things created in heaven and on earth, visible and invisible. He is before all, and by him all things consist."*

5. Christ is the supreme universal objective science; the supreme universal objective dialectic.

In the ontological order intelligibility and reality are one and the same thing; every thing real being by the very fact intelligible, and *vice versa*.

Now, Christ is the infinite and finite reality, hypostatically united together. He is, therefore, the infinite finite intelligibility, and consequently the universal objective science.

He is also the supreme universal objective dialectic; for he is essentially the type and the form

---

* St. Paul Colos. ch. v. 16.

of all reasoning. The form of all reasoning consists in the comparison of two terms with a third, with a view of deducing their agreement or disagreement. Christ is at once the infinite universal term, and the finite and particular term; both terms agreeing together in the oneness of his divine personality. He is, therefore, the type, and form of all reasoning, and the objective dialectic.

6. He is the light of all finite intelligences. Because, in the first place, he is the space of essences, so to speak; being the subsisting intelligibility of the Godhead.

Secondly. Because in his individuality there is the ontological agreement of all the problems of the human mind, and the solution of all the questions relative to the infinite and the finite, to time and eternity, to the absolute and the relative, to immutability and movement, to cause and effect, etc.

Thirdly. Because he is the incarnate Word, creating, supporting, elevating and perfecting all created intelligences, in force of his essential office of universal mediator of the cosmos.

7. Christ is the supreme universal and objective morality.

The moral perfection of the cosmos consists in the voluntary realization of the final perfection to which it is destined by its archetype.

Now, Christ is the archetype of the cosmos. Therefore, he is the supreme objective morality.

He is also supreme morality in the sense of his inciting and aiding the cosmos in the voluntary reproduction and realization of the type, in force of his office of mediator. Therefore, etc.

8. Christ is the supreme objective realization of the beautiful.

The beautiful lies in variety reduced to unity by order and proportion. Christ is the infinite and finite, the two beings most distant, brought together into the unity of his divine personality by order and proportion, as it is evident to every mind that has grasped the nature of the hypostatic moment.

He is, therefore, the supreme, universal realization of the beautiful.

9. Christ is the supreme and universal king and ruler of the universe.

For he is the medium of the creation, preservation, and action of the cosmos; he is its secondary end and exemplar; he is the type and light of intelligence, the law of morality and of the beautiful

The cosmos, therefore, is subject and dependent upon him for so many reasons, and consequently he is the supreme ruler of it.

10. He is the centre of all the other moments and persons of the cosmos; all things gathering around him as their chief, their exemplar, their mediator.

"I am the Alpha and Omega, the Beginning and the End." (Apoc. i. 8.)

CHAPTER X.

THE SUPERNATURAL OR SUBLIMITIVE MOMENTS OF GOD'S ACTION.

IN the hypostatic moment which terminates in the Theanthropos, created personality is absolutely left out; for that moment is limited to uniting only human nature to the infinite personality of the Word, in the bond of his single divine subsistence. Because, if the hypostatic moment had united also created personality to the infinite subsistence of the Word, the former would necessarily have ceased to exist; since the finite supreme principle in a being which is conscious of being its own, and of bearing the attribution and solidarity of its own acts, when united in the closest possible manner to an infinite personality, must necessarily yield its supremacy and cease to exist; and in the two natures united, one only can be the supreme and independent principle of action—the infinite personality.

It was, therefore, in order to preserve whole and entire created personality, that the hypostatic moment was limited to uniting human nature alone to the person of the Word. Yet this necessary limitation causes another dualism in the cosmos: on one side, all the natures of substantial creation, as recapitulated in human nature, elevated in the Theanthropos to an infinite life and dignity; on the other hand, all created personalities, the highest and the best elements of substantial creation remaining in the same natural state, and by no means partaking of the universal elevation of the cosmos consequent upon the hypostatic moment.

This dualism, which mars the harmony and beauty of the cosmos, which opens an abyss between one element and the other, must be reconciled and brought together. The moment which effects this, and which brings together the Theanthropos and created personality, is the *supernatural* or *sublimative* moment.

In this chapter, we shall define what is meant by the *supernatural*, show its metaphysical possibility, vindicate its imperative necessity in the plan of the cosmos, study its intrinsic essence and properties, and, finally, point out the relations which it bears to the Theanthropos and to substantial creation.

And in the outset we cannot but be aware that we undertake to grapple with a legion of would-be philosophers, who admit of nothing more than pure, unalloyed nature ; who reject peremptorily whatever is above or beyond the sphere of nature and the reach of the short span of their reason ; who are startled at the very utterance of the word supernatural, as something too imaginary, too arbitrary, too groundless, in fact, too absurd to claim any serious attention. We beg of such as these to read the chapter through, and to do nothing more than use their vaunted reason, and perhaps they will find that the supernatural is something too lofty and sublime, too necessary to the exigencies of the cosmos and the dignity of human personality, to be rejected.

What, then, is meant by the supernatural? So far as it is necessary now for the understanding of what follows, we may define the supernatural to be—*a principle of action imparted to and elevating created personalities ; in its cause, in its intimate nature and properties, in its acts or development, and in its end, superior to and above any principle of substantial creation, viewed in all these different relations.*

We shall in the course of the chapter explain every element of the definition. At present, we inquire, Is a principle of action, such as we have described it, intrinsically possible ; or otherwise, is there any intrinsic contradiction in supposing such a principle ? We find here, as we have supposed in all these chapters, that there is and can be no particular error; that there is only one universal error, *Pantheism;* and that there can be no medium between Pantheism and Catholicity: either universal error or universal truth, all truth or no truth.

Rationalism cannot logically hold the impossibility of the supernatural, except on pantheistic grounds; for the impossibility of the supernatural can only be supported on the ground that there is no possible distinction between the infinite and the finite; that all finite phenomena are but the intrinsic and necessary natural development of the infinite. On this ground only is it evident that the supernatural, as we have defined it, is intrinsically impossible; for, if there be no possible distinction between the infinite and the finite, if one only is the universal natural principle of action, the germinal necessary activity residing in the bosom of the infinite, it is a contradiction to suppose two principles, and a worse contradiction to suppose one superior to the other. If, as Hegel maintains, one is the supreme, absolute, solitary, universal principle of action—the *idea* which is identified with the *being*, which idea by unfolding itself becomes nature and humanity (the last expression and form of Pantheism)—it is evident that we cannot suppose a principle superior to any other.

From these remarks, it follows that the supernatural supposes the fundamental distinction between the infinite and the finite, as two distinct substances and acts, one absolute, the other relative; the one cause, the other effect; the one supreme and first, the other dependent and secondary.

How, then, the fundamental substantial distinction between the infinite and the finite establishes the possibility of the supernatural, we shall point out as briefly as possible.

The fundamental distinction between the infinite and the finite once admitted, it follows that on one side we have an infinite activity, which is not exhausted by the effecting of substantial creation, and its necessary principles of action; and which may consequently effect another principle of action, superior to any of the substantial moment. On the other side, we have the finite essentially and necessarily indefinite in its development, and capable, therefore, of receiving a higher principle of action, engrafted upon its own natural principle, and elevating its energy, and widening the sphere of its action. This higher principle would be the supernatural. Therefore, the possibility of the supernatural logically follows from the fundamental distinction between the infinite and the finite. In all these chapters we have proved this distinction. Therefore, the supernatural is possible.

In other words, between the infinite and the finite there is the indefinite, that is, a possibility on the part of the infinite to increase the amount of energy of the finite, and on the part of the finite a capacity of receiving it. When this increase of activity is beyond and above every principle of action of substantial creation, it is called in Catholic language the supernatural. Therefore the supernatural is possible.

We pass to the next question—the imperative necessity of the supernatural in the plan of the cosmos. This necessity arises from all the laws which govern the exterior action of God, and especially from the laws of continuity, unity, and communion.

First, the law of continuity. This law implies that, between one moment of the action of God and every other, there should be a kind of affinity and proportion, not so strong as to alter at all the distinctive natures of the moments, but strong enough to establish a certain agreement and propinquity between them. Now, without the supernatural this law would not be observed; since without it we should have only two moments, the hypostatic moment and the substantial moment; and between these two there is no proportion or affinity. For the first terminates in an individuality, the Theanthropos, who is absolutely, and in all the force of the term, God; the second terminates in numberless individualities, which are absolutely, and in the strictest force of the term, finite. Hence we should have the usual dualism, the infinite and the finite, and no proportion between them. It is true that, no matter how high the finite might be exalted by an increase of activity superior to any activity of substantial creation, we should always have finite and infinite, and no proportion or affinity between them. Yet the supernatural, as Catholicity teaches, causes this difficulty to vanish, and establishes a real proportion; for, without at all altering the two natures of the moments to be brought together, it makes the finite partaker of the infinite at the same time that it effects in it a superior principle of activity, and thus establishes the proportion required between the Theanthropos and created persons. Created persons will not, in that case, remain in their natural state, but will be raised to a union with the infinite, as close and as high as possible, short of the hypostatic. Thus we shall have all created natures raised to a hypostatic union with the Word, and resulting in the Theanthropos; all created persons raised to as close and high a union as possible, short of the hypostatic, thus forming one universal cosmic harmony.

The law of unity, also, would not be fulfilled without the supernatural; for this law requires a union between the moments of the cosmos, which is not apparent or fictitious, but real and living. Now, such a union is impossible without a principle which can bring together terms not only distinct, but separated from each other by an infinite distance. Hence, to unite the Theanthropos and created personalities, a principle of union is necessary; and this principle is the supernatural.

Finally, the law of communion claims this moment; for this law requires an interchange of acts between one moment of the cosmos and another. Now, it is evident that such interchange of acts is altogether impossible when the actions of the respective moments that are destined to this interchange are wholly disproportionate.

A principle, therefore is necessary which may establish this proportion, and thus render the communion of acts possible. This principle between the Theanthropos and created persons is the supernatural.

In the second place, the supernatural is required in order to enable finite personalities to attain that supreme end to which they were destined, in view of the hypostatic moment. We must explain this at a certain length.

God, in acting outside himself, has one universal end in view—the manifestation of his own infinite excellence. To attain this end, he is bound to effect a variety of moments, subject to those laws so often alluded to in these articles. Each one of these moments, and each species and individual within each moment, expresses, as it were, a side of the infinite comprehensiveness of

God. And all taken together shadow forth his whole infinite excellence in the most perfect manner possible.

Hence each moment, and every species under each moment, and every individual when the moment allows this variety, has a particular end —that side of the infinite which they are destined to express, subject to the universal end of the external action.

Now, because the terms of the external action are progressive and in the way of development,* it follows that both the universal end of the cosmos and the particular ends of each moment are subdivided into two moments, the germinal and inchoative end, when the terms are effected and launched into action; the final and supreme end, when the terms reach their highest and supreme stage of development.

In force of the existence of these two ends, one universal and cosmic, the other particular and subjective, it follows that, in order to determine the last and supreme end of each particular moment and of the species and individuals within each moment, we must take into consideration not only their nature and specific faculties, but also their relations to all the other moments of the action of God, and consequently to the universal end of the cosmos.

---

* Of the hypostatic moment this is to be understood in a particular manner.

For a moment, viewed in its nature and specific faculties, and considered in itself, and as it were isolated from all the other moments of the cosmos, might point as its destination to one kind of end; whereas, if considered concretely, and as forming a part of the universal cosmos, its end might be different from what it would be if considered in the abstract and isolated; for the evident reason that, when considered as an element of the cosmos, it bears altogether different relations.

Hence a moment, considered in its nature, and as it were isolated from the rest, might point, as its final destiny, to an end inferior to that which it would have when looked upon as an integral element of the universal cosmos.

This is the case with created personalities. Viewed in themselves within the extent of their nature and faculties, their final and supreme end would be that perfection to which the highest possible development of their essential faculties would naturally bring them. But if we regard them as forming a part of the cosmos, and one of its most important parts; if we regard them in concrete, and as belonging to the actual plan of the cosmos chosen by God, we find that their end is no longer the highest natural development of their faculties, but an end of a different and much superior nature; for the simple reason that the cosmos, having been elevated, not to its highest possible natural development, but to the highest possible sublimation in the sphere of the possible, and created personalities forming an integral part thereof, it follows that they must necessarily be exalted and elevated along with it. The cosmos which God selected includes the hypostatic moment which was effected, as we have seen in the preceding article, in order to elevate the whole cosmos, and especially created persons, to a society with the three persons of the Trinity, consisting in the immediate intuition and the closest possible possession of the infinite next to the hypostatic. In consequence of this, the end of created persons is no longer natural but supernatural;* that is, above and beyond the highest possible natural development which they could attain in its cause, in its nature, and in its properties. From all we have said, it follows that the end of created persons, in its final, last, and supreme moment, is altogether supernatural. Now, an end supernatural in its last moment must be supernatural also in its inchoative and germinal moment. Consequently, the existence of the supernatural is imperatively necessary to enable created persons to attain their final and supreme

---

* There has been a great dispute among theologians whether the end of man is natural or supernatural. The reader can see that the question is useless when we consider man in his relations to the universal cosmos. For the end of the cosmos being supernatural, the particular end of persons must also be supernatural, if the cosmos must exhibit one harmonious whole.

end. In other words, if the final end of created persons be superior to that which their natural energies would bring them, it is evident that they could never attain it without being endowed with energies superior to their natural faculties, and proportionate in nature to the end to be attained.

Before we conclude this part of the subject, we wish to make a remark to avoid misunderstanding. We have proved the supernatural to be imperatively necessary. Now, to this the well-known axiom might be objected, that the supernatural, or grace, is absolutely free and gratuitous on the part of God. How, then, are the two qualities of necessity and gratuitousness reconciled? Does not the one exclude the other, and *vice versa*? It does not. In what sense do we hold the supernatural to be necessary? We proceed from these principles—1. The external action is absolutely free; 2. The amount of perfection to be effected is absolutely free; 3. God chose to make the best possible manifestation of his grandeur, as more agreeable to the end of his action; 4. This best possible manifestasion is attained by the hypostatic moment, and by created persons, united in the Theanthropos in one universal palingenesiac society with the three divine persons; 5. To effect this society between created persons and the infinite, the supernatural is absolutely necessary.

Now, who does not see that the necessity of

the supernatural is here hypothetical and conditional, founded on the supposition that God chose the final end of the cosmos to be this universal palingenesiac society with himself?

He that wills the end must will the means. On the other hand, the Catholic principle, that the supernatural is free and gratuitous, by no means clashes with this hypothetical necessity. For what does that principle import? Does it imply that the supernatural enters into the system of the cosmos arbitrarily, and as an afterthought, a correction or addition, having no possible relation with all the other moments? Decidedly not. The principle means this much.

1. The supernatural is free and gratuitous, because not due to created persons, as an essential element of their nature or as an attribute or property claimed by the same nature.

2. That it cannot be attained by any effort of activity in the whole sphere of substantial creation, and therefore cannot be claimed as a merit.

3. It is gratuitous in the sense that, though in the general plan of the cosmos the supernatural is necessary, because God chose a cosmos, which necessarily demanded it, yet no single individual person has, in force of this necessity, any right or claim to be the object of it.

The same takes place in substantial creation. This, including the existence of created persons, is necessary in the plan of the cosmos, yet in force of this necessity no individual person can claim existence as a right.

4. The supernatural is gratuitous also in the sense that God is absolutely free to dispense it to each created person, in the time and degree which he may choose, and no created person has a right to object to the time, mode, or extent of such dispensation. The metaphysical reason of all these principles lies in the fact that the necessity of the supernatural springs altogether from the choice of God, and nowise from any right inherent in any created person.

It is evident, therefore, that the imperative necessity of the supernatural in no way clashes, but perfectly agrees, with its gratuitousness and freedom.

We come to the study of the intrinsic nature of the supernatural, and first of its cause. We said in the definition that the supernatural is a principle of action superior in its cause to every principle of substantial creation. In what sense is this to be understood? God's action is most simple and infinite. From these two attributes of the action of God springs the possibility of the numberless variety of the effects and of the absolute oneness of the action. Because the action being infinite, and the effects finite, we may suppose a numberless variety of effects, as terms of the action, and yet neither divide nor multiply the action; because in itself it is absolutely simple. And if our intellect were as infinite in its comprehension as the action is infinite in its energy, we should be able easily to comprehend how one simple action can effect a variety of terms without being divided or multiplied. But our mind, being finite, must necessarily conceive that action, not in its oneness and simplicity, but partially and mentally distinguish it, in order to grasp the causality of all the terms it effects. This is the first distinction which we attach mentally to the simple action of God; a distinction which gives rise to what we have called moments.

Again, variety implies hierarchy—that is, a superiority of one term of the action of God over another. Now, our mind, contemplating the hierarchical variety of terms—that is, a variety of perfection of being—naturally imagines in the cause a greater effort of energy in the production of a superior term than in the production of an inferior one.

This is another foundation for mental distinction in the action of God.

According to these principles, it follows that when we say the supernatural is superior in its cause to every principle of action of substantial creation, we do not mean to say that it has a cause distinct from or superior to God, or that the action of God in itself is distinct or different from that which causes substantial creation, but we merely wish to point out that partial conception of our mind of the same infinite action of God, corresponding to the supernatural term, which it effects; and we call it distinct and superior, not because it is so in itself, but because, considering its relation to the effect, we apprehend it as distinct and superior, without of course detracting from the absolute simplicity of the action in itself.*

The supernatural, therefore, is a moment of the action of God distinct from the substantial moment, and superior to it inasmuch as it causes an effect in perfection superior to substantial creation.

But what is the intrinsic and subjective nature of this moment? In order to acquire a complete idea of it, it is necessary to premise a few remarks.

1. As the supernatural moment is an integral part of the cosmos, it must be governed by the same laws which rule over all the terms of the external action. Consequently, in uniting created persons to the Theanthropos, and through him to the Trinity, it must not destroy the vari-

---

* Nihil prohibet intellectum nostrum intelligentem multa multipliciter referri ad id quod est in se simplex, ut sic ipsum simplex sub multiplici relatione consideret; et quanto aliquid est magis simplex, tanto est majoris virtutis et principium plurium, ac per hoc multiplicius relatione consideret; sicut punctum plurium est principium quam linea et linea quam superficies.—*S. Th. C. G.* lib. ii. c. 14.

ety of the moments to be united, but, whilst it establishes a continuity between them, must at the same time preserve their distinct natures and attributes. Hence, because it *is* a sublimation of created persons, it cannot destroy or injure their essence or attributes or personality. For, as every one can perceive, if the supernatural were to do so, it would no longer be a sublimation, but a destruction of created persons. Hence, every one can see how far from understanding it are those who attack the supernatural on the plea that it offends and injures nature. Catholic theology teaches that the supernatural would be impossible on the supposition of its at all offending the nature, attributes, or rights of created persons; because its possibility rests precisely on the supposition that it must establish a continuity between the substantial moment and the hypostatic union. Destroy nature, and one term only is left; and what union or continuity can then be established? The system of the cosmos appears to the eye of the Catholic Church like a lofty and sublime pyramid, consisting of the base, the pinnacle, and the middle part. The base is substantial creation; the pinnacle is the Theanthropos; the middle part, uniting nature and the Theanthropos, is the supernatural. Take away the base of this lofty structure, and what remains of it but scattered fragments?

The particular law, therefore, which governs

this moment is as follows: *To establish a continuity and connection between the Theanthropos and substantial creation without destroying or offending the variety of the distinctive natures, properties, and rights, of each moment to be united.*

2. We remark, in the second place, that created persons are of twofold nature: purely intelligent spirits or angels; spirits hypostatically united to a body—men. A glance at the nature of these beings. The blessed Trinity creates, in the first moment of his action, a spiritual substance endowed with intelligence and will—that is, an apprehensive faculty and expansive faculty, which by their explication unfold and perfect the substance. This general idea of spiritual beings admits an endless variety of species and a variety of gradations within the species. Hence, revelation and theology teach that there exists an immense number of angelic species, and perhaps an immense number of gradations within the species.* The human species, which is the lowest in the sphere of spiritual beings, and connecting the spiritual world with the inferior elements of substantial creation,

---

* The question depends upon the principle of individualization, which varies according to philosophical systems. St. Thomas, who holds that the principle of individualization is matter, admits that every angel forms a species, a part, because the angel, not being united to a body, cannot consequently be individualized from another except by forming a species in himself.

admits a great variety of gradations within the species.

We remark, in the third place, that the first moment of God's action, which we have called substantial creation, is also a union and communication. For it implies a necessary and essential relation between God and the terms of his action; and what relation can there be closer and more intimate than that which exists between the cause and its effects? Now, relation and union are one and the same thing.

Substantial creation implies, moreover, two subordinate moments between God and his creatures, necessary that they may continue in existence and be able to unfold and develop their nature. These are preservation and concurrence. The first implies the immanence of the creative act, without which the creature would fall into nothingness. The second is the immanence of the creative act in relation to the faculties and activities of the creature, which must be excited, moved, and directed by the action of God, otherwise their development would be impossible. These two subordinate moments of the creative act, being relations, must also be considered as unions.

Finally, we call upon the reader to remember.

1. That the Incarnation is the highest possible communication of the eternal Word to human nature, constituting of both terms one single in-

dividual Christ; 2. That human nature, thus elevated to the personal union of the Word, was thereby exalted to the highest possible likeness of God, partaking of all the attributes and perfections of the Word. For as a piece of iron, as various fathers remark, when put into fire becomes so heated as to partake of all the qualities and assume the very appearance of fire, so likewise the human nature of Christ, united so closely and so intimately to the person of the Word, is as much compenetrated by him, and made to share in his divine attributes, as it was possible without destroying its distinctive nature. Keeping these remarks always in view, we are able to approach nearer to the subject of our inquiry: What is the intrinsic nature of the supernatural?

It cannot be a new *substance*. For, in the first place, it would be confounded with the term of the substantial moment.

Secondly, the object, for which it is required, is to elevate created persons to a union with the Theanthropos, and through him with the Trinity, and thus maintain the law of continuity and unity of the cosmos. Therefore, if the supernatural were a new substance, there would enter into the cosmos a new species of substance, and the result would not be an elevation of the substances already existing, a continuation as it were between human persons and the Theanthropos, and thus the object would be frustrated. It must, therefore, be a *new principle of activity engrafted on the substance of created persons.*

For, substance excluded, nothing else could be communicated except a new principle of acting, adhering to, and leaning upon the nature of created personalities, higher than all the activities of which created spirits are essentially possessed.

And as the communication of such activity implies a new relation of created personalities with God, it follows that it implies a new and higher union with God. Hence the supernatural as to its term must be a new principle of activity and a new union with God, higher than all the activities and unions of substantial creation. We may now give the full definition of the supernatural in its cause, term, and properties. It runs thus:

It is a moment of the action of God, distinct both from the substantial and the hypostatic moment, required in order to bring created persons into union with the Theanthropos, and through him with the blessed Trinity; by which moment the three divine persons communicate themselves to created persons, and produce in them a new permanent germinal activity, superior to all the activities which created persons possess in force of their nature; an activity itself possessed of three subordinate faculties, which under the concurrence of God, and by communing with their proper objects, unfold that germinal activity, and bring it to that final completion, which is assigned to it in the order and harmony of the cosmos in the state of polingenesia.

Let us now explain each term of the definition.

The nature, then, of the term of this moment consists in its being a new activity, a more perfect likeness of God than that which we naturally possess. Every one is aware that there is in every substance an internal principle of action, which springs from the essence, and which is called its nature. Now, the supernatural is an internal principle of action superior to our nature, and engrafted upon it, elevating, strengthening, and corroborating the latter. It is, therefore, as it were, a superior nature added to the natural internal principle of an impulse to action.

It might be objected to this doctrine that what we call nature in a being is the necessary consequence of its being a substance; and consequently, by admitting the supernatural to be a new nature, we must necessarily admit a new substance. We grant that a nature is a necessary consequence of substance; in other words, that a substance must have an internal principle of action; but we do not grant that an interior principle of action, the consequence of a substance, may not be strengthened and elevated so as to endow the same internal principle with a definite, permanent, higher energy of action, embracing a wider range of activity and grasping higher and more comprehensive objects, without multiplying the substance. For we see no contradiction in the supposition, nor to a close observer will there appear to exist any. God, who created the substance, produces also in it that internal principle and impulse to action called nature. Now, who would attempt to prove that the same God, by a moment of his action distinct from the substantial moment, could not elevate and increase the energy of that internal principle, and make that elevation and growth habitual and permanent without multiplying the substance?

Ontologically speaking, this principle of action, the term of the sublimative moment, is nothing else but an habitual permanent modification. Now, it implies contradiction to suppose that a modification could exist in itself without leaning on a substance or having any support whatever. But it is no contradiction to suppose a modification leaning on a substance of which it is not the necessary development or attitude. Hence, if the term of the sublimative moment did not rest on the internal principle, the consequence of the substantial moment, but existed in itself, then it could not be conceived without supposing it to be a new substance; but, leaning as it does on the substantial principle, resting upon it, elevating and strengthening its energy, one can easily conceive its possibility without supposing a new substance.

The term, therefore, of the sublimative moment is an internal and permanent principle of action, superior in its cause and its essence to that which in created persons is the term of substantial creation, and consequently it is a higher and better likeness of God's infinite excellence.* However, we cannot determine how much more superior to the substantial principle of action is this term of the sublimative moment.

For, in the first place, the terms from which we try to obtain an idea of the medium term are mysterious to us. No philosopher has ever determined and fathomed the depth and extent of the nature of created spirits. Our very essence, so present to us, is known only by its acts. Then we are the lowest on the ladder of created spirits. Who can ascend so high as to determine the extent of the energy of the least of those pure intelligences which form the angelic choirs, and who can soar so high as to obtain an insight into the energies of those high seraphs who hover in endless rapture around the throne of the infinite and ever-living intelligence?

The other term, by which we try to obtain an idea of the nature of this moment, is the Incarnation, which is by far more hidden to us and mysterious. Again, this moment is subject to the law of variety, and admits of an endless number of degrees within its sphere, beyond the reach of every finite comprehension. We cannot there-

---
* Expressio et participatio diviniæ bonitatis.—*S. Th.*

fore determine the hierarchical superiorty of the sublimative moment over the term of substantial creation, but must rest content with knowing that it is distinct in its cause, in its essence and attributes, from the substantial term, and far superior to it.

In the second place, we have said, in the definition, that the term of this moment is a *germinal* activity. For every created activity is always finite, and, however high and exalted it may be supposed to be, it is always capable of further development. God's activity alone, being infinite, excludes all progress and further perfection. If, then, that activity is germinal, it must be possessed of subordinate faculties, which may bring it to its final perfection. Now, what is the nature of these subordinate faculties? A glance at the end of the sublimative moment will afford the answer. The object for which this term is effected is in order that created persons may be placed in real communication with the Theanthropos, and through him with God. Now, a being cannot be put in real communication with another except in a manner conformable to the specific faculties of its nature. The question here is about created spirits, who are to be put in real communication with Christ, and through him with God; and as the specific faculties of spirits are intelligence and will, it follows that the communication must be effected through intelligence and will.

Therefore, the primary activity which elevates the nature of created spirits must be possessed of two subordinate faculties in order to elevate the intelligence and the will of spirits. These are supernatural intelligence and supernatural will. Our natural faculty of intelligence being destined, in its inchoative state, to *apprehend* the whole system of God's external works, together with the interior genesis of his life, and not to stop at the apprehension of the first moment of the external action, which is substantial creation — to fit it for its final and supreme state, which is the immediate intuition of the infinite, must necessarily be elevated. For naturally, our intelligence being the term of the substantial moment, its power of apprehension is limited within the boundaries of this moment, and cannot go beyond it by the law of hierarchy. Now, the whole system of God's exterior works, including all the moments, is far superior to the substantial moment, and constitutes a higher and wider object than that of the substantial moment. Consequently, if our intelligence were not strengthened and elevated by a superior light habitually and permanently residing in it, it would never apprehend its supernatural object.

*This habitual and permanent light,** communi-

---

* We take the word permanent here not in the sense that it cannot be lost, because this could be done by a positive act contrary to it, but in the sense of St. Thomas and other theologians,

cated to our natural intelligence and distinct from, though leaning on it, and superior to it, in its cause, in its essence, in its acts, in its object, and springing from the primary germinal activity, the first term of the supernatural moment, is called supernatural intelligence, or, in theological language, supernatural faith. Faith, because that supernatural light, as it enables us to apprehend the whole system of the cosmos, with its cause, is not and cannot be so high and so powerful as to make us *comprehend* them. The reason is most simple: even our supernatural intelligence is finite, therefore it cannot comprehend the infinite and everything related to him. Supernatural intelligence, therefore, in the germinal and inchoative state, enables us to apprehend the whole system of the external action. Yet it is like a twilight, we see enough through it to admit it, to be attracted by it, to be in raptures with it, yet we see a dark and mysterious ground lying beyond our apprehension which we cannot reach. That part of the object which we cannot comprehend we admit on the authority of God revealing, and consequently supernatural intelligence takes also the name of faith.

What we have said of our natural intelligence must be said also of the will. Our natural will in

---

who say that this light remains even when not actually acting. The same must be said of other faculties and of the germinal activity itself, which may be lost by a created person freely renouncing the supernatural.

its inchoative state is destined to seek and love an object outside of and superior to its natural energy. It becomes, therefore, necessary to endow it with an habitual and permanent energy of expansion, corresponding to the object it is destined to embrace. *This habitual and permanent energy of expansion communicated to our natural will, and distinct from, though leaning on it, and superior to it in its cause, in its essence, in its acts, in its object, and springing from the primary activity and from supernatural intelligence, is called supernatural will or charity, in theological language.*

By it *alone* we are truly put in that communication with the Theanthropos and the Trinity which is called *sanctification*—a term which no philosopher ever understood before the advent of Christianity.

To understand the metaphysical reason of this, it is necessary to give a glance at that which constitutes the supreme practical transcendental realization of morality, because sanctification imports the subjective realization of morality.

Morality, in its highest transcendental acceptation, is the perfection to which a being is destined, wrought by the voluntary exercise of its action. It embraces a twofold element, an objective element and a subjective. The objective element is the typical idea of the highest perfection of a being. The subjective is the realization of that type as existing in the subject.

In created persons, for persons alone are capable of morality, it is the perfection to which they are destined in the plan of the cosmos, to be acquired by the voluntary and *free* development of their faculties. It is also objective and subjective. The objective is the type of perfection to which they are destined, residing intelligibly in God. The subjective is the realization of that type as residing in them. And because created persons are finite, the subjective element of morality in them is divided into two moments—the inchoative and the final. The inchoative moment of morality takes place when a person, by a voluntary and free development, performs a moral act, or begins to realize the typical objective morality. The final, when the persons reach its supreme realization.

Having premised these few notions, it is evident that the supreme transcendental realization of morality lies in the Infinite and in the eternal genesis of his life. For in the life of God we have the following elements which establish transcendental morality:

First, the infinite essence of God, containing in itself all possible transcendental perfection, under the subsistence of primary unbegotten intelligent activity conceiving that same infinite perfection—the Father. Second, the whole perfection of the Godhead, under the subsistence and constituent of conception or ideal realization of the Infinite, objective morality—the Son. Third, both the Father and the Son—the one as first principle, the other as mediating principle—both active, realizing practically and voluntarily* the whole perfection of the Godhead under the subsistence of love—the third person, the Holy Spirit, who completes the cycle of infinite life, and exhibits all the elements of transcendental morality, the practical realization of infinite perfection, subjective morality. Hence the Trinity is called in the Scripture three times holy, because they are the supreme transcendental morality.

Now, in order that created persons may be sanctified, they must become assimilated to and must realize practically this supreme transcendental realization of morality, which is also, as we have often remarked, their supreme and last supernatural end. And it is supernatural will which makes them voluntarily and freely embrace and love this supreme realization of morality, which takes hold of it and is united to it in an inchoative state. The supernatural activity conceiving this supreme realization of morality through supernatural intelligence, would not be sufficient to sanctify created persons, because it would not unite or assimilate them to that realization, and would not render it subjective. For there is this distinction between apprehensive

---

* The aspiring of the Holy Ghost, as all the internal processions, is necessary in the life of God, but no less voluntary.

faculties and expansive faculties, that the first are not assimilated to the object which they apprehend, but assimilate the object to themselves;* hence intelligence is not degraded or defiled by the apprehension of objects of inferior nature, or even evil. But expansive faculties are united and assimilated to the object which they love, and partake of the dignity or inferiority of the object; hence the Scripture says of men that they were made abominable as the objects which they loved.

The metaphysical reason of this distinction is that apprehensive faculties *take in*, as it were, and mould, the object to fit them. But expansive faculties *give themselves*, and are consequently moulded to fit the object.†

Therefore the infinite life of God, as the supreme realization of morality, as apprehended by our supernatural intelligence, must take a form fitted to the nature of the intelligence, but our supernatural will, in loving this infinite life, is drawn toward it, exalted, and assimilated to it, and thus realizes subjectively the supreme transcendental morality, its last perfection also, and is thereby made holy and sanctified.

Briefly, the supreme transcendental morality is the life of the infinite, and this is also the

---

* Omne quod recipitur ad modum recipientis recipitur.—*S. Th.*

† Amatum in voluntate existit ut inclinans, et quodam modo impellens intrinsecus amantem in ipsam rem amatam.—*S. Th.*

supreme supernatural end of created persons. When they realize subjectively and in inchoative state this transcendental morality, or are assimilated to it, they are sanctified.

Now, it is supernatural will and not intelligence which unites and assimilates them to this transcendental morality. It is therefore by supernatural will alone that we are sanctified.

Having spoken of the supernatural intelligence and will, we must speak of a third faculty which springs from the germinal activity of the supernatural moment, called in theological language the virtue of hope.

Every finite being, being contingent, exists as long as the creative act continues to preserve it in existence. Moreover, the sublimative term, being essentially progressive, can be developed by movement. This as we shall see, requires the aid of God, which must excite, direct, and complete the movement to render it possible.

Finally, no finite being can arrive at its final completion without an extraordinary action of God, as there is a necessary leap* between the inchoative and palingenesiacal moment.

These three different moments of the action of God, which the spirit elevated to the sublimative moment needs in order to develop itself and reach its end, though necessary when viewed

---

* We can find no other word to express the idea. It will be explained in the chapter on "Palingenesia."

with reference to the other moments of the cosmos, are free on the part of God, respectively to the individual spirit.

In order, therefore, that a created spirit may be morally certain that God in his infinite goodness and excellence will preserve its being, aid it in its development, and bring it to its final completion, the same three divine persons, in effecting the supernatural being in the spirit, draw from its essence a third faculty, which consists in an habitual and permanent sense of its dependence upon God in all these things, joined with a power of trust and reliance upon his infinite goodness.*

As these three faculties are bestowed upon created persons in a habitual state, which not only implies a permanency but also a facility and use to action, it follows that they can with reason be called *virtues*. We conclued: the essence of the hypostatic moment implies on the part of the blessed Trinity a particular communication distinct from and higher than that of the substantial moment, and respectively to created persons it implies a closer union with the Trinity, and consequently a partaking of the Godhead, together with a higher likeness, truly inherent in the spirit—a likeness which breaks itself into

---

* As we are considering the supernatural moment independent of sin, the theory of these three faculties is necessarily incomplete.

three permanent and habitual powers of supernatural intelligence, supernatural will, and supernatural reliance, in the state of habits or virtues.

To complete the idea of this moment, a few more remarks are necessary relative to its preservation, and to the manner according to which it can act and develop itself.

And first as to preservation. We have often observed that the supernatural, comprehending a principle of activity dividing itself into three supernatural faculties, is finite; and consequently, as such it requires the immanence of the effective action of God to maintain its existence. This is evident. Every finite being, by the mere fact of its existence, does not change its nature of contingent, and pass into that of the absolute; but its essence being immutable, it remains always contingent, that is, of itself, and in force of its nature, indifferent to be or not to be. Consequently, in order that it may maintain and keep its existence, it is necessary that the same action which caused it to exist subjectively keep its existence in all the moments of time or extra time; that is, it is necessary that the same action, which *determined* the native and essential indifference to be or not to be to the fact of being, keep it always so determined. In other words, the existence of a contingent being does not originate in an interior and essential principle, as it is in the absolute, but arises from an exterior and independent principle. Therefore, that same exterior principle which caused its existence must maintain it, else the contingent, having no interior principle of preservation, would necessarily cease to have any subjective existence.

We pass to the last question affecting the supernatural moment: how can it act and develop its faculties, or how and under what conditions is the development of the supernatural faculties possible?

The answer is, that God must *excite* the supernatural faculties to action, *aid* them in the course of the action, and *aid* them in completing the action. These three moments of the action of God required to render the development of the supernatural faculties possible, is called concurrence. Now, this concurrence must not be of a moral nature, as it were presenting before the supernatural intelligence reasons and motives to action, and before the supernatural will attraction to act; but it must be of an efficient nature, effectively and consecutively exciting and aiding these faculties in their development. In one word, God must effect in them the action. This most momentous statement, fraught with so many consequences, we are going to prove with three decisive arguments.

The first is drawn from the nature of finite beings. A finite being is essentially potential;

the infinite being alone is essentially actual. Therefore, in order that finite beings may act, it is necessary that they should pass from the power to the act. But no being can pass from the power to the act without the effective aid of a being not already in act. Therefore, no finite being can act without the effective aid of a being already in act.

But the supernatural term is a finite being. Consequently, it cannot act without the effective aid of a being already in act. This being already in act is God. Therefore, the supernatural term cannot act without the effective aid of God.

We are to prove two things to complete the argument: 1. That no being can pass from the power to the act without the effective aid of another already in act; 2. That this being in act in the case must be God.

As to the first. It is a contradiction to suppose a being at the same time to be in potentiality and in action with regard to the same action. Because, if with regard to any particular action I am in potentiality, I cannot at the same time be acting it; for, in that case, to be acting would exclude my being in potentiality in reference to it.

Now, if a being passing from the power to the act were not aided effectively by another already in act, this contradiction would take place, because it would be in potentiality with regard to the action supposed; it would be in act with regard to the same action, because it would be moving itself, and not be moved by another.

It implies, therefore, a contradiction to suppose a being passing from the power to the act without the efficient aid of another being already in act.

2. That this being already in act in the present question must be God is evident when we consider that this being already in act, moving the supernatural term to action, is either finite or infinite. If finite, it needs itself a being already in act to move it to act; and this one again, if supposed finite, would require another, and so on *ad infinitum*. Therefore, it must be infinite or pure act.*

The next argument is as follows: If the term of the supernatural moment could act of itself without the effective aid of God, God would no longer be the first, the universal, the independent cause of everything. For, if a finite being could act of itself independent of God's effective aid, it is evident that it would be the first cause of its action; it is likewise evident that it would be the only cause of its action, and the independent cause thereof. Now, this is in contradiction both to the essence of finite being and to the essence of the infinite being. The finite being is essentially secondary and dependent cause; to make it first, only, independent cause is not to suppose

---
* *S. Th. passim.*

it finite, but infinite; for to the infinite essence alone belongs to be first, universal, independent cause. Consequently, it is absolutely impossible that a finite being could act of itself independent of the effective aid of God. We say effective, because if this aid were not effective, but only moral, the same result would follow—because a moral aid is nothing else but the presenting of motives or reasons. When an agent is determined to action by the aid of moral influence, it is the agent, after all, which efficiently determines itself, and not the motives or reasons which determine it. Consequently, if the aid of God were only of a moral nature, the finite would still be the first, only, independent, cause of its action, because it would determine itself. Finally, if the finite could act independently of God, God would have no knowledge of the free actions of his creatures. Because, in the first place, God knows things distinct from himself only inasmuch as he is the efficient cause of them. For his infinite power, which he perfectly knows, is the only medium whereby he can know things distinct from himself.* But in an especial manner he could not know the free, contingent, and future actions of his creatures if he did not cause them.

For there are three possible mediums of knowledge—identity, ideality or perception, and causality. Knowledge implies three elements: a sub-

---

* S. Th. Summa, part i. qu. 14, art. v., *in corpore*

ject knowing, an object known, and a relation be-between them—a certain contact by which the object is apprehended by the subject. Now, this relation or medium of knowledge may be either identity, when the object is identical with the subject—God knows himself through this relation; or it may be a relation of causality, as an architect knows his building; or it may be a relation of perception, as we know bodies or anything that comes under our perception.

Now, if we exclude causality, God could never know infallibly and certainly the future contingent acts of his creatures, because he could not know them through the relation of identity. Nor could he know them through the relation of perception, because such actions, being future, could only be perceived in their cause, and the cause, being contingent, could only give a possible conjectural knowledge.

A contingent cause, says St. Thomas, is equally inclined to opposite things, and thus the contingent, as future, cannot be the object of any knowledge with certainty. Hence, whosoever knows the contingent in its cause alone, can have but a conjectural knowledge of it.

It follows, therefore, that if we do not wish to deprive God of an infallible and certain knowledge of the free contingent acts of his creatures, we must admit that he knows them through the relation of causality, and say of God only what Vico erroneously said of man also: God only knows what he does respectively to things distinct from him. Two objections are to be resolved before concluding the chapter. The first is that, if it is God who must effect the action in finite beings, it is impossible to perceive how they can be agents. In order that they may really be supposed to be agents, the action ought to emanate radically from the essence of the being, and consequently the being ought to be able to develop itself. We should grant the force of the objection if the question related to the first cause; but the objection has no value when we consider that it has reference to secondary causes. For what means a first cause? That agent who, of himself without the aid of any other, can act. With regard to him, his action must emanate from his essence, and from that alone. But it is not so with secondary causes. A secondary cause means a cause essentially dependent upon the first—dependent not in any undefined sense, but dependent as cause, as active principle, in other words, depending on the first cause for its action. And this dependence does not at all destroy their causality. Because, as Bossuet profoundly remarks, as a created being does not cease to be being because it belongs to another, that is, to God, but, on the contrary, it is what it is because it comes from God, so likewise created acting does not, so to speak, cease to be acting because it comes from

God; on the contrary, the greater the being God gives it, the greater is the acting. It is so far from the truth, then, that God in causing the action of the creature takes away its action or causality, that the contrary is true; it is action because God effects it in the creature.*

The second objection is that our theory does away with the liberty of will. Now, the same answer is to be given to this objection. For as God effects in everything the being and its perfection, if to be free is something and a perfection in every act, God also effects, in such acts, what we call freedom; and the infinite efficacy of his action extends itself, so to speak, even to this formation. And it must not be objected here that the proper exercise of free will must originate only in free will; because this would be true if the free will of man were a free will first and independent, and not of a free will derived.†

God then causes the supernatural actions in created persons, and, in doing so, far from injuring their elevated free will, causes it in its first act, and in its exercises, and it is free will just because God makes it so.

The consequences of this moment in the next chapter.‡

---

* Bossuet, *Du libre Arbitre*, ch. viii.
† *Ibidem*.
‡ It will not be amiss to point out in this note the common theological terms of the supernatural moment.

What in our theory we have called primary germinal activity

is called in theological language the grace of exaltation. The three supernatural faculties, virtues of faith, hope, and charity. We have placed in the virtue of charity, the essence of sanctifying grace.

The preservation of the germinal activity and of its powers is called habitual grace.

The concurrence which enables the germinal activity to develop its faculties is called actual grace—which is of various kinds. If it only gives the power without the action, it is called sufficient grace. If it gives the action, efficacious grace. When it excites to action, preceding grace, *gratia præcedens;* when it aids during the action, accompanying grace, *gratia concomitans.* When it completes the action, succeeding grace, *gratia subsequens.* When it is directed to supernatural intelligence, grace of illumination; when to supernatural trust and will, grace of inspiration.

CHAPTER XI.

RELATIONS BETWEEN THE SUBLIMATIVE MOMENT AND SUBSTANTIAL CREATION.

IT will be the aim of this chapter to point out some consequences which result from the essence and properties of the supernatural term, considered respectively to the term of substantial creation. They go to establish the absolute supremacy of the supernatural term over substantial creation. We shall give them in as many propositions.

1st. *In the general plan of the cosmos, the supernatural term in itself and in its application, forming that part of the cosmos which may be called the supernatural order, takes precedence of substantial creation, or the natural order.*

This proposition is easily proven. The greater the intensity of perfection in a being, the nobler is the being; or, in other words, the greater amount of being a thing contains or exhibits, the higher is the place which it occupies in the ordinate location and harmony of the cosmos. The principle is too evident to need any proof, and we assume it as granted. Now, we have shown that the supernatural term in itself and in its application is by far more perfect than substantial creation; because it is a higher and more perfect similitude of Christ and of the Trinity; because it is the complement and the perfection of nature, and enables it to be joined with the Theanthropos, and through him to be ushered into the society of the three divine persons, communicating with their life, and thus arriving at the palingenesiacal state. Consequently, the supernatural in the cosmic plan must take precedence of substantial creation, and in the intention and design of the creator must precede nature.

2d. The supernatural is the end of substantial creation, and third end of the exterior action of the infinite.

In a series of means co-ordinate with each other, and depending one upon another in order to attain a primary object, that which in force of the excellence and perfection of its nature precedes others, is to be considered as end in respect to those means which follow next to it in dignity of nature; otherwise the means could have no relation whatever with each other, and the primary end could not be attained. In a series of means co-ordination implies dependence, and this dependence is established by the superiority of the one, and inferiority of the other. Hence the superior means in the series becomes *end* respectively to inferior means in the same series. Now, we have demonstrated that the supernatural term precedes nature in excellence and intensity of perfection; it becomes, therefore, in the harmony of the cosmic plan, the end of the substantial moment; as the Theanthropic moment is end in reference to the supernatural, and as God's manifestation of his infinite excellence and perfections is the end of the Theanthropos, the primary end of the cosmic plan is thus obtained.

"All things are yours," said St. Paul of those in whom the supernatural term is realized: "you are Christ's; Christ is God's."

3*d*. *The supernatural term is the exemplar and type of substantial creation.*

For it is the end which determines and shapes the nature of the means. The creative intelligence of the infinite, by contemplating the end which it has in view, and the essential laws of being residing in his nature, which is *the Being*, shapes and fashions mentally the nature and properties of the means. Hence it is evident that, the supernatural term being the end of substantial creation, it stands towards it as the exemplar and type to its copy.

4*th*. *The supernatural term is the mediator between the Theanthropos and substantial creation.*

This last proposition is a consequence of the

preceding ones. For, if the supernatural term precedes substantial creation in excellence and perfection of being, if it is its end and its type, it is evident that, in the general order and harmony of the cosmos, its natural place is between the Theanthropos and substantial creation. Consequently, it is mediator between them. Of course, the intelligent reader will easily understand that this mediatorship is not one merely of place and location, but a mediatorship of action; since the terms here in question are all agents.

These four properties of the supernatural moment, which, we flatter ourselves, have been demonstrated and put beyond the possibility of doubt will enable our readers to see the philosophy of various other truths held by Catholicity, and denied by rationalism, Pantheism, and Protestantism.

And first, the possibility of miracles follows evidently from these principles.

A miracle is a sensible phenomenon superseding, or contrary, to the established laws of corporal creation. A body left to itself by the ordinary law of gravitation should fall to the ground. Suppose it should hover between heaven and earth without any support, it would present a phenomenon contrary to the natural law of bodies. It would be what is called miracle, from the word *miror*, to wonder or to be amazed, because our intellect is always astonished when it cannot see at once the cause of an effect.

The possibility of such phenomena contrary to the established laws of nature has been denied by Pantheists and rationalists, both for the same reason, though each drew that reason from a different source. The Pantheist, who admits that the cosmos is nothing but that primary indefinite something which is continually developing itself by a necessary interior movement, denies the possibility of miracles on the ground that the development of the infinite being necessary, and being performed according to the necessary laws of being, the development must necessarily be uniform, and the phenomena resulting from it always the same.

The rationalist, though not admitting the germinal primary activity of Pantheism, asserts the absolute immutability of the laws of creation, and consequently cannot concede the possibility of any contravention to the result of those laws, without supposing their total overthrow.

We hold that the possibility of miracles follows clearly from the properties of the supernatural moment; for, if the supernatural moment precedes nature in force of its intrinsic excellence and perfection of being, if it is the end and type of the natural order, it is perfectly evident that the whole natural order is dependent upon and subject to the supernatural order by the law of *hierarchy;* and consequently it is evident that the laws governing the sensible order are also dependent upon and subject to the supernatural order, and must have been determined and fashioned in such a manner as to serve every purpose of that same order.

Hence, if the supernatural term, in order to assert itself before created spirits, to prove its own autonomy, its necessity, requires a phenomenon contrary to the established law of sensible creation, those laws must necessarily give way before their hierarchical superior, otherwise the whole order of the cosmos would be overthrown. This consequence is absolutely inevitable; and any one who has followed us in the demonstration of the intrinsic superiority of the supernatural term over substantial creation, cannot fail to perceive it. But to make it better understood we shall enter for a moment into the very heart of the question.

Let us take, as an example, the law of gravitation. Why do bodies left to themselves fall to the ground? The natural philosopher, with a look of profound wisdom, will answer at once, because of the law of gravitation. Now, if our philosopher claims to give no other answer but that which is within the sphere of his researches, the answer is correct; because his science of observation can carry him no further. But if by the word gravitation he should pretend to give a satisfactory ultimate reason of the phenomenon of the fall of bodies, his answer would make a metaphysician laugh. The law of gravitation! Indeed! But what is that law? Does it exist in the body, or in God? or has it an existence independent of both? If it exists in the body, how can it be a general law, when each body is an individuum? If it exist in God, how is it broken or altered, or destroyed, when the phenomenon of a miracle affects only a particular body? If it has an existence independent of both, what is it? Is it a god, or a Platonic idea, and, if so, whence does it derive the force to assert itself over God's creation?

These few questions, and many more which we could bring forward, show that to account for the fall of bodies by the law of gravitation, is to give no particular or satisfactory reason for the phenomenon.

We have already given one theory, the theory of the most profound metaphysicians of the world, that no finite beings can act without the aid of God; that God must really and effectively excite them to action, aid them during the action until it is accomplished; because he is necessarily the first and universal cause. Therefore, bodies as well as higher beings are absolutely dependent upon God for their action; and that which natural philosophers call the law of gravitation, or any other law, such as attraction, repulsion, and so forth, in itself is nothing more than the action of God upon bodies. Now, God in acting in and upon bodies has certainly a plan and an order marked out in his mind, according to which he acts in and directs them. This order he has derived from the infinite laws of being, which are his very essence, and consequently, in this sense, that order is stable and immutable. But it must be borne in mind that this order marked out in the mind of God, according to which he acts in and directs bodies, is *not the whole order of the cosmos.* It is only a part, a moment, and the most inferior of all. Consequently, it is an order subject to and dependent upon the order of the other and higher moments, and upon the universal order of the cosmos. Hence the same divine essence, the eternal model and type of everything, at the same time that it marks out the order for the acting in and directing of bodies, subjects it to the order of higher moments, and to the cosmological, universal order. In the application, therefore, of this eternal order marked out by his infinite essence, God acts in and directs bodies according to the stable and immutable order proper to this moment, until an exception is necessary. But when the order of higher moments and the universal order demand an exception, the order of the direction of bodies, being inferior, must necessarily yield to the superior, and the sensible order must, so to speak, be suspended for that occasion. We have said, so to speak, because even then the sensible order is not altered or broken, as rationalism imagines; it is the application of the general sensible order to a particular body which is suspended. It is not the objective order, but the subjective particular realization of it, which is superseded. Let us take as example the law so often mentioned. The general order established in the mind of God with regard to acting in bodies is to make them gravitate toward the centre of the earth. Suppose an exception of this law becomes necessary to assert the supernatural order. God, upon that particular occasion, does not apply the general law in a particular body, but acts in it contrary to that law. Is the law of gravitation broken or altered in consequence of that exception? If the law were an essential property of bodies, a natural consequence of their essence, it would be. But the law in its general and objective essence exists in God only; it does not exist in the body; and consequently it cannot be altered by a suspension of its application in a given case.

Were God to act otherwise than to admit such exceptions in the subjective application of the order of sensible creation, he would go against reason, and act contrary to his essence; for in that case he would prefer a particular and inferior order to the general and superior order of the whole cosmos. The true principles, then, in the present matter are the following:

1st. The laws according to which bodies act and are directed do not exist in bodies, but are an order marked out in the mind of God as derived from his infinite essence.

2d. This order is an element, and inferior one, of the universal order of the whole cosmos, and consequently, by the law of hierarchy, is subject to that same universal order.

3d. This sensible order is always stable and permanent in itself and in its objective state, but in its application to particular bodies is subject to variation when this variation is demanded by a superior order, or by the universal order of the cosmos.

The reader will observe, after what we have said, how futile is the argument of rationalists that a miracle is impossible because the laws of bodies are immutable. Certainly, if the laws exist in the bodies. But the laws of bodies, as we have said, are nothing more than the order marked out in the mind of God, according to which he acts in and directs them, and, this order being universal and objective, is never changed or altered. Only its application in particular bodies on a particular occasion is not made, or made in a contrary sense, because such is the requirement of the universal order. If this be kept in view, every difficulty will vanish in reference to this matter; for this is exactly that which prevents rationalists, from understanding the possibility of miracles—their want of perception that it is God who acts in every single body. They imagine a general principle, as if it were self-existing, which pervades all the bodies, which ought to be destroyed to permit the exception. Now, this is a mere phantom. It is God, we repeat it, who applies the order marked in his mind in every single body, which in his mind *only* is universal and objectively immutable, but subjectively, in its application, it need not be constant, except so long as no exception is required. Our natural philosophers of the rationalistic school imagine the law of bodies to be a sort of demigod, stern and immutable, particularly loth of and averse to being disturbed, and consequently cannot see the possibility of a miracle.

The second truth which follows from the attributes of supernatural moment, is that *prayer governs the universe.*.

Prayer, taken in its strictest acceptation, is the universal mode of action of spirits elevated to the supernatural moment. To understand this rightly, it is necessary to observe that every moment of the action of God, considered in its term, is possessed of a particular mode of action resulting from and befitting its essence and attributes. Thus, substantial creation, or the whole aggregate of being included in this moment, acts as it were by *apprehension and volition*. In spiritual beings, this manner of acting is strictly and properly so; in inferior beings, like the brutes, it is less so, but bears a great resemblance to it, for the animal has apprehensive faculties, though wanting in the power of generalization and abstraction, and confined within the concrete and in the individual; and he has also instincts and tendencies leading towards the object apprehended. The vegetable kingdom acts according to the same manner, though more materially; for it apprehends the elements required for its growth from the earth and the atmosphere, and, assimilating them to itself by an interior force, is able to develop itself. Every one is aware that the general laws of matter are those of *attraction and repulsion*, which bear a resemblance, though a faint one, to the law of apprehension and volition.

Now, the particular mode of acting in persons elevated to the supernatural moment is by *prayer*, which is composed of various elements according to various relations under which it is considered.

It may be considered in itself, its essence and nature, and in the persons to whom it has reference. The persons are the infinite and the finite. In itself, prayer is divided into two moments—a deprecatory moment, and a life-giving moment.

A deprecatory moment—because the effect of the prayer, resting absolutely on the free will of the infinite, cannot be claimed by the finite as a right, but as an effect of an infinite goodness yielding to a supplication; and in this sense it implies the following elements on the part of the finite:

1st. An acknowledgment, theoretical and practical, of the infinite as being the absolute and universal source of all good; and of the absolute dependence of the finite upon the infinite in all things; this acknowledgment arising in the finite from the consciousness and feeling of its finiteness both in the natural and the supernatural order.

2d. A gravitation, natural and supernatural, on the part of this finite towards the infinite, as the origin and the preserver of the being in both orders, as the mover of its natural and supernatural faculties, and as the final complement of both.

3d. A cry to the infinite for the satisfaction of this aspiration.

4th. A firm and unshaken reliance of being satisfied in this aspiration, founded both on the intrinsic goodness and on the personal promises of the infinite.

These four elements on the part of the finite are absolutely necessary to constitute a prayer in its deprecatory sense; and they are either implicitly or explicitly to be found in every prayer. The spirit who bows before the infinite must acknowledge theoretically and practically that God is the Master and Lord of all things, the infinite eternal source of all being and all perfection; he must acknowledge and be conscious freely and deliberately that his being comes from God, and that that same divine action which created and elevated it must maintain it in existence, aid it in the development of its faculties, and bring it to its final completion. He must freely and deliberately yearn after all this, and have firm reliance that the infinite will maintain his being, aid it in its growth, and bring it to its full bloom in the palingenesia.

On the part of the infinite, prayer in this same deprecatory sense implies an action of God assisting and aiding the finite in producing the aforesaid four acts necessary to constitute a prayer.

If we regard prayer in its life-giving moment, it implies two elements: one on the part of the infinite, the other on the part of the finite. On the part of the infinite, it implies a real actual and personal communication, a giving of himself by a personal intercourse to the finite; and, on the part of the latter, a personal apprehension of the infinite, and an assimilation of and transformation into the infinite. We cannot refrain here from quoting a beautiful page of a French writer in explanation of this last element; " When man's will, lifted by an ardent desire, succeeds in putting itself in contact with the supreme will, the miracle of the divine intervention is accomplished. Prayer, which *renders God present to us,*[*]

---
[*] Orig. *De Orat.*

is a kind of communion by which man feeds on grace, and assimilates to himself that celestial aliment of the soul. In that ineffable communication, the divine will penetrates our will, its action is mingled with our action to produce but one and the same indivisible work, which belongs whole and entire to both ; wonderful union of grandeur and of lowliness, of a power eternally fecund, and of a created activity which is exhausted by its very duration, of an incorruptible and regenerating element with the infirm and corruptible elements of our being; union, which believed in invariably, though conceived in different manner by the savage tribes as well as by the most civilized nations, has been under different forms, and in spite of the errors which have obscured it, the immortal belief of humanity.*"

Now, we maintain that prayer, understood in all its comprehension, besides the effect which it produces in its own natural sphere, is also the hierarchical superior of the action of the whole substantial creation; and that, consequently, the latter must yield to the former, whenever they should happen to come in conflict with each other; and thus, under this respect, it may be said that prayer governs the world.

This may be proven by two sorts of argument; one as it were exterior, the other intrinsic to the subject.

---

* Gerbet, *Le Dogme Générateur de la Piété Catholique*.

The first is drawn from the properties of the supernatural moment. For, if this moment is superior to substantial creation, if it is the end and type of it, every one can see that the mode of acting of elevated spirits—spirits in whom the supernatural moment is realized and concreted—must necessarily precede and be superior to the mode of action of substantial creation, and that the latter must necessarily be subject to the former—unless we abolish and deny the universal law of hierarchy presiding and ruling over all the moments of the exterior action of God, and founded on the intrinsic and respective value of beings. *Actio sequitur esse* is the old axiom of ontology. If the being of the supernatural moment is superior to the being of substantial creation, the mode of action in the first must also, in force of that action, be superior to the mode of action of the latter. When, therefore, a natural law, a law of substantial creation, comes in opposition with a true prayer, a prayer made with all the conditions which its nature requires, the natural law must yield and give way to prayer.

The second argument is drawn from the essence of prayer as a life-giving agent. What is prayer in this sense? It is an actual communication of the finite with the infinite, an actual participation of the infinite and his attributes; it is a possession which the finite takes of the infinite, the appropriation, the assimilation of the infinite. It is the finite transported and transformed into the infinite. For in it the mind of the finite takes hold of the mind of the infinite, and is, as it were, transformed into it; the will and energy of the finite grasps the will and the almighty power of the infinite, and is changed, as it were, into it; the person of the finite is united to the person of the infinite, and is assimilated to him. Now, it is evident that prayer understood in this sense is no longer an act of the finite alone, but an act of both the finite and the infinite; it is the result of the energy of both. Its efficacy and energy therefore must be superior to the energy of all substantial creation as the infinite is superior to the finite. Consequently, it is evident that when a natural law pregnant with finite energy comes in conflict with a prayer impregnated, so to speak, with infinite energy, the former must yield to the superior force of the latter.

Prayer governs the world also in a sense more general than the one we have hitherto indicated for it. The sum of all the actions of substantial creation has been so disposed, and is so ruled and governed, as to be always subject to the sum of all the actions of the supernatural moment, and this for the same reasons developed above.

Here it can be seen with how much reason those philosophers who call themselves rationalists sneer and wax indignant at the fact, constant in time and place, of the importance which mankind has attached to prayer for physical reasons, as for rain, for fair weather, for a good harvest, and the like. They show evidently how far they are from understanding the sublime hierarchical harmony of the cosmos, which the simple ones of the earth, who have faith in God, instinctively feel and acknowledge. For if God did not create the cosmos at random without a plan or design, he assuredly must have followed and maintained the necessary relations of things. Now, if substantial creation and its mode of action is hierarchically—that is, in comprehension of being—inferior to the supernatural term and its mode of action, if the latter is the end and type of the former, and if they are not to be kept apart, but to be brought together into unity and harmony, and must thus harmoniously act, it is clear to the rudest understanding that the one mode of action must be subject to the other, and that consequently, when a prayer is in opposition with the realization of natural law, the natural law must yield, and the prayer must prevail.

Nor will it do to say that if such were the case the natural order would no longer enjoy any stability or permanence, because some prayer or other might come continually in opposition to it. For the whole series of actions of substantial creation is marked out eternally in the mind of the infinite. Likewise the whole series of actions of the supernatural moment is marked out in the same mind; they are brought together in beautiful harmony in the same divine intellect from all eternity. God has foreseen when and how a prayer would require the suspension of the natural law, and has willed and decreed it, so that no suspension of natural law, consequent upon a prayer, can take place which has not been foreseen and arranged harmoniously from all eternity; and if we could for a moment cast a glance into the mind of the infinite, we should see an infinite series of actions of substantial creation; an infinite series of actions of the supernatural moment, all intertwined in a most harmonious whole, and the different exceptions here and there only linking together the two orders, putting them in bolder relief, and enhancing the beauty and harmony of the whole cosmos. The theory which we have been vindicating explains also a phenomenon so frequent and so common in the history of the Catholic Church—the saint who works miracles, or the *Thaumaturgus.*

A saint is one in whom a certain fulness of the supernatural term resides, and hence a certain fulness of the particular mode of action belonging to that moment. A saint can pray well; therefore he can work miracles, and does oftentimes. Protestantism has not only denied most of the miracles not recorded in the Bible, but has gone so far as to deny the possibility of such miracles ever occurring after the establishment and propagation of Christianity, on the plea that they are no longer necessary. It was but a logical consequence of its doctrine of justification. If man is not really made holy in his justification, if he does not receive in his soul the term of the supernatural moment as really inherent in him, it is clear he cannot have or possess the mode of action of that moment, still less a certain fulness of it. Consequently, neither is he elevated above substantial creation, nor is his mode of action superior to the action of that same moment, and therefore he cannot exercise a power and an efficacy which he has not. In other words, a man justified according to the Protestant doctrine cannot be a saint intrinsically, and cannot consequently pray. And how could he work miracles? It was natural to deny such possibility.

But endow a man with the supernatural term in a certain fulness, and hence suppose him possessed of a fulness of its mode of action intrinsically superior in energy to the mode of action of substantial creation, and you may suppose he is likely to exercise it, and work miracles oftentimes.

As to the plea of necessity, it is absolulely futile. A miracle would be necessary even after the establishment of Christianity in all times and places, which, by the bye, has not been accomplished yet, if for no other reason, in order to assert and vindicate from time to time the existence and the supremacy of the supernatural over the natural.

The third truth emanating from the qualities of the supernatural moment is that those created persons in whom the term of that moment is realized are essentially mediators between the Theanthropos and substantial creation.

The principle follows evidently from the fourth quality essentially belonging to the supernatural term, that of being mediator between the other moments, the hypostatic and substantial.

For if the term of that moment in intensity of being and perfection hold a place between the other two moments, it is evident that those in whom the moment is realized must hold the same middle place and be, consequently, mediators. Hence, it appears how the Catholic doctrine of the intercession, and by logical consequence, of the invocation, of saints, is a cosmological law, as imperative as any other law of the cosmos. For what does the word mediator mean? Limiting the question to location or space, it signifies a thing placed or located between two others; in a hierarchical sense, confining the question to being an essence, it expresses a thing in essence and nature inferior to one and superior to another; in the same sense, confining the question to action and development, it exhibits a thing in its action and development inferior to the action and development of one and superior in the same to another. The person, therefore, in whom the supernatural term is realized is mediator in the sense of being in essence, nature, attributes, action, and development, superior to the same things of substantial creation, and inferior to those of the Theanthropos. Now, as the cosmos is not governed by the law of hierarchy alone, but also by the law of unity and communion, and as these laws imply a real and effective union and communication of being and action between the terms of the cosmos, it follows that the person in whom the supernatural term is concreted is in real and effective communication with the Theanthropos, as inferior, and in real and effective communication, as superior, with substantial creation; he is in communication with the former as subject and dependent, with the latter as superior, and with both as medium; that is, a recipient relatively to the Theanthropos, as transmitting what it receives from the Theanthropos relatively to substantial creation; both relations being exercised by the person elevated in every sense, either as receiving from the Theanthropos and transmitting to substantial creation, or as representative of substantial creation before the Theanthropos.

And as we are speaking of moral persons, that is, free, intelligent agents, in what can these relations consist but in this, that elevated persons, acting as mediums, may intercede and obtain favors for created persons from the Theanthropos, and these may invoke their intercession in their behalf?

The doctrine, therefore, of the intercession and the invocation of saints is a cosmological law, resulting from the law of hierarchy, unity, and and communion, and governing the relation of purely created persons with those elevated to the supernatural moment.

It must be here remarked that the mediatorship of persons elevated is not confined only to persons in their mere natural state, but it extends also to persons elevated to the supernatural moment, because the supernatural term admits of variety of degree, some persons being endowed with a certain fulness of that moment, some with much less. Those in whom the fulness is realized are hierarchically mediators between the Theanthropos and other elevated spirits possessing a less amount of that term, and can consequently intercede for the latter.

It must be remarked, in the second place, that the law governs the cosmos not only in its germinal state, but also in its state of completion and perfection; and we cannot possibly discover or imagine by what logical process Protestantism, which admits this law in the germinal and incipient state of the cosmos, denies it to exist between persons elevated to the state of palingenesia and those who are yet in the germinal state. This denial, so far as we can see, could be supported only by the supposition that as soon as an elevated person reaches its final development, every tie of union, every bond of intercourse is immediately broken asunder between him and other persons living yet in the germinal state of the cosmos. But how false and absurd this supposition would be is evident to every one who at all understands the exterior works of God. The cosmos being measured by time, is essentially successive; in other words, all the elements of the cosmos cannot possibly reach their final completion at one and the same time, the law of variety and hierarchy necessarily forbidding it. It is absolutely necessary, then, that some elements should reach their final perfection first and some afterwards, in proportion as they come to take place in the cosmos successively. If, therefore, by one element of the cosmos reaching its final development all intercourse were to be broken between it and all other elements which have not reached so high a condition, it would follow that the cosmos would never be one, never in harmony, until all had reached their final completion and the creation of more elements entirely ceased. It would be a continual disorder and confusion until the end of the world. Now this is absurd, since unity and harmony must always govern and adorn

God's works. Nor can we see any intrinsic reason why it should be broken. The only plea alleged by Protestants in support of this suspension of all communion between the spirits in palingenesia and those living on earth, is that there can be no possible means of communication between them. They express this idea commonly by saying that the saints in heaven cannot hear our prayers. How philosophical this plea is we leave it to the intelligent reader to determine. Suppose we had no direct answer to give to this plea, the absolute necessity of the cosmos being one and harmonious, would make a true philosopher infer that the infinite must have found a means whereby to keep up this communication, though it might be unknown to us what that means actually is.

But the direct answer is at hand. The Word of God is essentially the life of the cosmos. He is the type of all the essences, of all the natures, of all the personalities, of all the acts composing the cosmos. The cosmos, in all these respects, is reflected in the Word. "All that was made in him was life." (St. John.)

Now, all elevated spirits are united to and live in the Incarnate Word. The spirits or persons in the germinal state are united to his person by the supernatural essence and the supernatural faculties of intelligence and of will. This forms the essential union between them and the Theanthropos. The spirits in the final state are united to him in the same substantial sense, with the exception that their supernatural essence has reached its utmost completion, their supernatural intelligence is changed into intuition, and their supernatural will has immediate possession of God.

The consequence of these principles is that the spirits in the germinal state produce acts of invocation to the spirits in the final state, and these acts are reflected or reproduced in the Theanthropos as the type and the intelligible objective life of the cosmos.

The spirits in the final state see, by intuition, in the Theanthropos all those acts of invocation of the spirits in the germinal state, and thus come to know what the spirits on earth claim from them. As orator and audience, living in the same atmosphere can hold intercourse with each other, because the words uttered by the orator are transmitted by the air to the ears of his audience, so the spirits on earth and the spirits in heaven hold intercourse with each other, because they live in the same medium.

The spirits on earth making acts of invocation to their brethren in heaven, these acts are reflected or reproduced in the Theanthropos, and from him reverberate and reach the eyes of the spirits in heaven living in him, and thus they come to the knowledge of the wants and prayers of their brethren on earth.

But why such interposition of persons when we could go directly to the Theanthropos? Does this not detract from the mediatorship of Christ?

Why, but because the cosmos must be one? Why, but because all the elements of the cosmos must communicate with each other? And how can this doctrine detract from the mediatorship of Christ when *he* is made the source, the origin, the end of everything? If Catholic doctrine claimed this intercourse independently of the Theanthropos, it would certainly detract from his mediatorship. But do we not establish and centre this mediatorship of the saint entirely in the Theanthropos?

The last truth which follows from the essence of the supernatural term is what is called the worship of saints. This truth is not only a cosmological law, but an ontological principle, since, considered in its simplest and most ultimate acceptation, it implies nothing more than the duty incumbent on every moral agent to acknowledge, theoretically and practically, the intrinsic value of being. Suppose a certain being is possessed of a hundred degrees of perfection, so to speak, I cannot, without a flat contradiction to my intelligence, which apprehends it, deny or ignore it; I cannot, without a flat contradiction to my expansive faculty or will, which is attracted by it, fail to appreciate it practically. Now, the worship of saints, against which Protestantism has written and said so much, is founded entirely on that ontological principle. The saint is possessed of a certain fulness of the supernatural term. The supernatural intelligence of other elevated spirits apprehends this fulness, and the supernatural will of the same spirits cannot fail to value it. This theoretical and practical appreciation is esteem, and when expressed outwardly is honor and praise. By the ontological principle of recognizing the value of being, therefore, it is evident that the Catholic theory of the worship of saints is not only theologically lawful, but eminently philosophical. Protestantism, in denying this worship, follows the same principle without being aware of it.

It starts from its own doctrine of justification, which consists, as we have seen, not in the interior cleansing of the soul from sin and in its elevation to the supernatural moment, but in an external application to it of the merits of Christ. The example of the cloak is most appropriate. Suppose a man, all filthy and loathsome; cover him with a rich and splendid cloak, so as to hide the filth and loathsomeness, and you have an example of Protestant justification. It is all foreign, outward, unsubjective. Now, apply the ontological principle of the value of being to a saint of this calibre, and it is evident that you cannot esteem and value him because he is worth nothing subjectively, and hence the denial of the worship of saints is a logical consequence of the Protestant doctrine of justification, and an application, in a negative sense, of the ontological principle of the value of beings.

On the contrary, admit the Catholic doctrine of justification, whereby a man is not only cleansed from sin, but elevated to a supernatural moment, receiving as inherent in him a higher and nobler nature and higher and nobler faculties, and it is evident that you must acknowledge *this*, value, esteem, and honor it.

CHAPTER XII.

THE COSMOS IN TIME AND SPACE.

THE supernatural moment unites created personalities to the infinite. By the moment of substantial creation the first duality is established between the infinite and finite. This duality is brought into harmony and unity in the Theanthropos, who knits together the finite and the infinite in the oneness of his single personality. But as the hypostatic moment united only created natures to the infinite, another moment was necessary, namely, a medium between the Theanthropos and substantial creation. This is the *supernatural*, which, by raising created persons above their natural sphere, enables them to arise, as it were, to the level of the infinite, and establishes a communication and intercourse between them. This we have shown in the preceding chapter. The question which now remains to be treated of at present is the following: *Who or what is to be the medium of com-*

municating the term of the supernatural moment to created personality?

Although God, in acting outside himself, might have effected everything immediately by himself, without allowing any play to second causes, yet, following the law of his wisdom, he exerted immediately by himself as much power as was required to set second causes in action, and then allowed them to develop themselves under his guidance. The law of wisdom is the law of sufficient reason, which implies that no intelligent agent can, in acting, employ more power than is absolutely necessary to attain its object; for acting otherwise would be to let the amount of action not necessary to attain the object go to waste, and be employed without any possible reason. Hence the necessity on the part of the infinite to admit secondary agency in the effectuation of this moment, whenever that was possible, in order to observe the law of wisdom. Applying this theory to the external action, we see that the substantial and the hypostatic moments were effected immediately by God himself, because no secondary agency could be employed therein; but the supernatural moment was effected by God through the agency of the Theanthropos, who merited it by his own acts of infinite value.* Hence, as the Theanthropos is the meritorious cause of the supernatural moment, he is pre-eminently its medi-

---

* Council of Trent.

ator, and therefore the medium of communicating it to created personality. This consequence of Christ being the medium of the communication of grace, in force of his being its meritorious cause, is so evident that we know of none who has ever disputed it. The only question which remains to be solved—a question of the greatest importance—is this: When the Theanthropos was living on earth, he would communicate the term of the supernatural moment in the personal intercourse and intimacy in which he lived with his followers; but as he has withdrawn his visible presence and intercourse from the earth, how is the term of the supernatural moment to be communicated to human persons in all time and space?

We answer by laying down the following principle: *This medium must be such as will preserve the dignity and the prerogatives of the Theanthropos, as will befit the nature of human personality, as will fulfil the object which the supernatural term is intended to attain.*

Because, if the medium which is chosen does not fulfil these conditions; if it does not maintain the dignity and prerogatives of the Theanthropos; if it does not befit the nature and constitution of human personality; if it frustrates the ends of the supernatural moment instead of attaining them, it is evident that infinite wisdom could never have chosen it without contradicting itself. The principle is, therefore, evident. Now, what can this medium be in its nature which fulfils all these conditions? It can be nothing else than *the sacramental extension of the Theanthropos in time and space.* In announcing such a principle, the reader is at once aware that we require some kind of presence of the Theanthropos in the cosmos extending to all time and to all space.

But what is meant by sacramental extension, and why should it be so?

To answer this question, let us get first a true metaphysical idea of the sacrament. The term sacrament in theological language is applied as conveying the idea of an instrument of grace. Hence, to get at the idea, we must inquire into the idea of instrument. Now, what is an instrument? It is an organism which contains a force. And what is force? It, being one of the first elements of our thoughts, can be defined but imperfectly, less by its essence than by its effects. It might be defined to be the energy of a being retaining its existence through the means of an effort of concentration, or diffusing it outwardly by a movement of expansion. Every act of force must be reduced to this two-fold movement: either we shut ourselves, as it were, in ourselves to concentrate our life, and give ourselves the highest possible sensation; or we expand ourselves to communicate our life to others, and according to the degree of this double tension we exhibit the phenomenon of force. The hand contracted or closed is the symbol of the force of concentration; the hand open to give is the image of the force of expansion. The force of concentration in its highest possible act is eternity—the possession of interminable life all at once. He alone possesses it who in an instant—one, indivisible, and absolute—experiences in himself and for ever the plenitude of his being, and says, *I am who am;* the sublimest idea ever conceived and ever uttered. The force of expansion at its highest possible act is the external action; and he alone possesses it who, absolutely sufficient to himself in the plenitude of his being, can call to life, without losing of his own, whomsoever and whatsoever he lists—bodies, spirits, worlds, and for ever in ages without number, and in space without limits. (Lacordaire.)

Now, God, in giving us being, has given us force, without which a being could not conceive itself, and has given us this force in its double element of concentration and expansion: the one, which enables us to continue its existence, and to develop ourselves; the other, which enables us to propagate ourselves: the one, by which we tend to the act of eternity; the other, by which we tend to the act of creation.

But there is this difference among others between us and the infinite, that *he* possesses in himself and by himself the force of concentration and expansion, whereas our force is borrowed and communicated to us by means of *instruments*, which his infinite wisdom has prepared. Life is kept in us by something *forcing* to us the *instruments* to which God has communicated the power of sustaining and repairing it.

We subsist by the invisible force contained in an organism. The same must be said of the force of expansion. We cannot act outside ourselves, on any being at all capable of resistance, by the simple direct act of our will, but must make use of instruments, among which our body is the first.

Now, the reasons of this are, that, if we possessed the force of concentration and expansion in ourselves and by ourselves, it would follow that, as these two forces constitute the essence of life, we should have life in ourselves and by ourselves, we should be to ourselves the reason of our being and subsistence, and consequently we should be infinite and not finite. Hence, Pantheism, which admits the unity of substance independent and self-sufficient, and all else as phenomena of this substance, rejects all idea of instrument in metaphysics, and all idea of sacrament in theology.

Nor would it do to say that God might communicate that double force to us immediately by himself without the aid of any instruments. For two reasons we must reject such a supposition:

First, the law of secondary agency, which requires that created substance should act, and it would not for any purpose do so were God to do everything immediately by himself. Second, the law of communion, so necessary to the unity of the cosmos, which is founded exclusively upon the action of one element upon the other, else the communion would be merely imaginary and fictitious.

We conclude: An instrument in its metaphysical idea is an organism containing a force of concentration and expansion. A sacrament, being an instrument, must therefore be an organism containing a force of concentration and expansion; and, as an organism is something outward and sensible, it follows that a sacrament must be also outward and sensible. And as the force which the sacrament is designed to convey is altogether supernatural, it follows that a sacrament must be an instrument of conveying supernatural force. We may, therefore, define a sacrament to be a sensible instrument or organism containing a supernatural force of concentration and of expansion.

But it is evident that no instrument, no organism in nature, is capable of conveying a supernatural force of concentration and of expansion; for that would imply an act superior to its nature, which is a contradiction. It follows, therefore, that this supernatural force must be communicated to the organism by the Theanthropos, otherwise it could never fulfil its destination and office. The Theanthropos, in order to be the means of communicating to all human persons in time and space the supernatural term, which is nothing else but a supernatural force of concentration and expansion, must communicate and unite his infinite energy and action to an external organism, and thus himself convey through that organism the supernatural life. And this union of the infinite energy of the Theanthropos with an outward organism must not be successive or temporary, but permanent and stable; since the object is to convey the supernatural force to all human persons in *all time* and in *all space*.

This is the sacramental extension of the Theanthropos in time and space, the continuation upon earth of the hypostatic union, the filling up, as it were, of his incarnation, a second incarnation; not of the Word with human nature in the unity of his personality, but an incarnation of the Theanthropos, the Word made man, with visible, outward, external instruments, in the unity of one sacramental being, to convey to men in all times and spaces the supernatural life of grace.

This sacramental extension of the Theanthropos must be divided into various moments, owing to the requirements of the object for which it is intended. The object of the supernatural moment is to reproduce the Theanthropos in all human persons by a similitude of his nature, perfections, and attributes, and by a real union with, and transformation into his life.

The infinite, from all eternity, under the subsistence of primary, unbegotten activity and principle, begets and conceives intellectually a similitude of himself absolutely perfect under the subsistence of intellectual expression, *Logos* or Word. This action of the *Principle* begetting the Word, exhibiting all the essential requisites of generation, constitutes the Principle—*Father;* and the begotten—*Son.* In his works *ad extra*, the infinite, in effecting the mystery of the hypostatic moment, does nothing less than exalt the cosmos, as recapitulated in the human nature of the Word, to the very same dignity which arises in his bosom when in the day of his eternity he begets his eternal Son. For the Theanthropos, or the Word made man, is not the Son of God figuratively, or by adoption, or by any other action than that which begets him from eternity. He as man-God is the Son of God really, naturally, and by the same identical action which eternally engenders him. Hence, the cosmos, as abridged in the human nature of Christ, in force of the hypostatic moment, is really, naturally, and by the same eternal action of the Father, the Son of God Almighty.

The infinite wishes to extend this divine *Son-*

ship of the cosmos, as recapitulated in the human nature of Christ, to the human persons also. This of course cannot be effected except by an adoption founded upon the following elements:

1. A perfect similitude of the nature, properties, attributes, and virtues of the Theanthropos.
2. A real union with him.
3. A communication of his life.
4. A communication of his beatitude.

In other words, a reproduction of Christ and his nature, his attributes, his life, and his bliss.

To effect this reproduction are required: First, a similitude of the nature of Christ; a similitude of his intellect; a similitude of his will; a sharing in his feelings. Second, a real and substantial participation of his life, in order that this similitude may be sustained, and that, initial and germinal as it is in this world, it may grow and develop itself by communing with its proper object, and thus become perfect and able to attain a participation of his bliss in palingenesia.

Thus the eternal Father, seeing all human persons bearing the image of his Son, having his mind, his will, his feelings, communicating with his life, extends to them the feeling of a father and the inheritance of children.*

Hence, the different moments of the sacramental extension of the Theanthropos:

---

* "Quos prescivit et predestinavit conformes fieri imagini filil sui, ut ipse sit primogenitus in multis fratibus." Rom. viii. 29.

1. A moment of supernatural generation by which the Theanthropos attaches his infinite energy to a visible instrument, permanent in time and space, and through which he confers a similitude of himself and the other divine persons; a similitude in essence, in intellect, in will, in feeling, in aspirations, in an initial and germinal state, and which establishes the incipient and germinal union of human persons with the Trinity.

2. A moment by which the Theanthropos attaches his infinite energy to a visible instrument, and through which he carries that initial and inchoative similitude and union to a definite and determinate growth.

3. A moment by which the Theanthropos attaches his infinite energy to a sensible instrument, in order to communicate to human persons the power to perpetuate his sacramental extension in time and space.

4. A moment by which the Theanthropos communicates his infinite energy to human persons, to exalt their natural force of expansion, and enable them to propagate the human and supernatural species.

5. A moment by which the Theanthropos attaches and unites the *real substantial presence of his person*, that is, of his humanity and divinity, both subsisting in his single divine person, to a sensible instrument, in order to communicate to human persons his real, substantial, theanthropic

feli, in order to put all human persons of all time and space in real living communion with each other, by meeting in him and through him as a common centre, and in order to reside continually in the visible cosmos.

The third and fourth moments follow necessarily from the others, both having the like office.

The first of them is intended to perpetuate the sacramental extension of Christ. An organism to be set in motion requires the agency of human persons; consequently, the supernatural organism or the sacramental extension of Christ, in order to be applied to human persons, requires the agency of human persons, appointed and fitted for such office by another visible instrument to which a particular theanthropic energy is attached.

This third moment is demanded also for another object, that is, the transmitting whole and entire, and without any error, by a personal intercourse, of the whole body of doctrines which are the object of the supernatural intelligence bestowed by the first moment. No other possible way can be thought of transmitting whole and entire the whole body of doctrines, the object of the supernatural intelligence, than a personal intercourse, the only safe, natural, philosophical manner of transmitting doctrine. Hence, for this object, also, a moment was required by which the Theanthropos, attaching his infinite energy to a particular instrument, would fit human persons to teach infallibly the whole body of doctrines he came to reveal, and to put in act his sacramental extension.

The fourth moment relates to the natural union of sexes in reference to generation.

Human persons being exalted by the first moment to the supernatural order, their personal acts must necessarily become supernatural; much more the highest possible personal act of expansion, which is the transfusion of their united life into a third. Consequently, it was befitting that the Theanthropos should attach a particular supernatural energy to the union of the sexes with a view to the act of generation, in order to exalt and sanctify it, and thus enable them not only to generate as persons exalted to a supernatural state, but to bring up the offspring in the same supernatural order.*

All the moments of the sacramental extension of Christ but the fifth imply a personal action of the Theanthropos, attached to each particular instrument constituting the moment.

The fifth moment alone implies a real substantial presence of the whole person of the Theanthropos under the visible instrument. This requires explanation and proof, since it has been denied

---

* There are two other moments, but as they imply the question of evil, shall be treated of when speaking of that question.

with a fierceness and rage of an opposition which did not and could not comprehend the grandeur, the sublimity, the magnificence of the elevation of the cosmos, by the fact of the hypostatic moment. Catholicity holds: 1. That, though the Theanthropos has withdrawn his *visible* presence from the cosmos, he remains in it still, not by a spiritual, figurative, phenomenal presence, but by a real, substantial presence of his *whole person*, that is, of his body, blood, soul, and divinity—a presence hidden under the modifications of bread and wine.

2. That the manner according to which this real, substantial presence of the Theanthropos is obtained, is by a change of the substances of bread and wine into the substance of the body and blood of the Theanthropos, not still and dead, but as vivified by his soul and divinity; a change effected by the sacramental words impregnated with the infinite power of the Theanthropos, and uttered by the minister over the elements to be changed.

Now the question arises: Is this substantial presence of the Theanthropos necessary? Is it metaphysically possible in the manner that the Catholic Church admits it?

As to the first question, we observe that such a presence is not absolutely necessary when considered of itself, independent of, and previous to, the adoption of the present plan of the cosmos by the infinite intelligence of God. But considered in relation to the present plan of the cosmos and as a complement of it, it *is* necessary. Infinite intelligence might have selected another plan, but, having once chosen the present plan of the cosmos, the real presence becomes absolutely necessary as a complement bringing it to perfection. This we shall endeavor to prove by the following arguments:

First, the end of the action of the infinite outside himself is the highest possible manifestation of his infinite excellence. To attain this end, an infinite effect would have been necessary. But as an infinite effect was a contradiction in terms, infinite wisdom was to find means whereby to effect the highest possible manifestation of himself, in spite of the ontological finiteness of the cosmos to be effected. This means was to produce a variety of moments; to bring the whole variety of moments to the highest possible unity in the person of the Theanthropos,

1. To produce a variety of moments, in order that the *infinity* of the perfections of God, which could not be expressed by the terms effected in *intensity* of being, might be expressed in *extension* and *number*.

2. The highest possible unity, in order that the infinity, simplicity, and oneness of God might be portrayed.

3. In the person of the Theanthropos, in order

that, if this variety brought into unity could not be ontologically infinite, it might be infinite by a union and communication the highest possible.

These are the three leading principles, according to which infinite wisdom resolved the problem of the end of the external action: highest possible variety, highest possible unity, highest possible communication.

Now, let us see if and how the effectuation of real cosmos was governed by these principles.

In view of these principles, God effected substantial creation and the hypostatic moment, by which the whole substantial moment was united to the person of the Word in the bond of his divine personality.

Was the problem of the highest possible variety and the highest possible unity and communication in the person of the Theanthropos resolved? It was, so far only as nature and substance were concerned; because the hypostatic union only wedded *human nature*, and through it all inferior natures, to the person of the Word. But this unity and communication excluded, and had to exclude, all human personalities. It excluded them in the fact; it had to exclude them, otherwise human personality would have ceased to exist. Here the problem must be resolved anew— how to raise human personality to the highest possible union and communication with the Theanthropos. Another moment was effected to initiate the solution of the problem; and this was the supernatural moment. By it human personality by being endowed with a higher similitude of the Trinity and the Theanthropos, and by receiving higher faculties, is brought into a real and particular union with the Word, and through him the other persons of the Trinity. But the supernatural moment does not resolve the problem yet; because the union which results thereby is union between human persons and the Word as God, not a union between human persons and the *Theanthropos*, the Word made man.

A real and efficient union between two terms requires a real relation between them. Now, the supernatural term establishes a relation between human persons and the Word, but not a relation between them and the Theanthropos, because it is wholly spiritual and incorporeal. A true relation between persons composed of body and soul must be a contact, not spiritual only, but also corporeal.

Hence, if we exclude the real substantial presence of the Theanthropos as such, we have a union of human persons united to the Word, but not a real efficacious union of human persons united to the *Theanthropos*. On this supposition, the cosmos would lack the highest possible unity and communication, and would fail to realize the end of that external action. But, admit the corporal presence of the Theanthropos in time and space, admit that presence incorporating and individualizing itself in human persons, and the whole wisdom and beauty of the design flashes at once upon your mind—the whole cosmos, as abridged in the human nature of Christ, made infinite by the hypostatic union with the Word; all human persons incorporated body and soul into the body and soul of the Theanthropos, built up into his body and soul, transformed, as it were, in them and through them, and in them coming in the closest possible communication with the divinity which a *person* can attain. In this plan only everything holds together and presents order, harmony, and beauty.

But, if the real substantial presence of the *Theanthropos* was necessary in order to bring human personality to the highest possible union and communication with the infinite, and thus realize the end of the external action, it was also required that the being and actions of human personality, might be elevated to the dignity, excellence, and value of *theanthropic being and acts*. In the hypostatic union, human nature and all the inferior natures which it eminently contains, as connected in the person of the Word, are deified, and their acts have the value and dignity of divine acts.

Hence, so far, the end of the external action which is to raise the cosmos in its nature and acts to an infinite dignity by union and communication, is attained. But human personality, not being an element of the hypostatic union, could not acquire in its being and in its acts the dignity and excellence of divine being and acts, and consequently the end of the external action could not by the hypostatic moment be realized as regards the same personality. Here another problem arose in the divine mind—how to raise human personality to such a union with the Theanthropos as, without infringing upon its nature, to raise its being and its acts to the value, excellence, and dignity of theanthropic being and acts, and thus to exhibit in it the most perfect image of the infinite. This problem was resolved by the incorporation of the Theanthropos, under the modifications of bread and wine, in human persons. This plan does not imply an hypostatic union, which would do away with human personality, but a union so strict, so close, and so intimate, as merely to fall short of the hypostatic. For, in it, and by it, the Theanthropos, the God made man, in his whole person, composed of body, soul, and divinity, is incorporated in human personalities by the act of eating, and his body pervades their bodies, his blood circulates in their blood, his soul inheres upon and clings to their soul, his divinity purifies, sanctifies, ennobles, exalts their whole being, and, like food, results in a transformation — a transformation not indeed of the Theanthropos into the flesh and blood of the human person, as it happens with ordinary food, but a transformation of the human person into the body, blood, soul, and almost divinity of the Theanthropos. "Cresce et manducabis me, nec tu me mutabis in te sed tu mutaberis in me."* The fathers have endeavored to express the intimacy of the union by adopting various similitudes. Some have likened it to a piece of glass when impregnated by the rays of the sun and appearing like a smaller sun. Others have compared it to the action of fire upon iron, which, when heated and become red hot, looks exactly like fire, and could fulfil the functions of fire. St. Cyril of Alexandria has chosen the similitude of two distinct pieces of wax, which when melted and mingled together are so intimately united as to form one single piece, defying every possible recognition of their former separation. But all these similitudes, plausible as they may be, can never express the mysterious intimacy and closeness between human personalities and the Theanthropos in the eucharistic banquet.

Now, how does this resolve the problem? Most perfectly. The infinite intends to exhibit in human personalities an image, an expression of himself as pure and as perfect as possible—an image of his being and of his life or action in obedience to the end of the external action, always preserving the conditions of human per-

---
* St. Augustine.

sonalities. Now, what does the cosmos of personalities, when united to the Theanthropos in the mystery of the Eucharist, when pervaded by him, when so closely and so intimately united to him as to feel his flesh come in contact with their flesh, his blood glowing in their blood, his heart beating against their hearts, his mind illumining and guiding their minds, his will captivating and mastering their will, his divinity ennobling and exalting their whole being and faculties—I say, when the cosmos of personality is thus united to the Theanthropos, does it not represent most vividly the infinite being of God? Does the infinite in looking at such a cosmos see anything but as it were one Theanthropos filling and pervading all?

As to expressing the action of the life of the infinite, and thus raising the acts of a human person to the dignity and value of theanthropic life, it will appear evident if we recollect that the life of the infinite establishes the eternal religion in the bosom of God which expresses itself in the mystery of the ever blessed Trinity. For the Father, in recognizing himself intellectually, and as it were theoretically, produces an intellectual image of himself, absolutely perfect in every sense. Both in recognizing themselves aspire a practical acknowledgment of themselves, the Holy Ghost, who completes the cycle of infinite life, and perfects the eternal religion.

Now, this eternal religion are human persons

destined to express, to realize in themselves, that they may be a most perfect image in their action and life of the life of the infinite. This they could never do either naturally or supernaturally. Naturally, because such acknowledgment requires an infinite intellect to apprehend the infinite excellence and perfection of God, and an infinite power of appreciation to value, esteem, and love it practically. Now, naturally these faculties of human persons are simply finite. Even the light of grace, which strengthens the natural intelligence, and the supernatural force, which corroborates the will, cannot do it, because in their nature also finite. It is, therefore, the infinite intellect and will of the Theanthropos which alone can appreciate him intellectually and love him as he deserves. Now, the mystery of the Eucharist enables human persons to partake of this intellectual and volitive recognition of the infinite by their union with the Theanthropos. When, after the solemn and happy moment of feeding upon the flesh and blood of the Theanthropos, I turn myself to adore God, to render him the homage of adoration which I owe him as a creature, then I am not alone with my limited understanding and will. It is with the intellect of the Theanthropos, which pervades and illumines my intellect, that I recognize theoretically his infinite perfections. When at the same moment I turn to him to offer him the tribute of my love, I cling to him then, not with the finite, limited, circumscribed power of my natural or supernatural will, but of a will under the guidance, the mastery, the possession, the infinite power of expansion of the will of the Theanthropos, under the immense weight of his love; and when I yield my heart to exuberant joy and complacency in his infinite loveliness and bliss, it is not the little vessel of a heart, which can contain but a finite joy, but a heart under the pressure of infinite jubilee, which gushes up from the heart of the Theanthropos and overflows into my heart, and makes it swim in a joy and a delight known to those alone who have tasted it. Thus, with the Theanthropos in my bosom, pervading my mind, my soul, my heart, my flesh, and drawing me toward him even as the bridegroom draws his bride to him, even as the mother presses her offspring close to her bosom in the intensity of maternal love, I know and I feel that I am adoring God as perfectly as a human person could possibly do, and the finite personal act of my adoration becomes infinite because mingled with the infinite act of the Theanthropos.

Hence the Eucharist is necessary, because it resolves the problem, how to elevate human persons to the most perfect image of God by incorporating the Theanthropos in human persons, and sharing with them his perfections and his acts.

So far, we have proved the necessity of the real presence, because, in force of the end of the external action, the cosmos, not only in the natures which it contains, but in the personalities also, required to be brought to the highest possible union and communication with the infinite.

We shall prove the same necessity from the requirements of supernatural life.

The supernatural term conferred upon human persons, consisting of a superior essence engrafted on their natural essence, and of supernatural faculties, must live, that is, act and develop itself.

Now, life, in the highest metaphysical acceptation of the term, consists in communion—the communing of a subject with an object. In the infinite, this communication is active. For the first principle lives inasmuch as he communicates his life to his conception, and both transfuse it into the spirit. But as the finite cannot contain life in itself, it must communicate with an object in order to appropriate it to itself. A person elevated to the supernatural moment cannot therefore live, except by communion with the objects proper to that moment. Now, what is the proper object of the supernatural faculties of intelligence and of will? For the intelligence, it is an actual apprehension of the infinite and the finite in all their relations, inasmuch as they are intelligible and inasmuch as the faculty is able to apprehend them. For the will, it is the infinite and the finite in all their relations, inasmuch as they are lovable. Hence, the supernatural intelligence must apprehend and come in contact with the infinite, his nature, his perfections, the mystery of his life and of his bliss, with the infinite, inasmuch as he acts outside himself, and, hence, with all the moments of his action and their terms. The same must be said of the supernatural will. This communication must be real and effective, otherwise the life which would flow from it would not be real, but fictitious and unsubstantial. But how to put the supernatural faculties of elevated persons in real, actual, substantial communication with the infinite and the finite in all their relations, so that the supernatural term may live, be unfolded, and transformed into them? By the real substantial, presence, and communication of the Theanthropos, who in his single individuality realizes the infinite and the finite in all their relations to each other. By communing actually and substantially with him, the essence of the supernatural moment comes in contact with the essence of the infinite, with his attributes, the eternal mystery of his life; it comes in contact with all substantial creation as abridged in the human nature of Christ; it comes in contact with the supernatural term, as Christ contains the fulness of it in his soul. Supernatural intelligence comes, therefore, in contact with all the objects which it is intended to appropriate, that it may expand, grow, and become perfect. The same happens to the supernatural will. Thus, in union with the Theanthropos by the eucharistic presence, they come in communion with all the objects which are to bring them to perfection by a gradual development and transformation.

Take the corporal presence of the Theanthropos away, and the supernatural faculties would only be in communication with the infinite, but not with the finite; with God, but not with his cosmos; because these faculties could never come in contact with the whole cosmos, except inasmuch as it exists and lives in the Theanthropos.

This argument introduces us to another. Every elevated person, to live fully and perfectly, must be in communication not only with the infinite and the finite as to nature, but also as to personality. Every elevated person must commune in a real, living, actual, quickening manner with elevated persons in time and space. The perfection of unity of the cosmos claims this communing, as it is evident; and the fulness of life of each particular person demands it, because life in its plenitude* results from communing with all proper objects.

Now, how to bring together all elevated persons living at a distance of time and space—some in the initial and germinal state, others in the state of completion and palingenesia? We come

---
* We speak of initial plenitude.

into communion with things and persons distinct and separate from us by time, space, or individuality, by a *medium* common to us and those things or persons we wish to enter into communion with. Thus, I come into communication with persons at a certain distance from me by the mediums of light and air, which are between me and them, and common to both. Suppose I was speaking, the air which exists between me and my hearers would be the common medium of communication. In articulating, I would strike the air which surrounds me, and the strokes would be transmitted from particle to particle in every direction until they would reach the ears of my audience, and thus a communication by speech would be established between us. If, therefore, all elevated persons must come in contact with each other, there must be something which will bring them together—a medium common to them all—to make them commune with each other. Now this medium is the real substantial presence of the Theanthropos incorporating himself in all elevated persons. I commune with the Theanthropos, with his divinity and his humanity, with his intelligence, his will, his heart, his body: I appropriate him to myself; another communes likewise with the Theanthropos; and thus we are brought together, we come in contact, we are united in the same life, intelligence, will, heart, body; thus we meet and live in one common theanthropic life. This is the foundation partly of that sublime, magnificent, ennobling doctrine of Catholicity, the *communion of saints*—communion of all persons elevated to the supernatural moment. Communion! What is the medium which brings them together? It is the real, living, substantial, presence of the Theanthropos incorporated in them, and on which they have fed and shall feed from eternity.*

How beautifully, how divinely was this communication of the Theanthropos given to us in the shape of food and at a banquet! Men in all times and in all places, by a prophetic instinct implanted in them by the Creator, have recognized the banquet as the supreme and the best expression of union and communication; because it was to appropriate, to drink life at one common source, from one common food. In the eucharistic banquet this is realized truly. Imagine a banqueting-hall as unbounded as space, and a banquet as long as time. Suppose millions upon millions of elevated persons entering the banqueting-hall to partake of the same repast. It is nothing less than the flesh and blood of the Theanthropos, not

---

* We hold that an elevated person once united to the substance of the Theanthropos, though not always actually united to his body, because this sacramental union only lasts as long as the species would naturally last, yet is continually so united in a spiritual though not less real manner.

dead, but living and quickening, by the indwelling of his soul and divinity, under the appearance of the simplest and most primitive elements of life—bread and wine. All partake of it; it penetrates and fills them all. A glow of theanthropic life runs through their supernatural being; their supernatural intelligence grows brighter at the flashes of his infinite, finite intelligence; their will expands at the embraces of infinite and finite loveliness; their hearts swell with virtues under the pressure of the heart of Jesus; their affections are purified, cleansed, ennobled, divinized at the contact of the affections of Jesus; their very flesh is spiritualized at the touch of his flesh; a seed, a germ of immortality is sown in it, to bud and blossom in the end of time. They live; not they, it is the Theanthropos who lives in them. And what wonder is it, then, that their natures, coming in contact in him, their intelligences meeting in him, their will harmonizing in him, their hearts beating together in him, their emotions mingling in him, their flesh touching in him and through him—what wonder, I say, is it, then, that they should communicate with each other, and that their virtues and their very merits should become common? Those who have never realized such a doctrine may often have marveled, on hearing a Catholic speaking of those who have passed from the initial and germinal state to the state of palingenesia, as if they were present to him, as if he were actually holding sweet converse with them. This doctrine explains it all. A Catholic feels truly that the life of the apostles and evangelists glows in his bosom, that the blood of martyrs runs in his very blood and ennobles it, that the guileless simplicity and innocent loveliness of the virgin's beams on his countenance, that the virtues of all the saints are transfused into him; because at the eucharistic banquet he can meet them living in the eternal mediator of all things, the Theanthropos, and in him and through him he mingles with them, associates with them, comes into the closest possible communication with them. Utopians have dreamt of a universal society, in which everything would be common. It is the eucharistic doctrine of the substantial presence of the Theanthropos which alone realizes this universal, sublime, ennobling society of all elevated spirits in one common medium, and having everything common in the only mediator, Jesus Christ, in all time and space.*

---

* We have given the real presence, and the communion of the flesh and blood of Jesus Christ, as the foundation of the communion of saints. To this might be objected that all the saints of the Old Testament, and many elevated persons, such as children dying after baptism, and grown persons who never could communicate, never were united to the Theanthropos in the Eucharist, and consequently would be excluded from the communion of saints. We answer, first, that we have only made the real presence *partly* the foundation of the communion of saints Second, we speak of the perfect state of the cosmos, and consequently not of the imperfect and incipient state, such as was the

We find that the arguments we have brought forward in vindicating the beautiful and sublime dogma of the real presence of the Theanthropos in his cosmos will have no effect on some minds, unless we remove the metaphysical difficulties which are raised against it, and show consequently its possibility. Therefore, we willingly hasten to the task. And as these objections are very popular, we shall put them in the popular form of a dialogue. The dialogue is between W. and D., the first a Protestant, and the other a Catholic.

W. I shall begin by a very strong objection. I cannot conceive the possibility of the body of a full-grown man being within the small portion of space filled by a wafer. Christ was a full-grown man. He is so now. How, then, can he reside or be contained in such a small particle of space as the host?

D. You will be kind enough to observe what the Catholic Church teaches, that it is the *substance* of the body and blood of Christ, which is under the modifications of bread and wine.

---

state of elevated persons in the Old Testament, who were united to Christ by faith and charity. As to children and grown-up persons who never communicated, we answer that we are giving the general law, and not accidental cases. The foundation, therefore, of the communion of saints is the union with Christ, real and actual, of the supernatural faculties. The perfection of the communion of saints is the real presence and incorporation.

W. Suppose it is; what difference does that make?

D. All the difference in the world. Pray, what is a substance?

W. It is that part of a being which remains immutable amid all the vicissitudes and changes of the being. These changes or vicissitudes are called accidents or modifications; that which remains always the same and immutable is called substance.

D. Right; and, pray, has substance any dimensions, has it length, breadth, height, or depth, or is it what philosophers call a simple being?

W. It must have no dimensions, because dimensions may change and vary, and the substance must be always the same.

D. Then substance is a simple being, that is, it has neither height, depth, length, nor breadth.

W. So it would seem, and so, if I recollect aright, all the metaphysicians worth the name hold it to be.

D. Right again; and, if you remember, Leibnitz calls it a *monas*, or a unit, and distinguishes two kinds of substances, the simple and the composite. The simple is one substance; the composite is an aggregate of simple substances or *units*. Thus, bodies are an aggregate of substances or units.

W. Well, suppose that bodies as to substance are an aggregate of simple units, what of that?

D. Why, then your objection is answered.

W. How?

D. Did we not say that the Catholic Church teaches that it is the *substance* of the body and blood of Christ, which is under the modifications of bread and wine? Did we not agree upon the theory that substance has no dimensions? Did we not admit that a body is an aggregate of simple units, as to substance, and that consequently in that respect it has no dimensions? Then it matters not how large or how small you may imagine the wafer to be, it cannot make the least difference; seeing that our Lord's body in the holy Eucharist is there in its substance, or as an aggregate of simple units, and consequently has no dimensions, and occupies no space whatever. And remark, that what happens in this particular case happens in every other being under the class of bodies. The substance or the number of simple units forming a body occupies no space whatever, and is whole and entire under each and every modification. What is particular to the Eucharist is that the substance of the body of Christ lies not under its own, but under foreign modifications. But I trust you see no difficulty in this?

W. Not much; the main difficulty of space being removed, I can very well conceive that God could easily cause a substance to appear under foreign modifications; for I see no contradiction to any essential attributes of a substance in appearing under the garb of the modifications of another. But what I cannot conceive is this: if we admit composite substances to be an aggregate of units, that is, of beings having no dimensions or parts, how do you account for the phenomenon of extension? A monas, or unit, is like a mathematical point, that is, a cipher with regard to extension; multiply, therefore, the units as much as you like, and the result will always be a cipher with reference to space. How, then, do you explain the phenomenon of extension?

D. First of all, you will be kind enough to understand that it is not the Catholic Church who is bound to explain the phenomenon of extension. It is the metaphysicians who hold the theory, though it is the only true one. It is enough for the church to say, Your best and most universal theory is, that a body is an aggregate of units devoid of extension. I show you that my dogma agrees perfectly with your theory. But it may be as well to mention the explanation which the metaphysicians just mentioned give to the objection. They hold that extension, as it falls under the senses and the imagination is not real, but phenomenal, and that the real objective extension is nothing more than the constant relation of all the units of a nature to produce in a sensitive being the phenomenon of the representation of space.*

W. But the greatest difficulty remains yet. No body can be in different places at the same time. You hold that the body of Christ is in as many places as there are hosts in the universe. This would establish the astounding phenomenon of a body in millions of different places at the same time. This is certainly absurd, and I conceive that you will find much more trouble in explaining away this difficulty than you did the first.

D. I must beg leave to call your attention again to the fact that the Catholic Church teaches that it is the substance of the body of Christ which is in different places at the same time.

W. Oh! you are there again with your sub-

---

* We have given here the theory of the best of modern philosophers. But any one acquainted with the scholastics will at once perceive that their theory agrees perfectly with the above. The fundamental idea of the scholastics in reference to matter is that it is something absolutely indeterminate, which they express by saying that it is neither quantity nor quality, etc., and that it becomes determinate by the form which is something altogether unique and devoid of dimension. Matter they compare to potentiality, something only possible, the form to the act or actuality. We subjoin a few extracts from St. Thomas:

"Materia prima aliquo modo est quia est in potentia. Sicut omne quod est in potentia potest dici materia ita omne a quo habet aliquid esse potest dici forma. Forma dat esse materiæ."

It is clear, therefore, that, according to the scholastic theory, what gives being to matter is the form, something altogether simple and unextended.

stance! I must own you have an ingenious way about you, and, if you succeed in making me see how this circumstance removes the objection, as it did the first, I give it up.

D. But it *does* remove it. And let me tell you that you Protestants, in fighting against the dogmas of the Catholic Church, commit two very serious faults: First, you do not provide yourselves with philosophy enough to cope with her. Secondly, you do not sound the depth of her statement. Then it generally happens that, when you think you are proposing your strongest objections, and you are very sure you have her in a corner, you are merely combating a phantom of your own imagination.

Now, let us see if the substance of the body of Christ can be in different places at the same time. To do this, we must examine the other question, How can a simple being reside in space? Metaphysicians teach that a body may reside in space in two ways, according as it is considered either in its phenomenal representation or in its real objective nature and substance. In its phenomenal representation, a body resides in space by contact of extension; in its real objective nature and substance, by acting upon it. I lay my hand flat upon the surface of a table, and suppose I consider both my hand and the table in their phenomenal extension. Under this respect, all the points and parts which form the phenomenal extension of my hand come in contact with all the respective parts of the table which my hand is able to cover.* Under this respect, a body naturally *cannot* be in different places at the same time without a contradiction, because the supposition would imply that the parts of my hand which are in contact with the respective parts of the table are also in contact with parts of other bodies at any given distance.

But if we consider a body not in its phenomenal extension, but in its real objective nature and substance, the case is different; because, as we have seen, the body as to its substance is simple and unextended, and therefore, as such, it cannot reside in space by contact of extension, inasmuch as its parts touch the phenomenal parts of space; for it has no parts which it may touch. Hence it follows that it resides in space as every other simple being, that is, by acting upon it.† In this case, a body in its substance and objective nature does not reside in space except by its action upon it.

Now, naturally, a body in its objective nature and substance is limited in its action to a certain defined space, and cannot extend its action beyond it. But there is no possible contradiction

---

* "Corporalia sunt in loco per contactum quantitis."—*St. Thomas.*

† "Incorporalia non sunt in loco per contactum quantitis sed per contactum *virtutis.*"—ID.

in supposing that a body may be endowed by the infinite with the power and energy to act upon any indeterminate amount of space at the same time.

Now, with regard to the body of our Lord, we have seen that it is in the holy Eucharist in its objective state, and consequently is there by its real action. The miracle in this case is, that the infinite power of the Word to which it is hypostatically united intensifies its natural sphere of acting upon space, and makes it extend to thousands of places at the same time. To conclude: The question, Can the body of Christ be in different places at the same time? resolves itself into this other: Can the substance of the body of Christ act really and truly in different places at the same time? Who could give a reason worth anything to show that it cannot? Who could prove any contradiction in the supposition? There would be a contradiction in saying that the phenomenal dimensions of the body of Christ, at the same time that they touch the dimensions of one definite space, touch also the dimensions of numberless other spaces. But there is no contradiction in saying that the substance of the body of Christ can act by virtue of the Word, to whom it is united, in numberless places at one and the same instant.

The completion of the theory of the cosmos in time and space will be given in the next chapter.

CHAPTER XIII.

THE COSMOS IN TIME AND SPACE—CONTINUED.

IN the preceding chapter we have seen that, in consequence of the sacramental extension of the Theanthropos in time and space, substantial creation in its highest and noblest element, which is personality, has received its last initial and inchoative perfection of being, by the union of human persons with the Theanthropos by means of his substantial and sacramental presence, and through that union the elevation to a higher similitude of, and communication with, the three persons of the infinite. Now, this last complement of the cosmos, this union of the Theanthropos, with human persons, through his sacramental extension in time and space, constitutes the Catholic Church, which may be defined to be:

The Theanthropos present in the cosmos through the sacraments, and through them incorporating into himself human persons in time and space, raising them to a higher similitude of and communication with the three personalities of the infinite, and thus not only realizing the highest initial perfection of the cosmos, but also unfolding and developing that initial perfection, and bringing it to its ultimate completion in palingenesia.

The Theanthropos, therefore, has placed himself in the very centre of the cosmos by his sacramental and substantial presence, as became his great office and prerogative of mediator. By those moments of his sacramental presence to which he has only attached his infinite energy and power, he disposes and fits human persons for the real incorporation into himself in the following manner: By the sacramental moment of order, through the moral instrument in whom this moment is realized, he propounds and explains his doctrine, the *gnosis* respecting God, and the cosmos which he came to reveal to men. By the sacramental moment of regeneration, he infuses into human persons the term of the supernatural order in its essence and faculties, and thus raises them to a higher state of being, and to a closer communication with the Trinity, but all this in an initial and inchoative state. By the sacramental moment, called confirmation, he brings that essence and its faculties to a definite and determinate growth. When human persons are thus fitted and prepared, he by his substantial presence incorporates them into himself, and enables their supernatural being to live and develop itself by being put in real, actual communication with all the proper objects of its faculties. Thus, the cosmos of personalities, perfected in its initial supernatural state, can act and develop itself—the Theanthropos himself, through his moral agents, organically constituted, governing and directing its action to the safest and speediest acquirement of its last perfection.

From this metaphysical idea of the church, derived and resulting from its very essence, it follows:

First, That next to the Theanthropos, the Catholic Church is the end of all the exterior works of the infinite. The supreme end of the exterior works was the highest possible communication of the infinite to the finite. This was primarily realized in the hypostatic union which bound all created natures to the infinite, and is realized next in the union of all personalities with the Theanthropos, and through him with the Trinity. Now, the very essence of the Catholic Church consists in this union. Consequently, as such it is the *last supreme imperative* law of the cosmos. The last, because with it closes the cycle of the creative act, and begins the cycle of the return of the terms to their principle and cause. Supreme, because no higher initial perfection of the cosmos can be realized after supposing its existence. Imperative, because it is a necessary complement of the plan of the cosmos.

Hence, without the Catholic Church the cosmos of personalities would have no aim or object. It would stand alone, and unconnected with the other parts of the cosmos, the particular end of each personality could never be attained, and the whole would present a confused mass of elements, without order, harmony, or completion.

It follows, in the second place, that the Catholic Church is fashioned after the hypostatic moment, and is its most lively representation. For as that moment implies the bringing together of a human and divine element, finite and infinite, absolute and relative, necessary and contingent, independent and subject, visible and invisible, in the unity of one divine personality, so the Catholic Church is the result of a double element, one human, the other divine; one visible, the other invisible; one finite, the other infinite; one necessary the other contingent; one immutable, the other variable; the one independent and authoritative, the other subject and dependent, in the union of the Theanthropos with the sacramental element. This union of the Theanthropos with the sacramental element, both moral and physical, is, as we have said, the very essence of the Catholic Church, and which endows it with that double series of attributes and perfections, one belonging to God, the other essentially belonging to the finite, but which are brought together in one being in force of that union; and all the difficulties brought against the church hinge upon that very thing—the sacramental union of all the divine attributes of the Theanthropos with the finite attributes of the sacramental element. All those who object to all or some of the Theanthropic attributes of the church object to the possibility and existence of that union.

But that union, as the last supreme imperative law of the cosmos, is such a strict consequence of the plan, is so connected and linked with all the other moments of God's action *ad extra*, depends so entirely upon the identical principle which originates the others, that once we deny it we are obliged to yield up all the other truths, and take refuge in nihilism, and proclaim the death of our intelligence. For once we admit the impossibility of the union of the attributes or substance of the Theanthropos with the sacramental element, on the plea that the attributes of each are opposite and contradictory, for the selfsame reason we must admit the impossibility of the union of the Word of God with the human nature, and sweep the hypostatic moment clean away; because, if it is impossible to bring together opposite attributes in one sacramental being, it is much more impossible, so to speak, to bring not only attributes but two natures quite opposite together, into one subsistence and personality, and entirely exchange attribution and names, and call man God, and God man, and attribute exclusively divine acts to human nature, and *vice versa*. But, having denied the hypostatic moment in consequence of that pretended impossibility, we cannot logically stop here. We must generalize the question, and deny all possible union between the finite and the infinite. For what can there be more opposite and more contradictory than these terms, absolute and relative, necessary and contingent, immense and limited, eternal and successive, immutable and changeable, universal and particular, self-existing and made, infinite and finite? And could they possibly be brought together into any kind of union? Nay, we must go further, and deny the very coexistence of both terms, because one certainly seems to exclude the other—the universal being, for instance, including all possible being, must necessarily imply the impossibility of the coexistence of any particular, circumscribed, limited being. Arrived at this, we must conclude that all finite things which come under our observation, not being able to coexist with the universal being, must be only modifications and developments of that same, and throw ourselves into Pantheism. But once Pantheism is admitted, we must, to be logical, suppose the existence of a universal something impelled by an interior instinct of nature to unfold and develop itself by a succession of efforts, one more distinct, marked, and perfect than the other. Now, taking this substance at one determinate stage of development, and going backward, from a more perfect development to one less perfect, and from this to one still less perfect, we must necessarily arrive at the most indeterminate, indefinite, abstract *something*, at the idea-being of Hegel—that is, at nihilism.

Nihilism is consequently the logical product of the denial of the union of the infinite attributes of the Theanthropos with the sacramental element, the very essence of the Catholic Church. *The Catholic Church, therefore—or nihilism.*

And we beg the reader to observe that this logical conclusion which we have drawn is simply the history of the errors of the last three hundred years, and consequently our conclusions receive all the support which the gradual unfolding of error for three hundred years is able to afford.

The impossibility of the union of the infinite attributes and substantial presence of the Theanthropos in the sacramental element was proclaimed in the sixteenth century by Protestantism, when on one side it denied the authority and infallibility of the church, and consequently denied the union of these Theanthropic attributes with the moral instrument, the hierarchy, and on the other side denied the real presence, and thus refused to allow a union of the substance of the Theanthropos with the sacramental elements of bread and wine. It did not then see the full meaning of its denial, but yet established the principle of the impossibility of the union of the Theanthropos in action or substance with the sacramental elements. Deism followed, and, making the Protestant principle its own, added a logical application to it, and asked: How can the uncreated, infinite, and absolute being be united to a nature created, finite, and relative? or, in other words: How could the finite and the infinite be united so as to form the God-man? And then, like Protestantism, in reference to sacramental union, not being able to conceive that possibility, deism denied the hypostatic moment. But the question did not stop here. Pantheism followed, and, being gifted with as much logical acumen as deism, generalized the question, and asked: How can the finite coexist with the infinite, which comprehends all? And not being able to see the possibility of such coexistence, it refused all existence to the finite, and admitted the identity of all things and the unity of substance, allowing the finite no other existence but one ephemeral and phenomenal. This was the pantheism of Spinoza and others. But Hegel, with more acumen than all the rest, saw clearly that it was impossible to admit an *infinite* substance subject to modification and development, unless it was supposed to be, previously to any development, altogether abstract, and shorn of all determination and concreteness, among which determinations must be ranked existence also; because development implies limit, definiteness, determination, circumscription; hence, that primitive something could not be supposed infinite, except it was shorn of everything, even existence. Consequently, he proclaimed nihilism as the principle of all things. And nihilism, and along with the death of the intelligence, we repeat, must be admitted, or the Catholic Church—all truth or no truth.

We conclude: Deny the Catholic Church, or the union of the attributes and substance of the Theanthropos with the sacramental elements, because those opposite things cannot be brought together, and you must deny the union between human nature and the eternal Word for the same reason. Deny the hypostatic moment, and you must deny every kind of union between the finite and the infinite for the same identical reason, and you must deny the very coexistence of the finite and the infinite, and throw yourself into Pantheism.

We defy any one to find a flaw in the logical connection of these conclusions, or to prove that we have misstated the genesis and development of error for the last three hundred years.

From the essence of the Catholic Church, it follows that she is necessarily divided into two moments—the active moment, and the passive moment.

The first is the Theanthropos acting through his moral instruments, proposing and expounding to all human persons, in time and space, the *gnosis* of the whole cosmos, in its cause, term, effect, and destiny, actualizing through the same moral instruments all the other sacramental moments in human persons, and through the same moral instruments governing and directing the whole elevated cosmos. This moment is called in theological language *ecclesia docens*, or teaching church. The second are all human persons to whom the doctrine is taught, and who are the recipients of all the sacraments and the subjects of the government of the church. This moment is called *ecclesia audiens*, or hearing church.

The first is essentially active, the other passive; the one communicates, the other receives—though some members, in different relations, belong to the one or the other.

Though in demonstrating the essence of the Catholic Church, as we flatter ourselves, quite in a novel aspect, we have at the same time demonstrated all the Theanthropic attributes belonging to and resulting from that essence, yet, for the sake of those who cannot see all the consequences included in a general principle, we shall dilate at some length upon all the essential attributes of the church, and those characteristic marks which constitute her what she is, and point her out from any other body pretending to the same name.

The first attribute, which evidently emanates from the essence of the church, is its externation, and capacity of coming under the observation of men. For, if the essence of the church consists in being the Theanthropos, incorporating his power, as well as his substantial presence, in physical as well as personal instruments, and through them incorporating all human persons unto himself, who can fail to perceive that church must be visible, outward, able to come under the observation of men, in that double relation of sacramental extension of Christ and of having men as objects of incorporation with him?

An invisible church would imply a denial of any sacramental agency, and would be absolutely unfit for men, who are *incarnate* spirits. Hence, those sects which hold that the saints alone belong to the church have not the least idea of its essence. Holiness being altogether a spiritual and invisible quality, the saints could not know each other, nor, consequently, hold any communication with each other; the sinners could not find out where the saints are to be heard of; and therefore there could not be any possibility of discovering the church or any moral obligation of joining it.

The next attribute essentially belonging to the church is its *permanence*, in theological language called indefectibility, which implies not only duration in time and space, but also *immutability* in all its essential elements, attributes, and rights. The church must continue to be, as long as the cosmos lasts, whole and entire in all time and space, in the perfect enjoyment of all its attributes, characteristic marks and rights.

The reason of this attribute is so evident and palpable that we are at a loss to understand how it could enter men's minds that the church could and did fail or change in essential elements. When Protestantism, to cloak over its rebellion in breaking loose from allegiance to the church of the living God, alleged as reason that it had failed and changed in its essential elements—when Protestantism repeats daily the same assertion, it exposed and exposes itself to an absurdity at which the merest tyro in logic would laugh. It is one of the first axioms of ontology that the essences of things are immutable and eternal: immutable, inasmuch as they can never change; eternal, inasmuch as they must be conceived as possible from eternity, whether they have any subjective existence or not. Essences are like number. Add to it, or subtract from it, and you can never have the same number; likewise add to the essence of a thing, or subtract from it, and you may have another thing, but never the same essence.

Now, what is the essence of the church? It consists in the Theanthropos incorporating his infinite power and his substantial presence in physical and personal instruments, and through them uniting to himself human persons, elevating them to a supernatural state, and enabling them to develop and unfold their supernatural faculties until they arrive at their ultimate perfection, and all this in time and space.

Now, how can we suppose the church to fail when its very essence is founded on the union of the Theanthropos with the sacraments? The only possible failure we can suppose is if the presence of the Theanthropos were to be withdrawn from the sacraments; and this could happen either because the Theanthropos may be supposed powerless to continue that presence or unwilling; in both cases, the divinity of the Theanthropos is denied; because the first would argue want of power, the second a senseless change. Protestantism would do much better to deny at once the divinity of its founder, instead of admitting the failure of the church he founded. It would be by far more honest and logical. We can respect error when it is logical and consistent, but we must despise obstinate nonsense and absurdity. The same attribute is claimed by the end of the church—which is, to communicate to human persons in time and space the term of the supernatural moment. As long, then, as there are men on earth, so long must the church continue to possess invariable and unchangeable those elements with which it was endowed by its divine founder. Should it fail or change, how could men after the failure be incorporated into the Theanthropos? Should it fail or change, how could men believe in the possibility of their attaining their end? Should it fail once and at one period only, men would no longer possess any means of knowing, when and how, and where it might not fail again, and therefore they could not but look upon the whole thing with utter contempt.

The next attribute is infallibility.

Certainty objectively considered is the impossibility of error in a given case. Infallibility also, considered in itself, is the impossibility of error in every case within the sphere to which that infallibility extends. This attribute is essentially necessary to the church, but before we enter upon its vindication we will say a word about its nature, the subject in whom it resides, the object it embraces, and the mode of exercising it. The nature of the infallibility claimed by the church does not consist in a new inspiration: because inspiration implies an interior revelation of an idea not previously revealed or known. Now, this does not occur, and is not necessary, in order that the church may fulfil its office. The revelation of the whole *gnosis* respecting God, the cosmos, and their mutual relations in time and in eternity, was made by the Theanthropos in the beginning. The church carries it in her mind, heart, and life, as she traverses centuries and generations. But as all the particular principles constituting that *gnosis* are not all distinctly and explicitly formulated and set in human language, so as it becomes the office of the church from time to time to formulate one of those principles. In this she is assisted by the Theanthropos in such a manner that she may infallibly express her mind in the new formula she utters. Again, an error may arise against the revealed gnosis she carries in her mind. Then it is her office to proclaim what her mind is upon the subject, and condemn whatever may be contrary to it. Again, she is assisted by the Theanthropos in such a manner as to effect both these things infallibly. Infallibility in the present case, therefore, may be defined a permanent assistance of the Theanthropos preserving the church from falling into error in the exercise of her office.

The object of this attribute is limited to these three :

1. She is infallible in teaching and defining all theoretical doctrines contained in the revelation, be it written or not, but handed down socially from the beginning.

2. In all doctrines having reference to morality.

3. In the choice and determination of the external means of embodying that doctrine, theoretical or practical; whether the external means which embodies the doctrine be used by the

church, or, used by others, must be judged by the church.

This last object of infallibility is so absolutely necessary that without it the other two would become nugatory and fictitious. If, in propounding a doctrine, the church could err in fixing upon such objective expressions of language as would infallibly exhibit her mind, men could never be assured whether the church had expressed herself correctly or not, and could never, consequently, be certain of her meaning. Likewise, if the church could err in teaching whether such and such expression of language, intended to embody a doctrine, contains an error or a truth, men would be left in doubt whether to embrace or reject it, and could never, in embracing it, be absolutely certain whether they were holding a revealed doctrine or a falsehood.

From this it follows that: First, the church is not infallible in things belonging exclusively to natural sciences, and in no way connected with revelation; second, she is not infallible in reference to historical facts, and much less in reference to personal facts, unless these are connected with dogma.

The subjects in whom this attribute resides are the following:

1. The supreme Pontiff, the head of the hierarchy, who, independent of the rest, enjoys this attribute, in reference to all the objects above

explained. Because, by the interior organism of the church, as we shall see, he is made the source of all authority in teaching and governing.

2. The hierarchy, together with the Supreme Pontiff, either assembled in council or agreeing through other means of communication.

We almost blush to have to remark that this infallibility, centred in the Pope or bishops, does not render them personally impeccable. The two things are as distant as the poles, and can only be brought together and confounded in minds who, according to the expression of Dante, have lost the light of the intellect, and live in a darkness which is little short of death.

The modes of exercising this attribute are three:

She is infallible as teacher, as witness, and as judge.

As teacher: when she proclaims and expounds to the faithful the revelation of the Theanthropos.

As witness: when she affirms what belongs or does not belong to that revelation.

As judge: when she pronounces final judgment on controversies and disputes which arise in relation to revealed doctrines.

Having thus given a brief idea of all that belongs to the subject of infallibility, it seems to us that no one who has understood the nature and essence of the church, and the object for which it was established, can fail to perceive not only the entire reasonableness, but also the absolute necessity of such a doctrine.

We have said that the church in its active element is nothing less than the Theanthropos himself, communicating the term of the supernatural moment, which includes teaching, through the agency of secondary agents, both physical and personal. The church, therefore, under the aspect from which we are now regarding her, is the Theanthropos teaching his revelation, expounding his revelation, affirming and witnessing to his revelation, declaring what agrees with it, and what is contradictory to it, through the agency of the Supreme Pontiff, or the Pontiff and the rest of the hierarchy. And can anything be more reasonable than the assertion that she is infallible? Protestantism has boasted, and boasts yet, of having emancipated reason, of having brought it to the highest possible degree of culture and development. But when will Protestantism begin to exercise its vaunted reason?

Is it reasonable to suppose that the Theanthropos, the God made man, the infallible wisdom of God, the very intelligibility of the Father, who established the church, that is, united himself, either as to action or substance, with a sacramental element, be it material or personal, in order, among other things, to teach all men in time and space what was absolutely necessary for them to know to attain their ultimate perfection—is it reasonable to suppose, we say, that the Theanthropos should, through his personal agents, teach anything but absolute truth?

Deny the divinity of the Theanthropos, deny that the Theanthropos ever did or could unite his activity with personal agents, deny the essence of the church, and then you would be logical, then you would be consistent, then we could understand you. But to admit that the Theanthropos *is* God, to admit that he *did* unite his infinite and divine activity to the sacramental element, to admit that he did so on purpose to teach all men in time and space, and then to affirm that the church is not and cannot be infallible—that is, that the Theanthropos cannot teach infallibly through his personal agents—is such a logic as only the highly cultivated reason of Protestantism can understand. It is above the reach of that reason which is satisfied with a moderate share of culture and refinement, and cannot claim to soar so high.

We beg the reader to reflect for an instant on this single question: Is it the Theanthropos, or is it not, who teaches through the agency of his personal instruments? To this simple question, a simple answer should be given. Say you answer, It is not. Then you deny that the Theanthropos united his infinite energy to a sacramental element. Then you deny the essence of the church, and, in denying that, you must deny every other union between the infinite and the finite, as we have demonstrated. If you say it *is* the Theanthropos who teaches through the agency of his personal instruments, then what can be more logical or more consistent than to say that he teaches infallibly? What is there more reasonable than to say that a God-man should know what is truth, and should express his mind so, should embody it in an external means so, as to represent that mind infallibly?

Then, why so much opposition against this plainest attribute of the church? Why so much obloquy, so much sneering except that the so boasted Protestant reason is nothing but a vile, unmanly prejudice, except that those who boast so much of exercising their reason resemble those innocent and unconscious animals of which Dante speaks:

> "As *sheep*, that step forth from their fold, by one
> Or pairs, or three, at once; meanwhile, the rest
> Stand fearfully, bending the eye and nose
> To ground, *and what the foremost does that do
> The others, gathering round her if she stops,
> Simple and quiet, nor the cause discern?"*
> —*Cary's Translation.*

The next attribute of the church is authority. This, like the rest, flows from her very essence. That essence consists in being the sacramental extension of Christ incorporating unto himself all human persons in time and space, communicating to them the term of the supernatural moment in its essence and faculties, and aiding them to develop those faculties, and to bring them to their ultimate completion. The church, therefore, as sacramental—that is, outward and sensible extension of the Theanthropos intended for men—is a visible, outward society of human persons with the Theanthropos. Now, what does a visible society require? That the external relations of the associates should be determined and governed by the authority legitimately constituted in the society. For, if those relations were not determined and directed by proper authority in a visible society, it is evident that no order could be expected, and that all the members could not form one moral body, by a proper external communication. The church, therefore, as a visible society, must have authority to determine all the external relations of the members, and to govern and direct them.

This authority or power of establishing the external polity in the church is, of course, essentially residing in the Theanthropos, who communicates it whole and entire to the Supreme Pontiff, and through him to the whole hierarchy and the rest of the active church.

Having vindicated the essential attributes of the church, we think it necessary to dilate at some length upon the interior constitution, the internal organism of the same, in order to exhibit a fuller and more adequate idea of this masterpiece of the infinite. And in order to do it thoroughly, we must give a cursory glance at its eternal type, the supreme exemplar of everything—the Trinity. The reader will remember that the genesis of God's life takes place as follows: There is in the infinite essence and nature a first subsistence, unborn, unbegotten, which terminates in the first person. This is the supreme, active principle of the second, and both are the active principle of the third. In this third termination closes the cycle of infinite life. The production of the second person is brought about by intellectual generation. For the primary unbegotten activity, being infinitely intelligent, can scan with his glance the whole depth, breadth, height, and length of his infinite nature. Now, to intelligence means to produce an intellectual image of the object which is understood. Consequently, the primary unbegotten principle, by intelligencing himself, produces an intellectual image, absolutely equal to himself, the act of intelligencing being infinite, and also distinct from him, inasmuch as they are opposed as principle and term. The first contemplates himself in his substantial image, and is attracted toward himself and his image. The second contemplates himself in his principle, and is attracted toward himself and his principle. This common, mutual attraction or love, being also infinite, is consequently substantial, and results in a third termination of the infinite essence.

From this brief explanation of the genesis of God's life, it follows:

1st. That the infinite, though one in nature, has three distinct terminations or persons.

2d. That, though these three persons are absolutely equal, because possessed of the same identical nature, we find in them a necessary subjection of order founded on the law of origin and production, the second being originated by the first, and being in this respect subject to him; the third being originated by both, and under this respect being subject to both.

3d. The three persons possessing the same identical nature and substance, possess, consequently, all the perfections and attributes flowing from the substance in the same identical manner. Hence they possess in common all the metaphysical attributes of the substance, such as infinity, eternity, immensity, immutability; all the intellectual attributes, such as truth, wisdom, etc., all the moral attributes of the substance, such as goodness, etc.

4th. As nature is the radical principle of action and life, it follows that, as the three persons possess the same nature, they possess one identical action and life. But as the termination is the immediate principle of action, and the three persons have a distinct termination, their one identical action receives the impress of the distinct termination of each.

5th. Finally, the essence being identical in all the three persons, and the second and third being originated by an immanent action, and all being essentially relative to each other, it follows that they all live in each other by a common indwelling.

Now, the interior constitution, the internal organism, of the church must be modelled, both in its active and passive moments, after this supreme type of everything; always granting the necessary distance of proportion intervening between the infinite and the finite. For, if the whole cosmos is and must be fashioned after that supreme pattern, how much more must the church, which is the inchoative and initial perfection of the whole cosmos, the cosmos of personalities! Consequently, we must find in its interior organism all the laws of the genesis of God's life—laws which in the whole cosmos are reflected in those of *unity, variety, hierarchy, communion.*

And, first, as to the active moment of the church. As in the infinite we find one nature and essence, the abyss of all perfections, the *Being*, so in the active church we must find one nature and essence, the reflex of the essence of God. And that one nature consists in the fulness of the priesthood of the Theanthropos, communicated to the whole active church in the sacrament of order, and in the fulness of his authority.

As in the infinite the divine nature is possessed in common by a multiplicity of persons, the three terminations constituting the Trinity, so in the active church the priesthood of Christ and his authority must be possessed in common by a multiplicity of persons, some possessing it in its fulness, some partially, because distinction in the finite is by gradation, and cannot be by perfect equality, but all having the same identical priesthood as to its nature.

As in the Trinity, we find the law of hierarchy absolutely necessary in organic and living beings, which hierarchy consists in this, that the three divine persons, though absolutely equal as to nature, are distinct as to personality—a distinction which arises from opposition of origin. Now, this opposition of origin necessarily gives rise to a hierarchical superiority of order; the Father as such being necessarily superior in order to the Son, and the Son as such inferior to him; both as the aspirants of the third person necessarily superior to him, and *vice versa*.

Now, this hierarchical law must be found also in the church, and we must find a superiority of one over the other, not merely of order, but of gradation; the finite, as we have said, not being distinct except by gradation of being. Hence, we find the Theanthropos to have established three distinct elements constituting the hierarchy, and organically brought together. The first, a primary principle of authority from whom all receive, and he receives from none—the Supreme Pontiff, his own vicar on earth, the visible head of the church. The second, who receive from the first in measure and limit—the episcopate who receive from the Supreme Pontiff their authority and its extent. The third, also, receive from both in a more limited manner—the priesthood.*

As in the Trinity the divine nature, being the radical principle of action and life, and the termination, the proximate principle, there is one common action and life, but the same bearing the impress of the constituent of each person; so in the church the authority being the same as to nature, the Pontiff, the episcopate, and the priesthood have one common life and action radically, but each one displaying it according to the degree resulting from his dignity—the Pontiff in its fulness, the episcopate within the range of their dioceses, the priesthood within the limits appointed by the episcopate—the second as holding it from the first, the third from both.

---

* We have said *authority* and not sacerdotal character, because as to that there is no difference between the Supreme Pontiff and the episcopate, but only between the episcopate and the priesthood.

The reader can see by the theory we have just explained, and which cannot be gainsaid, how the late definition of the infallibility of the Supreme Pontiff is in accordance with and flows from the principles we have laid down. The Pontiff in the church of Christ is the first and primary visible principle of all authority, as in the interior of infinite life the eternal Father is the first primary principle of authority over the Son and the Spirit, as we have explained above.

From the Pontiff all must receive authority, and he can receive from none, as the Father in the internal organism of the infinite communicates and receives from none. Consequently, the Supreme Pontiff being the first, primary, supreme, visible principle of authority in the church of Christ, is the first, primary, supreme, visible teacher—the office of teaching being essentially included in the fulness of authority communicated to him by Christ.

And as the office of teaching in the church of Christ would be of no avail except it were endowed with the attribute of infallibility, it follows that the Supreme Pontiff is the first, primary, supreme, *infallible* teacher in the church of Christ. He must teach all, and can be taught by none. He teaches by himself the whole universal church, and none has and can have any authority for disputing, objecting to, and gainsaying his teaching.

We cannot perceive how any persons holding the supremacy and independence of his authority could ever have reconciled with their logic the dependence of his authority with reference to teaching.

We come to the interior organism of the passive church, to which the active church also belongs in different relation, and we find in it also a reflex of the Trinity.

For as in the infinite there is one nature common to all, communicated by the first person to the second, and by both to the third, so in the passive church we find the same nature, the term of the supernatural moment, consisting in a higher similitude of and communication with the Trinity; this term communicated by the active church; primarily by the episcopate, and secondarily by the priesthood.

As in the Trinity, the nature being the same, the three persons partake of all the attributes flowing from the nature, likewise, and with due proportion in the church, the nature of the supernatural moment being the same, all the members partake of the same attributes and faculties flowing from that nature; hence they have one common supernatural intelligence, one common supernatural will.

As the Trinity, the nature being the radical principle of action, and the personality the proximate, all have the same action, but each acts according to the constituent of his personality; so in the church, the term of the supernatural moment, constituting its nature, being the same, all have the same supernatural action and life; but personally, some members belonging to the active church, and some to the passive, it follows that those who belong to the first display that life in that relation, and those who belong to the second display it in the second relation.

As in the Trinity we find an indwelling of all the persons in each other, and a living perpetual communication founded on the identity of nature and on the relation of personalities; so in the church of Christ we find a perpetual communication of its members with each other, founded on the identity of nature, the term of the supernatural moment, and on the relation of personalities, all members of the passive church communicating with and living, as it were, in the active church, because proceeding from it.

We see, therefore, what is the interior organism of the church. As to the active church, the fulness of the priesthood of the Theanthropos is given to the whole active church. The organism is constituted and established by authority. The fulness of his authority is communicated to one, the Supreme Pontiff, the visible head of the church. From him, and from him alone, all others must receive authority. And hence the unity of the whole active church, unity of authority, of action and life, and the proper hierarchical order. The passive church is established upon the bestowal of the supernatural nature and faculties and acts. The two are brought together by the community of the same supernatural nature, faculties, and acts; and, by the dependence of origin, the second proceeding and being originated by the first. Both have one common life and action, but hierarchically exercised, the passive being governed and directed by the one which originates it, and thus exhibiting a most perfect image of the Trinity.

We have only been commenting upon those words of the Theanthropos: "Holy Father, keep these in thy name whom thou hast given me, that they may be one, as we also are." Here we have the necessity of the church being modelled after the Trinity, the archetype of everything.

"As thou hast sent me into the world, I also have sent them into the world." The common nature of the active church, the mission and authority of the Theanthropos.

"And not for these only do I pray, but for all those who, through their words shall believe in me." The continuation of that authority.

"Sanctify them in truth." The common nature of the passive church, the term of the supernatural moment.

" That they may be one, as thou Father in me

and I in thee, that they may be one in us." The completion of the inchoative society brought about by the supernatural element of union, and by the incorporation with the Theanthropos.

To complete the theory of the church, we have now to point out the characteristic marks which distinguish it from any counterfeit institution of men. These marks are four: unity, holiness, catholicity, and apostolicity.

Unity. What is the church, viewed in its essence, attributes, and interior organism? It is the Theanthropos annexing his infinite energy and his substantial presence to a sacramental element, both physical and personal, and through them first elevating human persons to a supernatural being, with its essence and faculties of supernatural intelligence and supernatural will in an incipient and inchoative state; secondly, through his sacramental, personal element proposing and expounding his *gnosis* to their supernatural intelligence; by a second sacramental moment elevating this supernatural essence and faculties to a determinate and definite growth: by the sacramental moment of his presence incorporating all elevated persons unto himself, and thus putting them in immediate contact with himself, and through him with the Trinity on one side and with all the cosmos in nature and personality on the other side, and thus affording their supernatural faculties proper objects on which they may feed, expand, be developed, and arrive at their ultimate perfection. Finally, by the personal sacramental element governing and directing all their exterior relations and communication to one social final end; and all this not in any particular spot or period of time, but in all space and in all time. From this it is evident that the church of Christ is *one* in force of the unity of the Theanthropos with the sacramental element; *one* in consequence of the interior unity of organism, both of the active and passive church; *one* in consequence of the unity of the supernatural being and faculties, the end of the church; *one* in force of the unity of the object of the supernatural intelligence; *one* in consequence of the unity of the object of the supernatural will—God and his cosmos, in their relations to each other; *one* in consequence of the real communion and intercourse between the members of the church; *one*, finally, in consequence of the oneness of the visible government of the church, all emanating from one invisible and one visible head.

The second distinctive mark of the church must be holiness. For the end of the church is to impart to human persons in time and space the term of the supernatural moment, together with its faculties, and especially the faculty and habit of supernatural intelligence and supernatural will or charity, in which, as we have demonstrated in the tenth chapter, the very essence of holiness consists. If the church, therefore, were deprived of this distinctive mark, she would fail in that very object for which she was instituted.

But it is to be remarked that not any degree of holiness would be sufficient to constitute a distinctive mark of the church, but a certain fulness of it is required in some of its members, for a twofold reason.

Like every moment of God's exterior action, she is subject to the law of variety by hierarchy. This involves the necessity of the church ranging between the lowest degree of sanctity to the very pinnacle of sublimest and loftiest exhibition of it; otherwise, those two laws could not be realized.

Secondly, an ordinary degree of holiness can easily be counterfeited. But none could for any length of time or any extension of space assume a sanctity which soars far above the ordinary and common level, and which exhibits itself as such. *Nemo personam diu fert* could be applied in this case more than in any other.

The next distinctive mark is *catholicity* or *universality*. She is such not only because she contains all truth; not only because she embraces all the moments of God's action, as the finishing stroke of them all; but because she is intended for all time and all space.

Finally, the last mark is *apostolicity*. The first

members of the hierarchy chosen by the Theanthropos to communicate as moral instruments the term of the sublimative moment, with the power and authority to transmit to others that very same dignity of being moral instruments, were the *apostles*. Therefore, that church alone can be the church of the Theanthropos which to this day and for ever can show that her own hierarchy are the legitimate successors of the apostles, by an uninterrupted communication. For we have said that the essence of the church is to be the Theanthropos acting in time and space, through the agency of the hierarchy and other sacraments. Now, suppose a hierarchy who cannot claim or make good their claim to be the legitimate successors of the first ones who composed it, who could not claim any communication or union with them, how could we suppose them to be those very instruments in whom and through whom the Theanthropos lives and acts?

Before we draw the consequence which follows from all we have said concerning the church, it is necessary to recapitulate in a few words all we have written in these chapters.

We set out with the question of the infinite, and after refuting the pantheistic idea of the infinite, and showing that Pantheism in its solution of the problem destroys it, we gave the Catholic idea of the infinite. Here another problem sprang up—multiplicity in the infinite. No being can be conceived endowed with pure, unalloyed unity. It must be multiple, under pain of being inconceivable. What is the multiplicity which can be admitted in the infinite? We demonstrated that the pantheistic solution which says that infinite becomes multiple by a necessary interior development, destroys both terms, the unity and the multiplicity. We proceeded to lay down the Catholic answer to the problem, and explained, as far as lay in our power, the mystery of the ever-blessed Trinity. The question next in order was the finite. And we showed the finite to be the effect of an absolutely free act of infinite power, free both as to its creation at all and also with regard to the amount of perfection to be created; though we admitted and proved that it was befitting on the part of the Creator to effect the best possible manifestation of himself. Here we found ourselves in face of a duality which claimed reconciliation. How could the finite and the infinite be united together, so as to preserve whole and entire the two respective natures, and at the same time to effect the best possible manifestation of the infinite? We answered by laying down the Catholic dogma of the hypostatic union, which raised the finite to a hypostatic or personal union with the infinite, and elevated finite natures to the highest possible dignity. But as the hypostatic moment raised to a personal union only nature, and left out personality, another duality arose: how to unite human persons with the Theanthropos, and through him with God, and make them partakers as far as possible of the dignity and elevation of the nature hypostatically united to the *Word*. The sublimative moment answered the question. This moment, medium between the Theanthropos and substantial creation, by bestowing upon human persons a higher nature and faculties, enabled them to unite in close contact with the Theanthropos and through him with the Trinity. But what was the medium chosen to transmit the term of the sublimative moment to human persons in time and space? The Theanthropos himself, the essential mediator between God and the cosmos; and to that effect he united his infinite energy and his substantial presence to personal and physical instruments, and through them imparted to human persons in time and space the term of the sublimative moment; and thus the cycle of the procession of the cosmos from the infinite was perfected in its being and faculties, to begin a movement of return to the same infinite as its supreme end. The sacramental extension of the Theanthropos in time and space we have demonstrated to be the Catholic Church, and from its essence we have drawn her essential attributes of visibility, indefectibility, infallibility, and authority, and also its intrinsic marks of unity, holiness, catholicity, and apostolicity.

After this necessarily imperfect sketch of all our work, we submit to the reader this necessary consequence—*the Roman Catholic Church is the only true church of God.*

First, because it is in the teaching of the Roman Catholic Church alone that the life of the intelligence is possible. We have shown throughout our work that in every question which the human mind raises, there is no possible alternative—either embrace the Catholic solution, so coherent with reason; or the pantheistic solution, and the death of the intelligence. Now, when we speak of the Catholic solution, we mean of the solution which is given by the church whose head is the Bishop of Rome, for no other pretended Catholic Church gives all the true solutions.

Second, because it is the Roman Catholic Church alone which knows her own essence and attributes. All others are more or less ignorant of the essence and attributes necessary to the church of the Theanthropos.

Thirdly, it is to the Roman Catholic Church alone to which the essences, attributes, and marks which we have shown *à priori* to belong necessarily to the Church of Christ apply. Consequently, the Roman Catholic Church is the real cosmos of God in its perfection of being and faculties, and men have no possible alternative but to join it, to submit to its authority, under pain of the death of the intelligence, of being a creature out of joint with the whole system of God's works, of being in the impossibility of attaining their last end in palingenesia. The Roman Catholic Church or Pantheism—all truth or no truth—death or life here and hereafter.

END OF THE FIRST PART.